CU00747105

BRITISH AGRICULTURE IN THE FIRST WORLD WAR

BRITISH AGRICULTURE IN THE FIRST WORLD WAR

P. E. DEWEY

ROUTLEDGE

First published in 1989 by
Routledge
11 New Fetter Lane, London EC4P 4EE
29 West 35th Street, New York NY 10001

© 1989 Peter E. Dewey

Printed in Great Britain by
T. J. Press (Padstow Ltd), Padstow, Cornwall

British Library Cataloguing in Publication Data

Dewey, P. E. (Peter E), 1944–
British agriculture in the First World
War.
1. Great Britain. Agricultural industries,
1914–1918
I. Title
338.1'0941

Library of Congress Cataloging in Publication Data

Dewey, P. E., 1944–
British agriculture in the First World War / P. E. Dewey.
p.   cm.
Bibliography: p.
Includes index.
ISBN 0–415–02637–7
1. Agriculture—Great Britain—Military aspects. 2. Great
Britain—History—George V, 1910–1936. 3. World War, 1914–18—
Economic aspects—Great Britain. I. Title.
HD1925.D49 1989
338.1'0941—dc19

ISBN 0–415–02637–7

To Hilary

CONTENTS

PART III THE ACHIEVEMENT

ACKNOWLEDGEMENTS

Most of the research on which this book is based was done whilst the author was in receipt of a postgraduate studentship from the Social Science Research Council (now the Economic and Social Research Council), whose assistance is gratefully acknowledged. The Central Research Fund of London University provided a research grant for the consultation of the minutes of War Agricultural Committees held in county record offices. The Isobel Thornley Bequest (London University) provided a grant to defray the cost of converting the author's word-processor discs into a suitable format for publication. I am glad to acknowledge the assistance of Somerset Record Office in granting permission to reproduce the document from the Somerset RO on p. 117, and Routledge for permission to reproduce the map on p. 205.

ABBREVIATIONS IN TEXT

AWB	Agricultural Wages Board
CPA	Corn Production Act (1917)
CP(A)A	Corn Production (Amendment) Act (1918)
DC	District Committee
DORA	Defence of the Realm Act
EC	County Agricultural Executive Committee
EO	Executive Officer
FPD	Food Production Department of the Board of Agriculture
IHC	International Harvester Company
WAC	County War Agricultural Committee
WLA	Women's Land Army
WWAC	Women's War Agricultural Committee

The term 'billion' signifies million $\times$ million throughout.

Chapter One

INTRODUCTION

The First World War posed enormous problems for the agricultural systems of the belligerent nations. In most cases, these problems were insurmountable. As labourers went off to war, and machinery, fertilisers, and horsepower became more scarce, the consequence was usually a substantial decline in production. This was particularly marked in the countries of central Europe such as Austria-Hungary and Germany, which were subject to blockade by the Entente powers. In continental Europe as a whole, agricultural production fell by about one-third.[1] In these difficult circumstances, Britain has long been recognised as an exceptional success story. During the war, the supply of food was maintained almost intact. At its lowest point, in 1917, the calorie value of the average UK diet was only 4 per cent lower than in 1909–13.[2]

In assessing the reasons for this success, contemporaries and historians have emphasised the success of the food production policy implemented by the Lloyd George government in 1917–18. This aimed, by ploughing up grassland, to produce more food from home agriculture. The scientific rationale behind this policy was sound; for physiological reasons, more human food per acre of land can be produced if it is devoted to crops for direct human consumption rather than livestock. Large claims for the success of the 'plough policy' were made after the war. These were put forward by Sir Thomas Middleton, who had been closely connected with the policy. His claim was that home agriculture increased food output in 1918 by 24 per cent over that of pre-war. In his view, this represented a signal success, which contributed to the satisfactory final result of maintaining food supplies.[3]

The policy of food production was widely felt to be successful, and provided the model for the policy of the Second World War, whose success is not in doubt. However, concentration on the policy of 1917–18 has led to a neglect of the history of British agriculture over the whole period of the war. One of the most compelling reasons for studying the period is that so far we have not known what British farmers actually produced during 1914–18. The first census of agricultural production was taken in 1908; the next one not until 1925. In between those dates we have to rely on the annual agricultural statistics, which have their limitations. This neglect of what was actually happening to agricultural production in 1914–18 has had two consequences; it makes it difficult to judge how effectively farmers coped with the wartime shortages of factors of production, and to judge the effectiveness of the plough policy in 1917–18.

The lack of a yardstick against which to set the performance of agriculture has led to confusion. This may be seen in the case of labour supply. Only in mid-1917 was farm labour fully protected against the demands of the Army. Thus until then, farmers could expect to lose a large proportion of their labour. The official view was that agriculture had lost about one-third of its labour by the end of 1916. This view was based on information whose validity we shall question. But it seems to have escaped notice at the time (and subsequently) that a loss of this magnitude, if true, had serious potential implications for production. To put it simply, how could farmers cope with a sudden loss of this size, and still maintain output?

There were also by this time losses of other factors of production to take into account – of fertiliser, feedstuffs, and machinery, as well as the supply of labour for maintenance and repair work, and of local services such as those of blacksmiths. Yet the authors writing on the experience of agriculture in wartime have not seriously considered the possibility that production might have fallen by the middle of the war; Middleton compared the production achieved in 1918 with that of pre-war, and so far there has been no clear estimate of what British farmers were actually producing between 1914 and 1917. This is a serious omission in itself, and has implications also for judging the success of the food production programme of 1917–18. A reconsideration of the history of wartime agriculture from the fundamental viewpoint of what factors of production were available, and how successfully farmers were able to employ them, will hopefully shed some light on the efficacy of policy in the second half of the war, as well as giving some idea of how farmers reacted to shortages of essential factors of production in 1914–18 as a whole.

In considering how successfully wartime agriculture coped with the loss of essential factors of production, it may be noted that the nature and situation of agriculture in Britain was radically different from that of other countries. Indeed, British agriculture could with some justification, be described as having unique features. Three in particular stand out: the virtual disappearance of the small peasant owner-occupier; the absence of protection from foreign competition; and the dominance of the system of landowner and tenant.

For a variety of reasons, which have never been entirely explained, English agriculture had for centuries witnessed the gradual disappearance of the small peasant farm. The process, which may be said to have begun in the years immediately after the Black Death in the fourteenth century, was hastened by the general development of English society until the late eighteenth century. On the eve of the agricultural and industrial revolutions of 1750–1850 English agriculture was already distinguished, in comparison with that of continental nations, by a high average farm size, and the degree to which landholding was in the hands of landowners rather than owner-occupiers. These features were accentuated by the enclosure movement of 1750–1850, which swept away the remnants of the old open-field strip farming system, and stimulated further the tendency towards large holdings.[4]

At this point a new development took place: the coming of Free Trade. The import duties enshrined in the Corn Laws were repealed in 1846, and not reimposed thereafter. This commitment to free trade in agricultural products even survived the depression of the last quarter of the nineteenth century, when pressure from farming interests caused most continental nations to revert to protection. By the early twentieth century, countries such as France and Germany imposed duties on both cereals and livestock products of the order of one-third by value.[5] The political commitment to free trade was one factor in the steady decline of British agriculture as part of the national economy. Whereas in 1851 it had employed one-quarter of occupied males, it employed barely 12 per cent by 1901.[6]

The decline of agriculture as an employer was echoed by its relative decline as a provider of human food. In the late eighteenth century it had fed the whole British population (about 8 millions), and still had a surplus of grain for export. By the 1840s, population growth had proceeded faster than the growth of agricultural productivity. The latter had grown quite impressively, however, so that 13 million people were now fed from home agriculture.[7] In the ensuing decades, especially after 1870, imports grew rapidly. The largest and most rapidly growing trade was in cereals, so that British farmers retreated from grain growing *en masse*. Over the next 30 years the tillage area in Britain fell by around 3 million acres. Meat and dairy imports also rose, due to the introduction of refrigeration. The result of this huge surge in imports was that by 1914 Britain, alone among the major nations, was dependent upon imports for the greater part of its food supply. Overall, about 60 per cent (reckoned in calories) of the UK food supply was derived directly from imports, and a further unknown amount was indirectly derived from imported fertiliser and animal feeds.

Other nations tended to see British reliance on imports as a source of potential weakness in time of war. These misgivings barely surfaced in Britain before 1914. The only major enquiry into the matter was the Royal Commission on the Supply of Food and Raw Materials in Time of War. This reported in 1905 that, although it might be prudent to take some minor practical steps such as building up a reserve of wheat, and introducing a scheme of insurance for shippers, the chief policy should remain what it had always been – to rely on the carrying capacity of the merchant fleet, and the ability of the Royal Navy to keep the sea-lanes open. The submarine, which was to so seriously upset this policy in the war, was as yet not sufficiently developed technically to pose a threat, and did not receive a mention in the report of the Commission.[8]

Although the structure of British agriculture, and its significance as a part of the economy and supplier of food, was greatly different from that of other countries, it faced similar problems during the First World War. The expansion of the armed forces generated a demand for manpower, money and war material, as had been the case in all wars. But the problems were different in the First World War because of the scale and nature of the conflict. This is best illustrated by considering recruitment to the forces: by the end of 1914, over one million men had volunteered for the Army in Britain, and by the end of 1916 the total size of the armed forces was over four million men. Nor did this mean that the war was merely an old-style war on a larger scale. The very nature of warfare had changed, as a result of the industrial revolution in Britain and other major nations. The consequence was that the demands made by the armed forces on the industrial sector of the economy were much more substantial and wide-ranging than ever before. The new warfare demanded immense amounts of metals, chemicals, and transport, so that the industries concerned expanded enormously to meet the demands of the forces. By May 1918 it was estimated in a report presented to the British Cabinet that 3.1 million men were directly employed by the government on the war effort, either for the British or allied governments.[9]

The consequences of this new warfare for agriculture was a loss of essential factors of production, as the armed forces expanded and industry turned its attention to supplying the enormously increased demand for military material. It was a paradox of the war that, whereas governments were eventually forced to consider as 'essential' for the war effort a wide range of industries which would not normally have been thus categorised, they were reluctant to apply this classification to agriculture. As long as the supply of food seemed to be maintained, little action was called for. Thus the supply of factors of production was curtailed as a result of the expansion of the forces, and no real attempt was made (in any of the belligerent countries) to safeguard these supplies. As far as the British economy is concerned, there is the further important point that military service was voluntary until 1916, so that there was no control over the types of labour lost to the forces.

Loss of the main factors of production was thus the great problem facing agriculturalists in the war. There was one further change which affected agriculture, and that was the high rate of inflation, induced by wartime shortages of all kinds and by the fiscal and monetary policies of governments. In Britain, the pre-war inflation rate had been about 2 per cent a year, but by mid-1915 it was about 25 per cent, and remained at roughly that rate for the next two years. Whilst farmers might expect that, as producers of essential commodities, this would prove advantageous, it was not certain. Much would depend on what happened to the prices and supplies of factors of production. It would be a sanguine view to expect that inflation would automatically benefit farmers rather than other sections of the community.[10]

Loss of factors of production and inflation therefore constituted the environment in which British farmers had to work during the war. In order to gain some idea of the impact that these had on farming, we must first examine the agricultural system which prevailed in 1914.

NOTES

1 D. H. Aldcroft, *The European Economy 1914–80* (1978), 22.
2 (Sir) W. H. Beveridge, *British Food Control* (1928), 314.
3 T. H. Middleton, *Food Production in War* (Oxford, 1923), 322.
4 On the meaning of 'peasant' in the English context, see J. V. Beckett, 'The peasant in England: a case of terminological confusion?' *AgHR* 32 (1984).
5 M. Tracy, *Agriculture in Western Europe: challenge and response 1880–1980* (2nd edn, 1982), 75.
6 B. R. Mitchell and P. Deane, *Abstract of British Historical Statistics* (Cambridge, 1971), 60.
7 In 1831–40 UK agriculture fed 21 million people, of whom 8 million lived in Ireland; Middleton, *Food Production*, 92–8.
8 *Royal Commission on Supply of Food and Raw Material in Time of War* (1905), PP 1905, XXXIX, I, paras. 129–33 and Part IV.
9 J. M. Winter, *The Great War and the British People* (1985), 46.
10 Calculated from the Ministry of Labour index of retail prices in Mitchell and Deane, *Abstract*, 478.

Chapter Two

FARMING AND FOOD SUPPLY
BEFORE 1914

PRE-WAR FARMING

The distinguishing features of British agriculture – its comparative lack of a 'peasantry', the dominance of the landowner and tenant system, and its minor role as a supplier of food – formed the framework within which it had to operate in meeting the particular problems posed by the First World War.

The lack of a peasantry in the continental sense did not mean that the small farmer was extinct in Britain. Exactly how many small farmers existed was a matter for conjecture, since there was no clear definition in the official enquiries of the time of the terms 'farmer' or 'farm'. The first census of agricultural production, in 1908, attempted an all-embracing survey, by considering all 'agricultural holdings' over one acre. These were not necessarily coterminous with farms, since many of the smaller holdings would be parts of larger farms, or held for purposes which would not be recognised as strictly agricultural – market gardening, horse breeding, keeping the horses of the local carrier, or the cattle of the local butcher. Thus the half-million holdings recorded in 1908 did not amount to an equivalent number of farms; the 1911 census of population found only 290,000 persons who described themselves as farmers. But the 1908 census was a fairly reliable guide to the size-structure of British farming (Table 2.1).[1]

Small farms were therefore still important in terms of numbers, although not in terms of total acreage. However, 'small' in the British context had a different meaning from that in other European countries. In France, for example, about two-fifths of all holdings were under 2.5 acres.[2] It was the lack of such a large number of

Table 2.1: British farm size-structure, 1908

Size (acres)	No. of holdings	% of holdings	% of farm area	Total (million acres)
1–5	108,094	21.20	0.01	0.35
6–50	231,819	45.60	14.67	4.72
51–300	151,002	29.70	58.88	18.97
300+	17,714	0.03	25.39	8.18
Total	508,629			32.21[a]

Note: [a] Rounding adjustment

Source: Board of Agriculture, *The Agricultural Output of Great Britain* (1912), Cd. 6277, PP 1912–13, X, 62

micro-holdings, and its large average farm size (63 acres) which made the British agricultural system outstanding in comparison with continental systems. But there were considerable regional variations. Generally, a broad distinction could be drawn between the land south of a line from the Bristol Channel to the Wash and that to the north of it. This divide, which roughly corresponded to that between highland and lowland Britain, was also that between smaller- and larger-scale farming. Including the south-western counties of England in the highland zone, it was apparent that, as one travelled east and south, farms became larger. In the small-holding areas of north-west England, Wales, and the west of Scotland, average farm size fell below 50 acres. In the regions of England classified by the Board of Agriculture as Eastern, North-Eastern, South-Eastern and the East Midlands, it was above 70 acres. The dividing line was not entirely reliable; the average size was highest of all in East Scotland (81 acres), but the general principle held good.

Apart from the large size of the average farm, British agriculture was unique in that the ownership of land was largely divorced from its working. The system of landlord and tenant had evolved over centuries and, by 1914, had reached its apogee. In 1909, it was estimated that only 13 per cent of all holdings, comprising 12 per cent of all farm land, were owner-occupied in England and Wales.[3] It was also remarkable that land ownership was highly concentrated. Enquiries made in the 1870s by John Bateman had led to the conclusion that some 4,000 persons owned slightly more than half the total land (of all sorts) in England and Wales – 18.5 out of 34.5 million acres.[4] In spite of the subsequent depression in the late nineteenth century, the landowner and tenant system survived intact down to 1914.

The corollary of the landlord and tenant system was the provision of capital by landlords and the receipt of rent in return. The general rule was that landlords provided fixed capital – buildings, fences, roads, ditches and drains. This accumulated capital represented a considerable sum, estimated in 1907 at £12 an acre.[5] In return for this the landlord received rent, which at the time was about £1 per acre in England and Wales. This represented a yield of 8.3 per cent. However, the costs of maintenance reduced this gross rent to 5.2 per cent net. Since the landowner could have received interest of 3.3 per cent on his capital without risk by investing in government securities, a deduction must be made for the income thus notionally forgone. Finally, the landowner was left with a sum which represented the economic rent of the land itself. This residual sum was only 4s 7d an acre, or 1.9 per cent of the original £12.[6]

This comparatively small return became even smaller when set against the cost of buying a farm, and joining the ranks of land-owners. In the years 1909–13, the average sale price of farms in England and Wales was £24 an acre, so that the net economic rent on new land purchases fell to 0.95 per cent.[7] That landownership was still a popular occupation is reflected in the high price of agricultural land. But clearly it was not economic inducements alone which attracted men to purchase land. The comment of G. C. Brodrick in 1881 was still valid:[8]

> a very large proportion of the purely agricultural land now possesses a value entirely independent of its rent-producing capacity. It has been purchased at a fancy price, not for the sake of the interest which it may yield, but for the sake of the social position, territorial influence, and legal privileges, which attach to ownership of land in this country, and the competition for which seems to be ever on the increase.

In contrast to the landlord, the tenant has attracted little atten-tion from historians. Like the landlord, he was a creature of infinite variety. At one extreme he might be a collier or cottager renting several acres for the sake of keeping a cow or producing vegetables. At the other extreme were such men as the father of A. G. Street, renting 630 acres in a fertile river valley in South Wiltshire, and employing 23 men. In the middle lay those such as Joseph Ashby, who, beginning as a farm labourer, managed eventually to rent a small farm in his Oxfordshire village of Tysoe, making the transition into the rural middle class with some success.[9]

Whatever the origins of the tenant, he traditionally provided the working capital of the farm, in the form of seed, livestock, implements, machinery, and any purchased feeds or fertilisers. The continued technical development of farming in the nineteenth century meant that tenants' capital requirements had risen substantially. By 1914, the large tenant of a mixed arable/pasture farm would possess working capital worth perhaps £10 an acre. This was the estimated cost of equipping a farm from new.[10] For the aspiring farmer there were cheaper ways of doing things; he might start by milking or fattening a few cows, increasing numbers out of retained income. On the arable side, there were second-hand implements to be had at farm sales; since their physical rates of depreciation were low, these represented good value for the budding tenant.

In order to carry out their work, British farmers cultivated some 32 million acres of improved agricultural land ('crops and grass' in the agricultural statistics), to which may be added some 13 million acres of 'rough grazings', which were relatively unproductive. There were considerable differences in the broad categories of land use in the three countries (Table 2.2).

Table 2.2: Land use in Britain, 1914 ('000 acres)

	Total area	Cultivated land	Rough grazing
England	32,389	24,368	2,448
Wales	4,750	2,746	1,333
Scotland	19,070	4,786	9,148
Totals	56,209	31,900	12,929[a]

Note: [a] Rounding adjustment

Source: *Agricultural Statistics*

Whereas some 75 per cent of the English land area had been brought into cultivation, the Welsh percentage was only 58, more or less the British average. But Scotland had far less; only a quarter of its total area was cultivated, and the cultivated area was only just over half of the area of rough grazing. In fact, Scotland accounted for about 71 per cent of the total British rough grazing. Even the comparatively small area of Wales managed to account

10

for about 10 per cent of all British rough grazing. The high ratio of rough grazing in Scotland and Wales meant that England was more important to the farming industry than it warranted by mere size; occupying 58 per cent of the total British land area, it contributed 76 per cent of the area of cultivated land.

The uses to which farmers put this supply of cultivated land may be most conveniently pictured by imagining Britain divided into plots of 1,000 acres, each reflecting the average pattern of land use. To each hypothetical 1,000-acre farm is appended the average quantity of rough grazing available per 1,000 acres of cultivated land (Table 2.3).

Table 2.3: Farmland use in Britain, 1914 (acres)

Land use	England	Wales	Scotland
Permanent grass	577	500	311
Rotation grass & clover	94	343	312
Grain	223	118	248
Potatoes	18	9	32
Roots, cabbage, etc.	63	27	93
Miscellaneous	11	1	2
Bare fallow	14	2	2
Totals	1,000	1,000	1,000
Rough grazing	100	486	1,911

Source: *Agricultural Statistics*

From this, it is clear that the main crop grown in Britain was grass. In all three countries it occupied over 60 per cent of the cultivated area; in Wales it was over 80 per cent. This tendency to favour grass was dictated by soil and climate, but there were differences in the balance between permanent pasture and temporary grass in rotation. In England, a high proportion of grass was permanent; in Wales and Scotland, more grass had to be brought into a rotation in order to maintain its fertility.

Grass apart, grain was the main crop; mainly wheat and barley in England, and oats in Wales and Scotland. The small proportion of cultivated land devoted to grain in Wales is notable, as is the high proportion in Scotland. The other major crops were roots (turnips, mangolds, and swedes), mainly grown for animal feed and forming an essential part of the arable rotation, and potatoes and cabbages for human consumption.

11

Certain national differences were also apparent in the provision of livestock (Table 2.4).

Table 2.4: Animals on farms, 1914
(numbers per 1,000 acres of cultivated land)

	England	Wales	Scotland
Horses	40	49	38
Cattle	210	276	254
Sheep	560	1,314	1,468
Pigs	93	81	32

Source: *Agricultural Statistics*

The horse was the universal provider of cultivating power. About three-quarters of horses were engaged in farm work, the rest being either too young, too old, or retained for other purposes. Yet in reality farms were overstocked with horses; in England the average horse was only called on to plough and cultivate about twelve acres annually, and in Scotland some fifteen acres. However, depending on local conditions, a team of two horses should have been able to plough between 30 and 50 acres. This imbalance reflected the indivisibility of horses, small farms (especially in Wales), and the fact that a plough team usually consisted of two (or, in difficult conditions, three) horses.

Cattle were, in terms of time, effort and sale value, the most important animals on the farm. The predominance of permanent grass reflected this, as did the need to purchase large amounts of feed, either manufactured or as a by-product of brewing and distilling. The cattle industry also imported large numbers of young animals from Ireland. In England, many cattle were kept for milking, although the milk industry was also important in south Wales and south-west Scotland. As well as providing milk and meat, cattle permitted the production of manure, and were thus important in the grain regions of southern England as well as in the more purely dairying districts of the west and north of Britain.

Sheep were unevenly distributed. This reflected the uneven distribution of rough grazings, which allowed Welsh and Scottish farmers to maintain large flocks at low cost, even if the animals were usually smaller than their English counterparts. But sheep were an essential part of many English farming systems, such as the sheep and corn districts of the southern downlands, and large numbers grazed on the Yorkshire Wolds and the Cheviots.

The pig was perhaps the least regarded of farm animals. However, the annual agricultural statistics did not include holdings of less than one acre, and so omitted the large numbers kept by cottagers and labourers – perhaps about half a million, to add to the 2.6 million in the official statistics.[11] The pig was especially useful as an omnivore, putting on weight rapidly, and producing two litters per sow each year.

The use made of land by farmers was reflected in the structure of production. By 1914, there is no doubt that livestock dominated British farming. This might surprise the public, accustomed to seeing considerable fields of corn, but the explanation was that a large part of the cereals went for animal feed. The first census of production in 1908 had estimated that the market value of all crops grown was £125 million, but that only £47 million of this was actually sold off the 'national farm', representing only about a third of the total farm income of £155 million. A recalculation of average farm income in 1909–13 confirms the extent to which it depended on livestock rather than crops (Table 2.5).

Table 2.5: Gross farm income in Britain, 1909–13 average (£ million)

Crops		Livestock	
Cereals	16.6	Animals	63.9
Hay	16.1	Milk	23.8
Potatoes	9.4	Wool	5.2
Straw	5.7	Dairy	4.4
Fruit	4.6	Poultry	3.8
Vegetables	3.3	Eggs	3.4
Hops	2.3	Horses	2.8
Totals	58.0		107.3

Source: Appendix D

The importance of livestock and livestock products was a consequence of the rising living standards of the later nineteenth century. A smaller proportion of the national food bill went on cereals and potatoes, and more on meat and milk. The new element in the situation was the raising of large numbers of the working classes above subsistence, a process which may be said to have begun with the rise in real wages from the middle of the century. Between 1880 and 1910 meat consumption per head in the UK rose from 102 lb to 114 lb per year, and consumption of wheat flour fell from 280 lb to 211 lb. Thus the basic market demand for the most important foods was changing substantially. When it is added that British farmers were in a better position to compete against imported meat (usually of lower quality than the native article) than imported cereals, the bias towards livestock output becomes explicable.[12]

In order to acquire this income, farmers had to meet current expenses (Table 2.6).

Table 2.6: British current farm costs, 1909–13 average (£ million)

Fertilisers	4.1
Feedstuffs	20.4
Machinery	3.5
Rent	33.3
Wages	38.3
Irish livestock	6.8
Miscellaneous	8.1[a]
Total	114.5

Note: [a] Machinery and implement repairs, veterinary, farrier and blacksmithing costs

Source: Dewey, *EcHR* (1984), 376

The importance of wages was notable, accounting for about a third of current costs. The other outstanding cost was rent. This rent estimate does not include that of rough grazings; no pre-war figures for this are available, but the second census of agricultural production (1925) recorded that they rented for about one-seventh of the value of cultivated land. On that basis, the rent for rough grazings would have added £5 million to the pre-war rent bill.[13]

Rent and wages together accounted for slightly over 60 per cent of current costs. Their dominance had undoubtedly been greater in the early nineteenth century, when agriculturalists purchased little in the way of productive inputs from outside the agricultural industry. However, the middle of the century had seen the beginnings of a significant change, which was to become even more marked after 1918. This was, in F. M. L. Thompson's expression, the change from an 'extractive' industry to a 'manufacturing' one.[14] Whereas agriculture had traditionally been concerned with exploiting its own natural resources, these were now joined increasingly by purchased inputs from the industrial sector of the economy – chiefly feed, but also fertilisers and machinery. This change was to have substantial consequences during the war. In particular, it is notable that one of these purchased commodities, feedstuffs, was of much greater importance (in financial terms) than fertilisers or machinery. A large proportion of purchased feeds, in the form of oilcake, was either imported or made from imported materials, so that this large input was potentially vulnerable to the interruption of overseas supply.

The reliance on purchased feeds, and the importation of Irish livestock, reflected the basic livestock orientation of British agriculture. To some extent this was also true of fertiliser usage; the most popular fertiliser was superphosphate, which accounted for about half of the total fertiliser bill. Only about a quarter of it was used on the three main cereals; the rest went largely on roots, and grass for the production of hay.[15] Something under £1 million each went on sodium nitrate and ammonium sulphate (both mainly cereal fertilisers), and about £0.5 million on basic slag, which was predominantly a grassland and roots fertiliser.

The machinery bill was similar to that for fertilisers. This was not due to lack of mechanisation. Most British farms were comparatively highly mechanised, but this had taken place before the turn of the century, and so the demand for new machinery and implements was largely a replacement demand. In addition, machines had low physical depreciation rates. There was, however, an unknown amount paid annually on the repair of machinery and implements.

THE PRE-WAR FOOD SUPPLY

The relative decline of agriculture as a part of the national economy had been accompanied by a substantial decline in its role as a supplier of food to the nation. In 1913, consumers in the UK had spent £669 million on food. At least £216 million of this had been imported.[16] Although the general degree of reliance on imported supplies was realised, no attempt had been made before the war to work out the implications of this for the nourishment of the British population. This task was first performed by the Food (War) Committee of the Royal Society in 1916, when the full pattern of dependence on imports was revealed (Table 2.7).

Clearly, British consumers relied on imports for the greater part of their energy supply. These estimates were later criticised by

Table 2.7: UK home and foreign food supply, 1909–13 average (billion calories[b])

	Home	Imported	Total	Home %
Wheat	3.05	12.69	15.74	19
Other cereals	0.65	0.30	0.95	68
Beef & veal	2.38	1.12	3.50	68
Mutton & lamb	1.07	0.71	1.78	60
Bacon	0.48	1.36	1.84	26
Pigmeat	1.26	0.16	1.42	89
Poultry & game	0.06	0.02	0.08	75
Eggs	0.17	0.17	0.34	50
Milk	3.22	0	3.22	100
Butter	0.91	1.64	2.55	36
Cheese	0.12	0.46	0.58	21
Margarine	0.47	0.46	0.93	51
Lard[a]	0	0.80	0.80	0
Fruit	0.17	0.91	1.08	16
Potatoes	3.76	0.25	4.01	94
Vegetables	0.30	0.51	0.81	59
Sugar (refined)	0	6.13	6.13	0
Other sugar	0	0.50	0.50	0
Cottage produce	2.23	0	2.23	100
Totals	20.30	28.19	48.49	42

Notes: [a] Imported lard only [b] million × million

Source: Royal Society, *The Food Supply of the United Kingdom* (1917), Cd. 8421, PP 1916, IX, Appendix Ia

T. H. Middleton; he considered that the estimates for the home production of meat (beef and mutton), potatoes, and especially cottage produce, were too high, and that the total estimate of home production should be reduced by 1.8 billion calories. If this suggestion were to be adopted, then the proportion of the national energy supply derived from home sources would fall slightly, to 40 per cent. However, he did not give the basis on which he makes the largest correction, that of cottage produce, and so it seems reasonable to adhere to the Royal Society estimate.[17]

A purist calculation would also attempt to identify the extent to which the national food supply benefited from imports of animal feed and fertiliser. Middleton calculated that, taking account solely of imported feeds, the degree of self-sufficiency would have been reduced to as low as 34 per cent. Consideration of the contribution made by imported fertiliser would reduce this still further. But even confining the discussion to foods produced, by whatever means, in the UK, the unique position of the British consumer becomes apparent.[18]

The reliance on imports was most striking in the case of wheat and wheat flour. Four-fifths of the wheat and wheaten flour consumed came from overseas, and wheaten flour contributed almost a third of the entire energy supply of the nation. The importance of wheat was due to the fact that bread was still a large item in the working-class diet, and that the British had long since developed a taste for the wheaten loaf. The meat supply was still mainly a home affair, but imports supplied a third of the beef, two-fifths of the sheep meat, and three-quarters of the bacon consumed. Of the main meats, only pork was still essentially home-produced.

There were, in fact, few commodities which were still largely home-produced. Where technical considerations permitted, foreign competition was present. Butter and cheese had long since become dominated by produce from Holland and Denmark. The fruit market was heavily geared towards tropical and semi-tropical produce. Sugar was entirely imported, and was in itself a major source of energy in the national diet, contributing some 14 per cent of the total. Even eggs were split evenly between home produce and imports. Of the major foods, only milk remained entirely immune to foreign competition, due to the difficulties of preserving it in transit. Potatoes were still largely home-supplied, due to the sheer cost of transport.

An alternative way of assessing the contribution of home agriculture to the national diet is to consider its importance as a provider of the three main components of food – protein, fat, and carbohydrate. The proportions of these supplied by home farming in 1909–13 were 52, 54 and 34 per cent respectively. In comparison to imports, the foods produced in the UK were thus of rather higher quality, with a greater concentration on protein (especially animal), fat (especially from meat and milk), and rather less on carbohydrate. This difference is reflected in the greater proportion of calories derived from imports rather than home produce.[19]

Pre-war agriculture in Britain may be summed up as follows: although relatively diminished as a part of the national economy and as a contributor to the national diet, it was still a large industry, employing a large labour force and a considerable amount of capital. Its structure varied geographically, but it was essentially a livestock industry, having failed to meet foreign competition in the supply of cereals (especially wheat). It was comparatively large-scale, and operated on a unique system of landowner and tenant farmer.

Finally, farming was characterised by political neglect. In spite of the controversies attending the 1909 Budget, political decisions hardly affected the farming structure or the operational decisions of farmers. The framework for both of these had been laid down in the later nineteenth century, as foreign competition had been allowed to proceed unchecked by such political influence as the landed interest retained. Thereafter, government played little part in the daily workings of the agricultural system. When its influence was felt, it was rather directed towards the social relations within the industry rather than to the technical or economic conditions under which it operated.[20] Few people in 1914 thought that this general state of disinterest in the basic functions of agriculture would ever change perceptibly.

NOTES

1 *Census of Population* (1911), *General Report*, Cd. 8491 (1917), 113.

2 J. H. Clapham, *The Economic Development of France and Germany, 1815–1914* (Cambridge, 4th edn, 1936), 165 (the figure is for 1908).

3 S. G. Sturmey, 'Owner–farming in England and Wales, 1900–1950', in W. E. Minchinton (ed.), *Essays in Agrarian History* (Newton Abbot, 1968), vol. II, 287.

4 *Return of Owners of Land* (1874); J. Bateman, *Great Landowners of England and Wales* (4th edn, 1883), 51.

5 R. J. Thompson, 'An enquiry into the rent of agricultural land', in Minchinton, *Essays*, vol. II, 79.

6 Ibid., 80.

7 J. T. Ward, 'A study of capital and rental values of agricultural land in England and Wales between 1858 and 1958', unpublished Ph.D. thesis, University of London, 1960, 44.

8 G. C. Brodrick, *English Land and English Landlords* (1881), 80.

9 A. G. Street, *Farmer's Glory* (1932); M. K. Ashby, *Joseph Ashby of Tysoe 1859–1919: a study of English village life* (Cambridge, 1961).

10 Agricultural Wages Board, *Report of the committee appointed by the Agricultural Wages Board to enquire into the financial results of the occupation of rural land and the cost of living of rural workers* (1919), PP 1919, VIII, Cmd. 76, 62.

11 J. B. Guild, 'Variations in the numbers of live stock and in the production of meat in the United Kingdom during the war', *JRSS* (1920), LXXXIII, IV, 544.

12 J. T. Critchell and J. Raymond, *History of the Frozen Meat Trade* (1912),

320–2: J. C. Drummond and A. Wilbraham, *The Englishman's Food; a history of five centuries of English diet* (rev. edn, 1957), 430.

13 Ministry of Agriculture, *The Agricultural Output of England and Wales 1925* (1927), Cmd. 2815, PP 1927, XXV, 113–14.

14 F. M. L. Thompson, 'The second agricultural revolution', *EcHR* (1968), 125.

15 Middleton's estimate of pre-war UK consumption, in *Departmental Committee on the sulphuric acid and fertiliser trades* (1919), Cd. 29, PP 1919, XXIX, 14.

[Since it is not possible to separate satisfactorily UK food imports from British food imports, the next section uses UK data on imports, production, and consumption as a proxy for British data.]

16 A. R. Prest and A. A. Adams, *Consumers' Expenditure in the United Kingdom 1900–1919* (Cambridge, 1954), 74; Mitchell and Deane, *Abstract*, 300.

17 Middleton, *Food Production*, 87–89.

18 Ibid., 88, 90.

19 Royal Society, *The Food Supply of the United Kingdom*, Appendix Ia.

20 Notably the Agricultural Holdings Acts passed between 1875 and 1914; see also the essays by H. E. Dale and A. W. Ashby in *Agriculture in the Twentieth Century; essays . . . presented to Sir Daniel Hall* (1939).

Part I

1914–16:
BUSINESS AS USUAL

Chapter Three

THE EVOLUTION OF POLICY

The history of agricultural policy during the war falls into two parts: the period up to, and the period after, the formation of the Lloyd George coalition government in December 1916. Before then, it could be said that policy was essentially laissez-faire; afterwards, it was highly interventionist.

The laissez-faire cast of mind of the government in 1914–16 did not prevent it from considering the question of food supplies at an early stage in the war. This took the form of the appointment of two committees: the Cabinet Committee on Food Supplies, and an Agricultural Consultative Committee, composed of experts to advise the Board of Agriculture. The former, whose deliberations are somewhat obscure, concerned itself essentially with imported supplies, and with seeing that reasonable prices were maintained. This concern did not amount to an approval of a system of controlled prices; it was realised that to control prices of imports would lead to the diversion of supplies away from Britain, and thus a deterioration of the food supply position. While the level of imports remained favourable, the Committee had little concrete advice to offer, and although it survived until the creation of the Ministry of Food in December 1916, it seems to have had little effect on policy.[1]

The deliberations of the Agricultural Consultative Committee began early in the war, and were embodied in press releases for the guidance of farmers. The policy favoured is illustrated in the notice of 18 August 1914, which thought that farmers should do all in their power to increase the production of food, chiefly by increasing the area under wheat, or other cereals if appropriate. They should also consider the breaking up of grassland, after consultation between owner and tenant where necessary. At the same time, there should be no reduction in the number of livestock kept, the slaughter of immature or breeding stock should be avoided, and, if possible, animal numbers should be increased.[2]

The committee did not suggest that any inducements in further-ance of this aim should be offered, contenting itself with suggesting that its advice, if followed, 'might prove to the financial advantage' of the farmer. However, the question of offering a financial guarantee was raised in the House of Commons on 9 September, when Mr Hunt (a member of the committee) suggested that a guaranteed minimum price of 35s (£1.75) a quarter should be offered for all wheat suitable for bread reaped in 1915.[3] However, the government did not feel justified in holding out a financial inducement to farmers to increase their cereal area, or their stocks of cereals.[4]

With this decision, any possibility of an interventionist policy faded away for some months. This was not necessarily due to a slavish adherence to the tenets of laissez-faire. The government proved capable of intervening in a substantial way with the normal course of trade when necessity demanded. This was clearly so in the case of sugar, imports of which were disrupted early on in the war (about two-thirds of the pre-war sugar supply had come from Austria-Hungary). The Cabinet Committee on Food Supplies had created a Royal Commission on Sugar Supplies on 20 August 1914, which effectively took over the entire sugar trade, although the government had been buying large amounts of sugar in the East and West Indies from 7 August. Steps were also taken to secure the supply of meat for the Forces; the Board of Trade made large contracts with South American meat companies from 28 August, and in 1915 took steps to secure supplies from Australia and New Zealand. Finally, efforts were made to build up a reserve of wheat, and to control the Indian grain crop.[5]

In spite of the government's decision not to take any positive steps to safeguard food production, the fact that the war was not going to be over as quickly as had been hoped was always liable to re-open the question. Protagonists of an interventionist policy were encouraged by the formation of the first coalition government under Asquith in May 1915. The new President of the Board of Agriculture was Lord Selborne, who was an advocate both of increased food production and of giving farmers guaranteed prices for cereals. In furtherance of these aims, he appointed a departmental committee in June, to enquire into the steps which should be taken to increase home food production, assuming that the war would last beyond the harvest of 1916.[6]

The division of ministerial responsibility for agriculture meant that separate committees had to be appointed for Scotland and Ireland, but the most influential committee was going to be that of England, in view of the size of its agricultural area. Chairing the English committee was Lord Milner, who was generally in favour of an interventionist policy. Of the other seven members of the committee, four could be classed as pro-intervention, since they all eventually occupied positions of responsibility in the food production programme of 1917–19: R. E. Prothero (Lord Ernle), C. W. Fielding, E. G. Strutt and A. D. Hall. In the circumstances it is not surprising that the interim report of the committee, which appeared only one month after its appointment, was unanimous.[7]

The central conclusion of the Milner committee was that a 'plough policy' was called for:

the only method of effecting a substantial increase in the gross production of food in England and Wales for the harvest of 1916 and later consists in restoring to arable cultivation some of the poorer grass land that has been laid down since the 'seventies.

This theme was to be the central tenet of policy in 1917–18; strangely, the report did not attempt to prove this assertion, and assumed that it was obviously true. Following from this principle, certain lines of policy were recommended. The main one was to offer farmers a minimum price for wheat for several years; 45s a quarter for four years was suggested. Farmers would then receive deficiency payments amounting to the difference betwen 45s and the official 'Gazette' price. To meet the objection that this would reward farmers for growing wheat which they would have grown in any case, it was suggested that it would only be payable if they had either increased their arable land by at least a fifth since October 1913, or had at least a fifth of their grass and annual crop area under wheat. By this means it was also hoped that they would increase production on their existing arable area, secure a good crop on their additional arable, and be prevented from substituting wheat for other crops on their arable land. The committee were unsure whether it was desirable to fix a maximum price, but thought that if one was imposed, it should not be less than 55s a quarter.

The committee thus came down firmly in favour of an interventionist policy, but one working via the market, and not by
compulsion. It was realised that other aspects of the situation should
be addressed. Thus it was hoped that landlords would not refuse
consent to breaking up grassland, although the committee thought
that restrictive covenants on this affected mostly the better grassland
pre-dating the 1870s, and not the poorer grass laid down in the
ensuing depression. It was also hoped that landlords would not
raise rents, and that farmers would offer higher wages, but none of
these points were to be the subject of legislation. Finally, it was
proposed to set up county committees, which would offer farmers
guidance on which crops to grow.[8]

The recommendations of the English committee were not echoed
by the Scottish and Irish committees. The former rejected a guaranteed price for cereals, although advocating the formation of district
committees to provide the farmer with guidance, and a means for
bringing his needs for labour and other factors of production to the
attention of the government. The Irish committee, while supporting
the idea of an extension of tillage, committed itself to a guaranteed
price (unspecified) for only one year for wheat and oats. A minority
report recommended guaranteed prices for three years.

In retrospect, the Milner report prefigured almost all the elements
of what became official policy in 1917. But for the moment its
recommendations were declined. On 5 August, the day after the
Cabinet had debated the report, Asquith reported to the King that:
'Lord Selborne's proposal found little favour and will probably not
be discussed again'.[9] Explaining the decision at a meeting of farmers
and agricultural experts at the House of Lords on 26 August,
Selborne cited four reasons: a reduction in the danger from German
submarines, an increase in the world's cereal acreage, an anticipated
increase in enlistment of agricultural labourers, and the expense of
the proposed subsidy.[10] Selborne had to confine himself to an appeal
to farmers to increase production by converting their poorer grass
to arable.[11]

For the moment, the only concrete result was the adoption by
the Board of Agriculture of the system of county committees
suggested in the report. The functions of these War Agricultural
Committees (WACS) were to organise the supply of labour
(especially female), to consider how food production could best be
maintained or increased, and to report on shortages in the supply

of fertiliser, feed, machinery, and other supplies. Their establishment was not mandatory, nor were they to have executive powers, yet they were to be of great importance as the basis on which the county Executive Committees were to be formed in 1917.[12] For the time being, they served as rather unwieldy channels of communication for agricultural opinion between the counties and the Board of Agriculture. Intended to be representative of the opinions of landowners, farmers, and labourers, they tended to be dominated by farmers and county councillors. Thus the Lancashire committee, which in form was a sub-committee of the county Education Committee, had 70 members, of whom 20 were from the Education Committee, 5 were from the Royal Lancashire Agricultural Society, and 33 were co-opted members of farmers' associations and farmers' trading associations.

This unwieldiness was to some extent overcome by the formation of district committees; there were 12 in Lancashire, and they were used to conduct a survey of agricultural opinion on a variety of topics, the results being passed on to the Board of Agriculture.[13] The early history of the 84-member Cheshire WAC was similar; it appointed 10 district committees, which considered the general ways in which food production might be encouraged, and made specific suggestions on the use of female labour, the encouragement of allotments and pig-keeping, the cultivation of waste land, a census of steam tackle, the destruction of rats and vermin, and other subjects.[14]

The government's refusal to give a guarantee to arable farmers did not commend itself to the Milner committee, which produced its final report in October. This reiterated support for a permanent 'plough policy' after the war, while accepting that it was not desired at the moment. However, as two of the committee (Inchcape and Verney) correctly pointed out in a dissenting minority report, the majority was going outside the terms of reference, which had been concerned with wartime only.[15]

At central government level, the possibility of an interventionist policy was for the time ruled out. But Selborne was still committed to a plough policy, and sought to promote it indirectly. The September 1915 issue of the *Journal of the Board of Agriculture* contained two articles on British farming by senior civil servants at the Board, R. H. Rew and T. H. Middleton; both papers had been read at the annual meeting of the British Association for the Advancement of Science. While Rew's paper was a discursive impression of the course of prices and production since the war had begun, Middleton's was a didactic exercise in favour of a plough policy. After analysing the relative output of food (in energy terms) from different agricultural systems, he showed clearly that arable led the way, and concluded:

> The question that forces itself upon us in the middle of this long and exhausting war is this – can the nation any longer afford to neglect the development of the resources now lying intact in its unproductive grass land?[16]

This leading question came from an Assistant Secretary of the Board, and related to a question of policy which had recently been considered and rejected by the Cabinet. It can only be assumed that Selborne encouraged the publication of the article. Middleton was an appropriate choice, since he was also in favour of a plough policy. A memoir published by him in 1920 shows that he was consciously trying to influence policy in 1915:

> In September 1915, in a paper read before the Manchester Meeting of the British Association, I contrasted the effects which the adoption of different systems of farming had upon the nation's food supply, and from time to time thereafter I urged the importance of breaking up grass land; but though a plough policy was widely advocated in the autumn of 1915, no active steps to secure the ploughing up of grass land were taken.[17]

In the government, Selborne continued his efforts to get support for a plough policy. In February 1916 he was corresponding with R. E. Prothero, MP, with a view to using the latter's press contacts to stimulate a newspaper campaign in favour of the policy.[18] On 2 March he sought instructions from the War Committee (the sub-committee of the Cabinet dealing with the prosecution of the war) on whether to take measures to increase food production in 1917, on the assumption that the war would still be in progress. The chief reason for concern was not so much an actual shortage of wheat, but of shipping. If the committee thought action desirable, Selborne thought that 'a good deal' could be done to increase home production, using the good offices of the WACs, backed up by a price guarantee to farmers; he suggested 40s a quarter for wheat, guaranteed for four years after the end of the war. Alternatively, a food production policy backed up by powers of compulsion could be adopted.[19]

The subsequent debate is of interest in that the plans put forward by Selborne prefigured closely the policy which was eventually adopted by the Lloyd George coalition in December 1916. However, for the time being they came to nothing, largely due to political opposition within the War Committee, but partly due to the dilatory nature of policy-making in the Asquith coalition. Asked by the War Committee to present his plans in more detail, Selborne responded with a memorandum on 16 March. This gave two possible lines of approach. If no compulsory powers were to be used, then all that would be needed would be a guaranteed price for wheat, and assistance for farmers with extra labour. If compulsion were to be adopted, it would be necessary to take legal powers, establish a new branch of the Board of Agriculture and increase the funds at the disposal of the WACs. Then a rapid survey would be made of the area 'which could advantageously be ploughed'. Land could then be tilled, using extra supplies of labour (e.g., soldiers, Irish or Portuguese labourers) and machinery. Further questions would arise such as the need to compensate farmers for loss, and the impact of state intervention on agricultural wages.[20]

Selborne's proposals were discussed by the War Committee on 23 March. His only effective supporter was Lloyd George, and they could do little against the laissez-faire members (McKenna at the Treasury, Runciman at the Board of Trade, and Arthur Balfour at the Admiralty). Particular outrage was expressed by Balfour at the suggestion that compulsory powers to enforce tillage might be adopted: 'Mr. Balfour thought that the proposals under Part I (of Lord Selborne's memorandum) were the wildest things ever proposed. It would be better to take over the land, and run it on socialistic principles.'

Apart from the question of compulsion, there were other considerations, which damaged Selborne's case. In particular, the question of whether the proposals were only for wartime, or were intended as a permanent policy confused the issue. Apart from that, the opposition of the Chancellor of the Exchequer and the President of the Board of Trade, who would have to find the necessary public funds and shipping, was fatal to his case. However, he seems to have been easily silenced, and did not even make the obvious point that the programme would save shipping space and foreign exchange.[21]

The discussion of 23 March was adjourned due to lack of time, and was not resumed for two months. By then the situation had changed considerably. During that time, much of Asquith's attention was on the aftermath of the Easter Rising in Dublin. It was not until the end of May that the discussion was resumed in the War Committee. This delay was galling for Selborne, who was more than ever convinced that a plough policy was required. Indeed, he had become convinced by May that a permanent plough policy was needed, since, in his view, the current war would not be the last conflict with Germany, and in future Britain would have to become more self-sufficient in food on military grounds.[22]

The ensuing correspondence provided a striking illustration of the ability of Asquith's government to procrastinate. It began with a letter to Bonar Law from Selborne (8 May), asking for the War Committee to instruct him on what to do about the 1917 harvest, since he had asked for instructions on 2 March, and had not received any. Law passed the request on to Hankey, the secretary of the War Committee, who wrote to Selborne on 15 March, enquiring innocently whether the subject was concerned with the buying of Australian wheat. This called forth a reply from Selborne which was a model of grim self-restraint. He reiterated the demand for instructions:

> I simply wish to know where I stand. Ten weeks have passed since I asked my question, and every day which passes makes it more difficult to do anything effectually supposing that the War Cabinet [sic] decided that something ought to be done . . .[23]

The correspondence ended with Hankey's reply, which was that he had asked Asquith whether the matter should be put on the agenda of the War Committee again, and Asquith had replied: 'not at present'. When Asquith should return from Ireland, Hankey promised to bring the matter to his attention.[24]

By the time that the discussion was resumed in the War Committee on 26 May, the situation had changed; the submarine danger appeared for the moment to have receded, stocks of wheat had remained stable for the past two months, and in any case it could be argued that the lapse of time precluded a policy for 1917.

Thus the committee decided not to pursue any further the idea of an interventionist policy.[25]

In June, Selborne resigned from the government, as a result of his disagreement with its Irish policy. However, he was to make a further contribution to the promotion of a plough policy. Whilst in office, he had asked Middleton to prepare a pamphlet on the relative food-producing capacities of Britain and Germany. This appeared on 1 June, with a foreword by Selborne. In it, Middleton had no great difficulty in showing that German agriculture contributed a much higher proportion of the nation's energy supply than did the British (90 per cent, as opposed to 40 per cent), that a much larger number of people were fed in Germany per unit of cultivated land than in Britain (70–75 persons per 100 acres, compared to 40–45), and that this was due to the higher proportion of arable land in Germany. Thus: 'The clear lesson which we may learn, if we wish to learn, from German experience, is that if we desire to make any considerable addition to our home-grown supplies of food we must as a nation adopt the old farming motto "Speed the Plough".'[26]

The sudden volte-face in policy, from laissez-faire to intervention, came in response to a sharp deterioration in food prospects in the summer and autumn of 1916. The greatest threat was the comparative failure of the North American wheat harvest. Just as the good harvest of 1915 had averted intervention, so the poor harvest of 1916 stimulated the interventionist case anew. Whereas in 1910–14 the average combined wheat harvest of the USA and Canada had been 25.1 million tonnes, it reached 39.5 million in 1915, but fell back to 24.5 million in 1916.[27] This threat was the greater since these countries had before the war supplied over half of British imported wheat, by a shorter journey than that from India or Australia, thus taking less of the increasingly scarce shipping space. However, the harvest in North America could only be said to be poor in comparison with the exceptional yield of 1915; a point which seems to have escaped attention at the time.[28]

There were other threats to the food supply. In particular, imports of sugar had fallen substantially from their pre-war level, in spite of the attempts made by the Sugar Commission to replace European by Caribbean sugar. In 1909–13 the average import of refined and unrefined sugar (cane and beet) had been on average 36.3 million hundredweight; in 1915 it had fallen to 29.6 million, and was only very slightly higher in 1916 – 30.7 million.[29] The shortage of sugar was of particular importance in view of its pre-war contribution to the national supply of energy.[30] A decline in the supply of sugar of about one-sixth was a serious matter, especially if there was little prospect of the supply reviving. At home, the 1916 potato crop gave cause for concern. The Scottish crop was a disaster, being only slightly more than half of the pre-war (1909–13) average. This largely accounted for the fact that the British crop was down by 16 per ceent in total.[31] As in the case of sugar, potatoes were an important source of energy in the national diet, and provided calories even more cheaply.

Underlying these supply considerations were others. In particular, the shipping situation was deteriorating from September, and in October the Germans intensified their (still restricted) submarine campaign, and the rate of tonnage loss rose sharply.[32] Finally, the rate of inflation, which showed no signs of abating, was causing continued political concern.

Initial reaction by the government was directed to importing problems. On 9 October, it took over responsibility for the importation of wheat, in the form of the Royal Commission on the Wheat Supply, headed by Lord Crawford, who was Selborne's successor at the Board of Agriculture. At the end of October, Crawford prepared for the War Committee a memorandum on food supplies, outlining the increasingly gloomy situation, which was largely due to the shipping problems. Even at this stage, however, he does not seem to have contemplated a food production policy, merely hinting that: 'It might be desirable to establish some central food department to supervise and coordinate the varied relations of the State with the import, purchase and distribution of food . . .'[33]

Crawford was in fact suggesting the appointment of a 'food controller', to supervise distribution rather than production. The call for a Food Controller was taken up by Lloyd George in a memorandum of 10 November. He also suggested that the food controller should direct his attention to the promotion of home production, increasing the acreage devoted to cereals, potatoes, and vegetables. This was the first time production of food at home had formed the subject of War Committee discussion since Selborne's failure in May, and Crawford concurred in the suggestion. However, in the ensuing lively discussion it was lost sight of, and the final conclusion of the meeting only referred to the approval of the appointment of a Food Controller, subject to the right man being found: 'to control the great organisation contemplated'.[34]

The search for a Food Controller had a higher priority in the War Committee than the need to increase food production. Apart from this, the coalition was on the verge of breaking up, and this increased the existing tendency to indecision. However, the basis for an interventionist policy was already being worked out within the Board of Agriculture. In November, Middleton prepared a memorandum for Crawford, emphasising the changes in the situation, and proposing an immediate effort to enlarge the area under oats and potatoes (these being the only products whose increase was feasible for 1917), and preparation for the 1918 harvest at once.[35]

In spite of the Middleton memorandum, little in the way of an interventionist policy emerged from the War Committee during its last days, although Crawford made a half-hearted attempt to put the Board of Agriculture view. On 24 November, the Committee was still discussing the appointment of a Food Controller, with no result. Two decisions, however, were taken concerning food production. On the initiative of the War Office, it was agreed to give Irish farmers a guaranteed price for oats, to stimulate production for the use of Army horses, and the Ministry of Munitions was authorised to begin producing agricultural machinery. Crawford attempted to argue that having guaranteed oats prices for Irish farmers, then the same guarantee should be given to Scottish farmers, and to English farmers for wheat. His intervention was unsuccessful.[36]

Crawford did make a last attempt to develop some form of interventionist policy, but it was on a small scale and rather half-hearted. He began by writing to the Chancellor of the Exchequer (McKenna), stating that he hoped shortly to be able to mount 'an extensive campaign for increasing our home-grown food supply', that he had been in negotiation with the War Office for many weeks to retain enough labour on the land, and that to develop the programme, he would need a grant of money; he could not specify the precise amount, but was anxious to be authorised to spend 'a considerable sum'.[37] This vague request was fleshed out shortly afterwards by the Board to a sum of £50,000 for staffing, agricultural machinery, fertiliser and seeds, the promotion of allotments, and extra farm labour.[38] The Treasury turned down this request, being particularly agitated about the need to import machinery, and thus incur foreign exchange liabilities. It also desired a more detailed analysis of the purpose for which the money was required. Nothing daunted, Crawford constructed a draft list on a much larger scale, amounting to £856,000 (of which £400,000 was for imported machinery). Whether this represented a realistic programme, or was, as the Permanent Secretary to the Board of Agriculture put it, 'an estimate with a sufficiency of specious details', is unclear. In any case, it had been overtaken by events. The political crisis which had been rumbling on since the end of November had come to an end on the evening of 7 December, when Lloyd George kissed hands as Prime Minister. This was to be the signal for a full-scale food production policy. The incoming President of the Board of Agriculture was R. E. Prothero, who was committed whole-heartedly to a plough policy. On 15 December he added a minute to Crawford's file on food production: 'Forward to me in a week when matters may have developed further.'[39]

NOTES

1 L. M. Barnett, *British Food Policy during the First World War* (1985), 20–3.
2 Ibid., 104–5.
3 The 1909–13 average price had been 33s 4d, and the 1914 price was 34s 11d; *Statistical Abstract for the United Kingdom 1905–1919*, (1921), 310–11.
4 House of Commons Debates, 9 September 1914.
5 (Sir) W. H. Beveridge, *British Food Control* (1928), 6, 10–15.
6 *Interim Report of the Departmental Committee appointed by the President of the Board of Agriculture and Fisheries to consider the Production of Food in England and Wales* (1915), Cd. 8048, PP 1914–16, V.
7 But see Barnett's comments (51) on some of the difficulties in getting unanimity.
8 Milner Committee, Cd. 8048, paras. 4–16.
9 Asquith to the King, 5 August 1915, CAB 41/36/37.
10 'Lord Selborne's food supply meeting', *JBA*, September 1915, 489–503. On the reasons for declining a guarantee, see Barnett, *Food Policy*, 52–60.
11 'Lord Selborne's Appeal, 28th September 1915', *JBA*, October 1915, 571.
12 Middleton, *Food Production*, 137, 167.
13 Lancashire Record Office, WAM/1, Minutes of the War Agricultural Committee, 4 Oct. 1915–31 Jan. 1916.
14 Cheshire Record Office; *County War Agricultural Committee; Review of*

work of the above Committee from date of appointment to 30th June 1918
(1918), 1–2.
15 Milner Committee, *Final Report*, Cd. 8095 (1915), PP 1914–16, V,
paras. 2–5, 11.
16 T. H. Middleton, 'Systems of farming and the production of food –
the need for more tillage', *JBA*, September 1915, 520–33.
17 T. H. Middleton, 'Farming of the United Kingdom in peace and in
war: the plough policy and its results', *Journal of the University College of
Wales, Agricultural Department*, IX (1920), 10.
18 Selborne Papers; Selborne to Prothero, 7 Feb. 1916.
19 CAB 42/10, G-60, 'Food Supply and Production; Note by the Earl of
Selborne'.
20 CAB 42/11, G-65, 'The Food Supply of the United Kingdom.
Memorandum by the Earl of Selborne', 1–5.
21 CAB 42/11/9, 79th War Committee meeting, 23 March 1916, 17–21.
22 Selborne Papers 83; Selborne to Vaughan Nash, 15 May 1916.
23 Selborne Papers, 80/167.
24 Ibid.
25 Barnett, *Food Policy*, 64–5.
26 T. H. Middleton, *The Recent Development of German Agriculture* (Board
of Agriculture, Cd. 8305, 1916), 6, 44.
27 Middleton, *Food Production*, 160.
28 The same point applies to comparisons made of the British cereal crop
in 1916 and 1915 – see Crawford's memo of 30 October 1916, CAB 42/
22, G-91, 1.
29 *Statistical Abstract* (1921), 132–3.
30 See above, p. 17.
31 Ministry of Agriculture, *A Century of Agricultural Statistics*; *Great Britain
1866–1966* (1968), 114–15.
32 A. Salter, *Allied Shipping Control* (1923), 328.
33 CAB 42/22/12, G-91, 'Food prospects in 1917', 30 October 1916.
34 Ibid.; CAB 42/24, G-95, 'Food Supplies. Proposals by the Secretary
of State for War', Minutes of War Committee meeting 13 November
1916.
35 Middleton, *Food Production*, 162.
36 CAB 42/25, War Committee minutes, 24 November 1916, 14.
37 MAF 42/11, L. 32316/1916, Crawford to McKenna, 27 November and
1 December 1916.
38 Ibid.; Olivier to Treasury, 4 December 1916.
39 Ibid.; memorandum by Olivier, 8 December 1916; L. 32645/1916,
memorandum by Olivier, 8 December 1916; Crawford to Olivier, 8
December 1916; minute by R. E. P., 15 December 1916.

Chapter Four

RECRUITING AND FARM LABOUR

The maintenance of the supply of labour was essential for the agricultural industry to maintain the pre-war level of output. Before we assess the evidence on the course of labour supply during the war, we may put it in perspective by looking at the supply of labour prior to 1914.

There are two sources of information on the pre-war labour supply. These are the 1908 *Census of Production* and the 1911 *Census of Population*. These give different results, partly because they covered different populations, and partly because they analysed their data differently. The 1911 census was based on occupation, so that persons not considering themselves as principally employed in agriculture were self-excluded. The 1908 census included all persons engaged on agricultural holdings (above one acre), whether working full- or part-time, and whether engaged on holdings run by a full-time or a part-time 'farmer'. The differences between the two surveys are apparent from Tables 4.1 and 4.2.[1]

In assessing the utility of these estimates, it may be said that the 1908 census represents a maximum, and the 1911 census a minimum estimate of the pre-war labour supply. The sources of over-estimate in 1908 are the large number of occupiers (some 200,000 more than the number of farmers returned in 1911), and the very high numbers of relatives. However, there is broad agreement that the most important single category of labour is the non-family male labourer.

Broadly, therefore, the industry was run before the war by well over a million persons, working about 300,000 farms. The core of the labour force was the 250,000 or so full-time male farmers, and about 700,000 full-time hired men. But there were also a large,

Table 4.1: Farm population of Britain at 1908 census of production ('000)

	Male	Female	Total
'Occupiers'[a]	508	–	508
Permanent family labour	313	189	502
Other permanent labour	576	95	671
Temporary labour	127	40	167
Totals	1,524	324	1,848

Note: [a] No sexual classification in the census; occupiers are here assumed to be all male.

Source: *1908 Census*, Cd. 6277, 16

Table 4.2: Farm population of Britain at 1911 census of population ('000)

	Male	Female	Total
Farmers, graziers, etc.	258	32	290
Relatives	109	63	172
Others	753	28	781
Totals	1,120	123	1,243

Source: *1911 Census of Population*

unknown number of part-time holdings, largely run by the labour of the occupier and his family.

Some idea of the distribution of tasks in the labour force before the war is gained from the 1911 census (Table 4.3).

Table 4.3: Occupation of male farm workers, 1911[2]

Farmers[a]	252,727
Relatives	114,316
Foremen[b]	29,391
Shepherds	29,879
Cattlemen	82,900
Horsemen	163,596
'Ordinary' labourers	447,323
Total	1,120,132

Notes: [a] Including graziers and (in Scotland) crofters
[b] Including bailiffs and (in Scotland) grieves

Source: *1911 Census of Population*

Specialisation of function was a feature of farms with hired labour, especially the larger farms in the south and east of England; elsewhere, the hired man might, like the Northumbrian hind or the Scottish farm servant, be more versatile. On the smaller farms without a hired labour force, men turned their hands to a variety of tasks.

In the hired labour force, the broad distinction was between men in charge of animals, and the 'ordinary' labourers not so distinguished. Cattlemen, horsemen, and shepherds were more highly paid than ordinary labourers, but worked longer hours (and on Sundays), feeding, cleaning, and tending their animals. Horsemen were something of an aristocracy, since their work was particularly demanding in terms of skill and physique; as well as looking after the horses they worked them in the fields and around the farm, in ploughing, cultivating, harvesting, and carting. The ordinary labourer was often referred to as unskilled, but that was erroneous, since his skills lay in a variety of tasks, from the field to the barn. Apart from lack of responsibility for animals, his distinguishing features were shorter, less flexible hours of work and lower pay than the other labourers.

During the first two years of the war, agricultural labour was vulnerable to the demands of the armed forces. Until the passing of the first Military Service Act in January 1916, recruiting was voluntary. Thus there was in theory no barrier to farm workers joining the forces. Like other workers, they were not immune to the call of patriotic feeling. Nor, since they were comparatively lowly paid, was there a financial disincentive to joining the forces; the existence of separation allowances for soldiers' and sailors' dependants ensured this. Nor did agricultural workers enjoy the steep rise in earnings which occurred in such sectors as engineering and chemicals, or high wages such as in the expanding munitions industries. Thus farm workers probably had more incentive to enlist than other groups of workers.[3]

That farm workers enlisted in very large numbers in the first two years of the war is well enshrined in the opinions of contemporaries and historians. Most authorities concur in stating that agriculture had by the end of 1916 lost between a quarter and a third of its labour force, although the rate of loss slowed appreciably for the remainder of the war. We shall later question the basis of these opinions. But it is worth noting at this stage that farm labour was not completely unprotected during the first half of the war, and the authorities gradually imposed restrictions on recruitment.[4] As early as May 1915, the War Office instructed recruiting officers not to accept skilled farm workers. This covered working bailiffs or foremen, head carters, horsemen and stockmen, waggoners, shepherds, and 'necessary' milkers. This might have given some protection, but it is noticeable that 'ordinary' labourers are not mentioned, and in any case, recruiting officers did not always follow these instructions.

The next stage came after the compilation of the National Register (a survey of the national labour force) in the autumn of 1915, which 'starred' workers considered indispensable as civilians. Certain farm workers were now to be 'starred'. The main ones were working bailiffs, shepherds, stockmen (including milkers), and horsemen. In addition, ancillary labourers such as thatchers, engine drivers, machinery mechanics, steam plough and threshing machine operatives were protected. This list seems to cover the skilled workers (although it is not clear whether waggoners and carters were still protected), but the 'ordinary' labourer is again omitted.

The final phase in the voluntary period was that of the Derby scheme. Under this, farm workers already 'starred' under the National Register scheme, or on the list of reserved occupations which had been prepared at the same time, would not be accepted for the forces. Although they could 'attest' their willingness to serve, they would be passed into the reserve, and stay in their occupations. Thus the skilled men continued to be protected. Although farmers, in common with other employers, had not been 'starred', they were urged by the Board of Agriculture to attest rather than enlist. 'Starring' would cease to apply for any man who left farming for other employment.

The Derby scheme was a failure, and conscription, in the form of the first Military Service Act followed. Operative from 2 March 1916, it applied to single men aged 18–41, who were now deemed to have attested, and passed into the reserve, even if they had not originally done so. The corollary of conscription was the promulgation of a list of 'certified occupations'; a necessary proviso if conscription was not to sweep away important civilian workers indiscriminately. The agricultural workers on the list were essentially those already starred or in reserved occupations, but with the important addition of farmers. The final list included all the types of labour recognised as skilled in Britain (including Scottish farm servants and hinds, if they were foremen or ploughmen). The two types omitted were farmers' relatives (unless they were covered in respect of their existing function) and ordinary labours (those not in charge of animals). In addition, ancillary machine operatives and mechanics were exempt.[5]

Thus some degree of protection was evolving in the period of voluntary recruiting. How much effect this had on the tendency of farm workers to enlist is uncertain. The official view was that recruiting losses had been considerable. The Director-General of Recruiting (Lord Derby) stated that England and Wales had by January 1917 lost some 180,000 men to the armed forces; this estimate was based on a survey by the War Office in December 1916. The Board of Trade estimated at the same time that 216,000 had left agriculture in Britain, either to join the forces or for some other reason.[6] A later estimate from the Ministry of National Service was that 273,000 men had left agriculture for the forces or for munitions work by April 1918.[7] The largest estimate came from the Board of Agriculture in October 1916; working from surveys by the Board of Trade, it calculated that some 350,000 men had left agriculture in England and Wales since the start of the war.[8]

In spite of the fairly wide differences in these estimates, they all agreed that the loss of labour was very serious. Both the pre-war censuses of population and production had indicated that the permanent male hired labour force in Britain was about 700,000–750,000 (farmers excluded), so that the lowest of the official estimates implied a loss of male labour of c. 23 per cent, the highest a loss of c. 45 per cent – both occurring about two years from the start of the war.

The idea that agriculture suffered such a serious loss of labour firmly entered into history after the war with the writings of Lord Ernle (R. E. Prothero) and others. Ernle, the President of the Board of Agriculture in the Lloyd George coalition from its formation in December 1916 until 1919, wrote in his history of English farming that, by the winter of 1916–17, '250,000 of the pre-war rural population of England and Wales' had gone into the Army. He later wrote that, again by the winter of 1916–17, 'one-third of the skilled men' had joined the forces – presumably also from England and Wales, although the area was not specified.[9] T. H. Middleton, who was the first Director-General of the Food Production Department, wrote later that the loss of labour was the 273,000 estimated by the Ministry of National Service.[10] The only other contemporary estimate was that of A. W. Ashby, who thought that 243,000 men had enlisted from agriculture up to July 1918.[11] These estimates by contemporary writers were broadly accepted by historians. Thus K. A. H. Murray, in his official history of agriculture during the Second World War, reviewed the events of 1914–18, and wrote: 'Ultimately one third of the regular male workers had left the land – for which the substitution of prisoner-of-war and female labour did not compensate'.[12] It would seem that Murray was following Ernle in his estimate of labour loss, although the rider about the inadequacy of replacement labour appears to be his own. More recently, E. H. Whetham has written that: 'about 300,000 agricultural workers in England and Wales joined the services in the four years of war, compared with a total of about 1¼ million men engaged as employers or employees in agriculture in 1911'.[13]

The fact that eminent contemporaries came to similar conclusions may obscure the fact that their opinions were based on shaky foundations. The apparent precision of such statements is misleading; the government had no means of knowing precisely how many men had left agriculture. There was no mechanism for counting men as they left for the forces, and the Director-General of Recruiting (Lord Derby) admitted this.[14]

The lack of any mechanism which would take a tally of men as they moved from industries to the forces, or to other industries, was a general problem for the government. In the early days of the war, faced with an unprecedentedly large demand for men for military service, it was realised that some effort to monitor such large flows of labour was required. In default of a head count, the government did the next best thing; it initiated a regular sample survey whose aim was to monitor the flow of men from civilian industries (including agriculture) to the forces. The task was performed by a section of the Board of Trade, the War Enquiries Branch, which seems to have been set up for this purpose. The method adopted was to send letters to a large number of employers, asking for details of their labour force, as compared with July 1914. These letters were sent every three months. Having received replies from employers in a particular industry, the current employee numbers were added up, and expressed as a percentage of the total pre-war labour force of those employers. This percentage was then applied to the labour force of each industry, using as a basis the total labour force recorded at the pre-war *Census of Production* (1907/8). The final result was an estimate of the number of employees in each industry who had enlisted since the outbreak of war. In all, the survey was conducted 19 times; 18 reports were prepared, and all but one have survived.[15]

The significance of the Board of Trade reports (usually referred to as the 'Z8' reports, after the code number of the War Enquiries Branch) is that they form almost the only quantitative evidence – and certainly the only regular evidence on any large scale – as to the impact of military recruiting on British industries. They have usually formed the basis for statements by historians on such matters as losses to the forces, and wartime contraction or expansion of individual industries. Yet it is not usually appreciated that such statements rest on a series of sample surveys, and that the degree of success in sampling varied greatly between different industries.[16]

In the case of agriculture, the relative size of the sample was very small. While in other industries it was usual for at least 10 per cent of the employers to be sampled, the proportion of farmers sampled in England and Wales remained between 1 and 2 per cent throughout the war. In Scotland the percentage was higher, being 4–6 per cent. While little information on how the sample was derived is available, one report mentions that the 'larger' farmer was sampled in Scotland. This is certainly the case, since the average farm size of employers in the Scottish sample was around 500 acres. In England and Wales the average size was around 340 acres. Clearly both are much above the average farm size, the British average before the war being about 60 acres. The disparity between the British average and the sample is so large that it would be tempting to hazard a guess as to the sampling method adopted. Such speculation may be inherently fruitless, but it may be relevant to point out that the annual Agricultural Returns classified holdings over one acre in size, and that the highest category was 'over 300 acres'. There were before the war some 18,000 holdings in that category in Britain, and the names and addresses of the occupiers would have been readily available to the Z8 branch of the Board of Trade from the Board of Agriculture. Did the sample consist of this category alone? Such a procedure would certainly commend itself on the grounds of administrative expediency. It would have had the additional advantage of accounting for a large proportion of the labour force with the minimum of effort; whereas the average agricultural holding in 1908 employed less than two permanent male labourers, the holdings in the sample (in England and Wales) employed over nine each. Whatever the basis of the sample, it meant that the statements as to recruiting from agriculture were based on replies from about 6,000 farmers, compared with the 0.29 million in the 1911 population census or the 0.5 million holdings above one acre recorded in the 1908 census of production.[17]

There is abundant evidence that the work of the Z8 department provided the basis for the statements on the degree of labour loss in agriculture which have been noted above.[18] The surveys show an increasing degree of labour shortage in the first two years of the war, reaching a peak in early 1917, and thereafter remaining almost unchanged. By July 1916, the surveys recorded an enlistment loss of 30.6 per cent of the permanent male labour force. Applied to a base for July 1914 of 800,000 men (derived from the data in the 1908 *Census of Agricultural Production*), the result was a loss of 245,000, which is very close to the figures put forward by contemporaries such as Ernle. However, this loss was to some extent offset by drawing fresh labour into farming, which reduced the loss to 22.2 per cent.

The pattern of labour loss shown by the Z8 surveys for the first two years of the war is shown in Table 4.4.[19]

Table 4.4: Board of Trade 'Z8' survey of agricultural employment, 1914–16

| | Permanent labour | | Temporary labour | |
	Male	Female	Male	Female
July 1914 ('000)	800	80	120	50
Per cent change:				
1915				
April	−14	−17	−31	−12
July	−12	− 5	−22	+11
Oct.	−16	−15	− 3	+56
1916				
Jan.	−20	−26	×	×
April	−23	− 3	−61	−29
July	−22	+33	−11	+80
Oct.	−27	+ 1	×	×
1917				
Jan.	−30	−18	×	×

× = unknown

Source: Board of Trade, *Report on the State of Employment* . . . (1914–17)

The January 1917 employment (and recruitment) loss was the highest recorded in the surveys, which show the labour force thereafter as almost static; the average employment of permanent male labour in 1917 and 1918 was 28 per cent and 27 per cent below that of July 1914.

In spite of the fact that the results of the Z8 surveys have been accepted by historians, they are inherently implausible. Firstly, they were clearly directed at the exceptionally large farm, with a very large hired labour force, and are thus not representative of the labour force (or farms) as a whole. Secondly, the notion that the labour force in agriculture fell by about a third cannot be accepted without also asking whether it had noticeable effects on agricultural output. This was not a question which contemporaries raised. But estimates in the present work (chapter 14) suggest that, whatever the actual size of the labour shortage, it had little effect *per se* on output. Thus, even without considering the shortcomings of the sampling procedure of the surveys, their conclusions should be treated with caution. Finally, the surveys expressly excluded farmers and their relatives, who formed a large minority of the pre-war labour force.[20]

Regardless of the shortcomings of the surveys, they may be used in order to obtain a better idea of the degree of labour shortage in agriculture during the war. This may be done by adopting the survey results in respect of the hired labour force (which was the population covered), and making certain assumptions about the propensity of the rest of the labour force to be recruited into the forces or to leave for other industries.

Farmers may be regarded as almost unrecruitable; whereas cases of farmers joining the forces did occur, the number of agricultural holdings remained almost unchanged during the war.[21] It is unlikely that this camouflaged an exodus of farmers to the forces and the maintenance of their farms by their wives and other relations; most British farms were rather too big for this to happen. The rapid rise in farm profits in any case provided a strong incentive to stay in business.[22] It can therefore be assumed that the male farmer population remained the same during the war.

The male members of the farm family must also have been less vulnerable than hired labour to recruiting and the lure of alternative employment. As one descended the farm size scale they became increasingly important, the smaller holdings having too low a marginal labour product to permit the payment of wages to hired labour. Thus family pressure would constrain those wishing to enlist. In addition, there was the need to help the family enterprise at a difficult time, and possibly the lure of eventual inheritance. This is not to say that some relatives did not join the forces, perhaps to escape tedious work, to seek excitement, or from patriotic feeling. That some did so is certain, but they have left few traces of their passage. We propose to rate the liability of family males to enlistment as half of the rate recorded in the surveys for hired labour. For female relatives, we have calculated changes in proportion to the losses of permanent female labour recorded in the Z8 reports, in default of other information.

Apart from the native labour, there was the special case of Irish migrant labourers. These were usually present in England and Scotland for about six months from spring to autumn. During the first two years of the war, their numbers were maintained. Thereafter, political difficulties in the aftermath of the Easter Rising, and the fear of conscription, seem to have effectively cut off the flow.[23] In addition, farmers who had perhaps had their sons conscripted resented the Irishman's immunity to military service.[24]

Having allowed for the different experiences of the main components of the labour force there are two further problems: the selection of a suitable pre-war base, and the measurement of the labour force in a common unit. The most suitable pre-war base is that supplied by the 1908 *Census of Production*, which, although giving a high estimate of the labour force, has the advantage of analysing it by family allegiance, age, sex, and whether permanent or temporary (i.e., seasonal). The unit of measurement ('man-unit') will be the adult male, types of labour being rated as:[25]

Male 20+ yrs = 1.0   Female 20+ yrs = 0.8
Male −20 yrs = 0.6   Female −20 yrs = 0.5

The only remaining problem is to determine the length of the working year of casual labour ('temporary' in the Z8 reports). The periods which saw the greatest activity were the hay and corn harvests, root thinning and hoeing, root and potato lifting, and hop and fruit picking. Since the time taken by these tasks was about three months, we may rate the casuals at a quarter of the permanent labour. Since the length of the Irish casuals' working year was about six months, we shall rate Irish labour at half that of permanent English labour. These ratios have been applied to the result of the Z8 surveys for juvenile, female, and casual labour.

The resulting estimate of labour supply in 1914–16 shows that, when account is taken of the whole labour force, and not just the hired man, the overall supply of labour fell in 1915 by some 7 per cent, and by 11 per cent in 1916 as compared with the pre-war level.[26] These figures should not mislead by a spurious precision; there are many elements of uncertainty in the calculation. In broad terms, it would be more acceptable to say that labour by the end of 1916 was deficient by about one-tenth, rather than by the one-third which has been traditionally assumed.

Given that (as we have assumed) some important elements in the labour force (farmers and male family members) were not as liable to recruitment as the hired male, and given that the female labour force was of some importance in the total supply, it seems that labour supply was not drastically impaired by the demands of the forces and of non-agricultural industries in the first two years of the war. Even so, the losses of 'permanent' adult males must have been large in themselves; our estimate here is that their numbers had fallen by the middle of the war by some 107,000, and the supply of juvenile males (under 18) by 16,000.

What can be said about the types of labour leaving agriculture? Patriotic feeling apart, the main factor was the age-grouping of the components of the labour force (Table 4.5).

Table 4.5: Male farm workers aged 18–44 in 1911

	Nos.	%
Farmers[a]	96,187	38.0
Relatives	78,747	68.9
Foremen[b]	15,581	53.0
Shepherds	15,529	52.0
Cattlemen	46,961	56.6
Horsemen	113,614	69.4
Ordinary labourers	215,058	48.1
Total	581,677	51.9

Notes: [a] Including crofters
[b] Including grieves and bailiffs[27]

Source: *1911 Census of Population*

Given that farmers on the whole did not enlist, and confining the discussion to hired men, horsemen stand out as the most liable to recruitment by reason of age. Since they were also the strongest and generally recognised to be the fittest physically, their propensity to enlistment was probably very high.[28] Cattlemen and shepherds were less liable to recruitment due to age, and the ordinary labourer the least of all. Yet, if the increasing degree of protection afforded in 1915–16 was effective, the skilled groups were less liable to recruitment as time went on. The ordinary labourer, although proportionately less liable to enlistment by reason of age, was unprotected. Since he was also the lowest paid of all, the lure of separation allowances may have acted as a spur. What can be said is that, in absolute numbers, the bulk of recruits up to the end of 1916 were likely to have been drawn from the ranks of the ordinary labourer.

This broad pattern is confirmed by the results of the only substantial wartime enquiry made into losses of agricultural labour, apart from that of the Board of Trade. This was carried out by the War Office in December 1916, but few county results have survived. Table 4.6 shows the losses for Hertfordshire.[29]

Table 4.6: Types of farm labour loss, 1911–December 1916 (Hertfordshire)

	Nos. lost	% loss
Cowmen	629	43
Ploughmen	1,022	60
Labourers	1,623	21

Source: Cd. 25, 112

Indirect confirmation from a more reliable source (the county WAC) is available from West Sussex, where male labour requirements in February 1917 were noted as:[30]

Carters and ploughmen	324	Stockmen	196
Shepherds	65	Labourers	743
Machinemen	26	Thatchers	63

These totals apparently did not include the anticipated labour needs of the plough policy, so reflected previous losses of labour only.

The shortage of labour was mitigated to some extent by the use of alternative supplies of labour, in the form of schoolchildren, soldiers, and women. From the earliest months of the war, there arose demand on the part of farmers that children should be released from school during term-time to help on farms. This pressure was not unsuccessful. That it was so was due to two factors: the legal background, and the cooperation of many county education authorities. The legal position was that, although the official school leaving age was thirteen years, it was open to the parents of any child who had reached the age of twelve, and who had attained a certain educational standard (and/or had attended school a certain minimum number of times) to withdraw the child from school. In addition, the 1870 Education Act made provision for the withdrawal of children from school in the case of sickness 'or any other unavoidable cause'. In an emergency it was permitted for local education authorities to pass by-laws giving blanket exemption under this provision.[31]

Most local education authorities agreed to release children for farm work in the first two years of the war, although the numbers involved were not considerable. Returns for England and Wales show that in the five months from September 1914–January 1915 inclusive, 38 authorities had released, at one time or another, 1,413 children for farm work. These numbers rapidly rose, and by 1916 most authorities were giving exemptions; on 31 January 1916, 8,026 were exempted by 54 authorities. On the last occasion on which a count was taken (16 October 1916), the number had risen to 14,915, exempted by 57 counties. By then only five counties were not giving exemptions.[32] Thereafter, such returns were not produced, and the course of juvenile employment can only be guessed. However, a later report noted that in five Midland counties child employment at the end of 1916 was 1,339, and that this had risen to 2,629 by the end of 1917.[33]

In encouraging the use of schoolchildren for agricultural work, a part was played by the War Agricultural Committees; the Oxford WAC resolved in January 1916 to remind the Education Committee of the importance of getting children out of school and onto the farms 'at certain periods of agricultural activity'.[34] The Wiltshire WAC passed a motion in February 1916 calling on the Education Committee to examine boys as early as possible, so that they might be employed in agriculture.[35]

Since the build-up of a large army, with considerable numbers of soldiers in camps in the UK, the use of soldiers as replacement labour was of obvious interest to farmers. The War Office first made them available for farm work for the hay harvest of 1915, when Home Defence men who wished to work on farms were given two weeks' furlough. No conditions were laid down as to the nature of the work, the area in which it was to be performed, or the rates of pay. These were all to be settled between the farmer and the soldier. After the corn harvest the supply of soldiers became subject to conditions. Whilst they would still be made available, the farmer had first to prove that there was a shortage of labour in the district, and detailed rates of pay were fixed by the War Office. These payments were to be made directly over to the War Office, the soldier continuing in receipt only of his army pay. For the autumn cultivation, the period of furlough was now extended up to four weeks.

Until the end of 1915, soldiers had been made available for specific seasonal tasks only, but in January 1916 the rules were altered to permit farmers to use them at any time of the year for up to four weeks, on application to the local Labour Exchange. This procedure was adopted, in spite of the well-known aversion of farmers to using Labour Exchanges, to ensure that unemployed local labour would receive first preference. The managers of the Exchanges were instructed to check that other types of labour were unavailable before passing on the request to the nearest camp. An exception was permitted in the case of short-term emergency, when farmers could apply direct to the nearest camp for soldier labour for not more than six days.[36]

Although plentiful and physically fit, soldiers were not cheap. The cost to the farmer was 4s per day (2s 6d if the farmer provided board and lodging), the hours to be those customary in the district. Since this worked out at 24s per six-day week, it was probably several shillings above that of the ordinary (southern) English labourer.[37] A further source of friction was the stipulation that wages should be paid regardless of the weather, so that farmers could not refuse to pay soldiers for 'wet time', when rain stopped work, as was the custom.[38] At the same time, the use of convalescent soldiers was permitted on broadly the same conditions, save that the pay was 6d a day less. Whether many convalescents were thus employed is unknown, but there was presumably a large potential labour supply; West Sussex WAC were informed that there were 6,000 in the county, many of whom were fit enough to do a few hours' work each day.[39]

For the 1916 corn harvest, the supply of soldiers was increased. For the first time, the War Office agreed to make available a specific number of soldiers for farm work (27,000). Wage rates and hours of work were fixed, and it was permitted for squads of soldiers to camp out in order to be more easily available for work.[40] While a certain number of soldiers was supplied under these arrangements, the 'total fell short of the available supply. Between 3 June and 28 July applications for over 33,000 soldiers were made to the Labour Exchanges, but only about 14,000 were provided.[41] Matters were not helped by the War Office sending out a circular which asked farmers to specify their labour requirements within five days; a proviso which had to be rescinded, but not before bad feeling had been caused.[42] Thereafter, from 12 August to 13 October, 28,805 were applied for, but only 16,690 were supplied. There seems no doubt that part of the blame for this failure lay with administrative confusion at the War Office. Farmers may have been mollified by the fact that 7,679 of the soldiers supplied had been specifically requested by name.[43]

During the first two years of the war, the use of soldier labour was on a comparatively small scale. Between 15 October 1915 and 11 August 1916, farmers had requested the services of 56,882 soldiers, and had been supplied with only 22,780. None of these had been employed for more than four weeks, and, deducting the 14,000 supplied in June and July 1916, it seems likely that, before the corn harvest of 1916, only about 8,000 had ever been employed in farming. The use of soldiers was subject to certain other drawbacks; comparative expense, lack of training, and military restrictions which made it difficult to use soldiers outside the eastern counties.

Given the constraints attending the use of soldiers, it was natural that farmers should turn to female labour. However, they were slow to do so before 1917. This was due to both supply and demand factors. On the side of supply, women whose husbands had enlisted were in receipt of separation allowances which were not, in the early years of the war, inadequate. For those who wished to find employment, there was a high demand for labour in occupations which paid better than farm work, and where the hours were shorter. Farmers were particularly aware that munitions factories provided more attractive conditions.[44] On the demand side, local women had by this time little experience of field work except in places like the Holland area of Lincolnshire, Oxfordshire, and Northumberland.[45] Nor were they suitable to replace, untrained, the skilled labour in charge of animals. Nor did farmers relish the prospect of getting their regular workers to work easily with women.

Finally, problems of accommodation would occur if the woman should need to 'live in'.

The evaluation of the role played by 'village women' in mitigating the wartime labour shortage is fraught with difficulty. Perhaps the main problem is the conflicting estimates of pre-war female employment. In addition, many women during the war entered agriculture without officials noticing the fact. Finally, official estimates are themselves suspect. Estimates of the number of women in pre-war farming vary widely. The 1911 *Census of Population* enumerated 70,000 in England and Wales, of whom the great majority (57,000) were farmers' relatives. There were also some 29,000 women in Scottish farming. The 1908 *Census of Production* had, however, showed a much higher level: 189,000 farmers' relatives, 95,000 full-time employees, and 40,000 part-timers, making 324,000 in all.[46]

There is no satisfactory way of reconciling these disparities.[47] For our purposes, the problem may be set on one side, since the Board of Trade decided to base its wartime surveys of the farm labour force on the1908 census. For reasons unknown, the Board modified the pre-war full-time female labour force to 80,000 and the part-time labour force to 50,000.[48] While, as already stated, the Board's survey results are not a good guide to the degree of labour shortage for agriculture as a whole, since they represent a sample of large farmers only, they may be used to indicate trends in employment. The results for female labour are shown in Table 4.7.[49]

Table 4.7: British female farm labour force, 1914–18

| | Average % change p.a. | | Nos. employed ('000) | |
	Full time	Part time	Full time	Part time
1914	–	–	80	50
1915	−12.2	−18.5	70	41
1916	+ 1.2	+25.3	81	62
1917	+ 5.6	+38.9	85	69
1918	+16.0	+12.9	92	56

Source: Board of Trade Z8 surveys

The main trends are clear; in the first year of the war, both full-time and part-time labour fell below pre-war levels. Thereafter both rose, but full-time labour did not rise appreciably above the pre-war level until 1918. Part-time labour, though, was substantially higher than pre-war in 1916–17.

The revival, and subsequent growth, of the female labour force in 1915–16 owed something to official action. The Board of Agriculture developed a scheme in 1915 for training women at agricultural colleges in milking and light farm work. The women were selected by the Labour Exchanges, which offered to find them work after the course (of 2–4 weeks). During the 25 weeks that the scheme lasted, 218 students passed through it, and 199 of them found farm work.[50] Some county councils took up the work. Nottingham had a training scheme for women by September 1915, and Cornwall also had a scheme, which involved setting up a women's committee in each parish, drawing up registers of women willing to be trained, and organising classes in milking and the preparation of animal feed. These were small affairs; the Nottingham scheme only catered for eight women at a time, and Cornwall only organised two agricultural gangs in 1915 and 1916.[51]

Official encouragement for women's work developed further in the autumn of 1915, with the formation of the WACs. Lord Selborne encouraged them to pay particular attention to organising women for farm work. The initial response was disappointing. As Sir Sydney Olivier, the Permanent Secretary to the Board, expressed it: 'Very few of them showed any disposition to move in this direction.'[52] As a result, a circular was sent in February 1916 to all WACs, ordering the formation of county women's farm labour committees, to work in concert with the WACs and any existing women's organisations.[53]

The setting up of the Women's War Agricultural Committees (WWACs) marked a new phase in the mobilisation of female labour. However, it was dependent for its effectiveness on local energy and initiative. Apart from enforcing the setting up of the committees, the Board had no powers of compulsion over the WWACs, and never acquired any. Local keenness was probably very variable. Thus the Oxford WAC was drawing up leaflets urging women to undertake farm work even before the formation of the WWAC, and West Sussex and Wiltshire had milking training schemes organised, also before February 1916.[54] Over the country as a whole, interest must have varied quite widely. When the Board of Agriculture came to draw up a report on the first six months' work of the WWACs, only 30 reports were received from the 63 WWACs then extant in England and Wales.[55]

The work of the WWACs in 1915–16 centred on drawing up a

register of women willing to work in agriculture, and promoting their employment by direct contact with farmers and the Labour Exchanges. The more active committees had impressive totals of women registered within a few months. By mid-May, Shropshire had 800, and by the end of the month there were 1,500 in Oxfordshire.[56] Wiltshire claimed 3,154 registrations by mid-October, and Durham had the highest number, with 4,938. Altogether, there were 57,497 women registered in England and Wales in August 1916, of whom 28,767 were working.[57]

As well as promoting employment, the committees tried to develop training schemes. In Hertfordshire, where the committee was very active, the county council already had a training scheme in operation; the committee opened a hostel for eight girls on the training scheme in June. The girls were trained by local farmers in milking, feeding stock, cleaning sheds, and general field work. Their work was periodically inspected by the committee: 'A.H.: Training with Mrs. Morgan at Waterford Hall. Milking and general work quite good. Conduct rather disappointing. Inclined to be flighty and rather noisy.'[58]

Certain inducements were offered by the government to promote the employment of women. In the spring of 1916, the Board of Agriculture arranged with the Cooperative Wholesale Society a supply of clothing and boots at wholesale prices. In addition, women who had worked on the land for not less than 30 days, or 240 hours, were entitled to wear an armlet of military appearance (khaki, with red crown). Women enrolling with the WWACs who had not yet attained this length of service received a certificate emblazoned with the Royal Arms, signed by the Presidents of the Boards of Agriculture and Trade, stating that women working on the land contributed as much to the war effort as did the soldier or sailor.[59]

In view of the limited inducements offered, it is rather surprising to find that the total number of enrolments was alleged to be quite considerable. It was recorded that 140,000 women registered in 1916, and that 72,000 certificates and 62,000 armbands were issued.[60] However, this would seem to be an overestimate of the number actually at work; the Board of Agriculture report cited above found less than 29,000 at work in August 1916. In addition, it was found that the registration system was defective. Many women engaged in agriculture did not register, and a proportion of those registered were already in farm work before the war.[61] In Durham, while in August 1916 there were 4,938 registrations, 1,048 were already working when registered, and only 383 were placed in agricultural work from the register.[62] Also, a lot of those at work were part-timers. The earliest reference to this is for Oxfordshire in July 1917; 674 of the 1,126 women were registered for full-time work, and the rest for part-time work. In Gloucester in October 1917, 2,080 women were at work, but 1,142 of these were part-time.[63]

Interest in increasing the employment of educated women in agriculture was for the first year of the war confined to private organisations. The first effective contribution came from the Women's Defence Relief Corps, whose aim was to utilise women in 'home front' work in order to release men for the forces. The type of workers which it desired to attract were educated women, especially teachers and students. These not being forthcoming in sufficient quantities, the scope of recruiting was widened to include clerks, shop assistants, and domestic servants. The work of the Corps was taken over by the Board of Agriculture in 1917; a few provincial centres (notably Manchester and Bolton) carried on without official assistance until the end of the war, after which the Corps was finally disbanded.[64]

The two other unofficial organisations of note were the Women's Legion, which formed an Agricultural Branch, and the Women's Farm and Garden Union. The former, in the person of the chairman, Lady Londonderry, managed to obtain an annual grant from the Board of Agriculture to assist in the running of training centres for women. These appear to have been of slight value, and the work of the Legion was marked by inefficiency and self-advertisement. The particular inadequacy of the Rutland branch brought matters to a head between the Legion and the Board. In November 1917, Lady Londonderry was persuaded that the Legion should henceforth confine its agricultural energies to fruit-bottling and horticulture.[65]

The Women's Farm and Garden Union was the most successful of the private organisations. It was the only one which existed to supply women to agriculture before the war, and became the basis for further official organisation during it. Before the war, its main business had been to promote the training of educated women for careers in gardening. When the war began, the basis of training was broadened to include purely agricultural work, and in February

1916 its work was recognised by the Board of Agriculture, which granted land for the founding of a training school.[66]

Simultaneously, the Board formed an organisation based on the WFGU, to which many of its members switched. This was the Women's National Land Service Corps. Although the WFGU was not disbanded until after the war, its history for the rest of the war was indistinguishable from what had been originally its offshoot, the WNLSC. The latter represented an interim stage between the voluntary effort of earlier organisations, and the fully-fledged official body of 1917, the Women's Land Army. Its aims were: to recruit women for seasonal agricultural work, to break down anti-feminine bias in agriculture, to organise 'village women' in gangs for farm work, and to generally help with official propaganda.[67] While fairly successful in obtaining agricultural work for its members in its first year, it was largely used thereafter by the Board to harvest industrial crops, in particular the flax harvests of 1917 and 1918.

In addition to the organised women, there existed an unknown number of educated women who entered farm work on their own initiative, and who may even have been unaware of the existence of such organisations. It is unlikely that the numbers were large, but the motives of the women must have been similar to those in the organisations – the desire to live in the countryside, to have a healthy occupation, or to 'do one's bit' for the war must all have played a part.[68]

In spite of the variety of organisations working to increase the employment of (largely educated) women in agriculture in 1914–16, comparatively little was achieved. The numbers involved were small; from 1914 until the end of 1916, the WFGU and WNLSC together provided only 3,437 women workers. For the entire war, all four organisations did not provide more than about 12,000.[69] Nor were the women particularly well trained. The early months of the war saw a rash of private initiatives by landowners, farmers, and women's organisations with the object of providing training for their members. The resulting training centres were uncoordinated and set up without reference to the prospects of the women finding work. By the end of 1916 they represented a duplication of effort, since the Board of Agriculture, some county councils, and the WACs had started their own schemes. The longest training (six weeks) was offered by the WNLSC, but this period was not really enough to do more than toughen the muscles, as the WLA were to find out.[70] The plethora of uncoordinated schemes led the Permanent Secretary of the Board (A. D. Hall) to comment irritably in December 1917: 'The country is full of these irresponsible training (?) centres for women, and they are doing great mischief...'[71] Finally, the bulk of the employees were from the WNLSC, so that they did not do much to repair the shortage of full-time labour, being largely employed on seasonal work.

On the whole, attempts to increase female employment on the land before 1917 were not very successful. The Board's report on the work of the WWACs to August 1916 devoted much space to explaining the relative failure to mobilise village women, and gave primacy to the system of exempting farm labourers from military service and the use of soldiers and schoolchildren. Difficulties were also noted in the refusal of women to work full-time, finding suitable accommodation for outside labour, and the hostile attitude of farmers.[72]

The overall impression left by a consideration of replacement labour flows in the first two years of the war is that they were comparatively small. An estimate has been made of the effective contribution made by replacement labour to overcoming the labour shortage in 1914–16. Making allowances for the lower efficiency of women and children (soldiers are counted as the equivalent of a male labourer), the contribution of replacement labour may be roughly estimated at 15,000 man-units in 1915, and 30,000 in 1916. When added to the estimate of the supply of conventional labour, the effect is to reduce the loss of labour to 6 per cent in 1915 and 9 per cent in 1916.[73]

Presenting the labour shortage in this light makes it easier to comprehend how farmers managed to cope with labour shortage during the first two years of the war; the shortage was simply not as severe as the traditional sources (derived from the Z8 returns) indicate. A telling comment is to be found in the Z8 report for January 1917 (for south-west England): 'On the other hand, farmers are, for various reasons, using neither substitute men, women, nor children, and apparently have not increased their machinery, but are carrying on as far as possible with a depleted staff.'[74]

NOTES

1 *Census of Agricultural Production 1908*, PP 1912, X, Cd. 6277, 62; *Census of Population (England and Wales) 1911*, X, Pt. 2, Table 13; *Census of Scotland 1911*, II, 272–5.

2 Ibid.

3 The influences on recruiting are discussed in P. E. Dewey, 'Military recruiting and the British labour force during the First World War', *Historical Journal* (1984), 199–223.

4 J. K. Montgomery, *The Maintenance of the Agricultural Labour Supply in England and Wales during the War* (Rome, 1922), 3–6, for this and subsequent paragraphs.

5 Ibid., and PRO, NATS I/53, R. 78, R. 79, *List of Certified Occupations*.

6 House of Lords, 5th series (1917), XXIV, 325–6.

7 Middleton, *Food Production*, 266.

8 PRO, MAF 38/180, memorandum on 'Agricultural Labour', 2–3.

9 (Lord) Ernle [R. E. Prothero], *English Farming Past and Present* (6th edn, 1961), 398; *The Land and its People: chapters in rural life and history* (1925), 104.

10 Middleton, *Food Production*, 266.

11 A. W. Ashby, *The Agricultural Labourer in Great Britain during the War*. This unpublished work (1921) was to have been one of the Carnegie series. I am indebted to Mr Andrew Ashby for its loan.

12 K. A. H. Murray, *Agriculture* (History of the Second World War. United Kingdom Civil Series) (1955), 15.

13 E. H. Whetham, *The Agrarian History of England and Wales*, vol. VIII 1914–39, (Cambridge, 1978), 71.

14 See n. 5.

15 On the Z8 enquiries generally, see Dewey, 'Military recruiting', Appendix 1.

16 Ibid., 201, n. 8.

17 On the methodology of the Z8 farm labour survey, see Appendix H.

18 PRO, MAF 38/180, 2–3.

19 Board of Trade, *Report on the State of Employment in the United Kingdom* . . . (1914–17).

20 Ibid., January 1917, 28.

21 See Appendix F.

22 See ch. 16.

23 Department of Agriculture and Technical Instruction for Ireland, *Reports Relating to Irish Migratory Agricultural and other Labourers*, PP 1914, LXXIX, 3–6; 1916, XXXIII, 3–5.

24 Agricultural Wages Board, *Report on Wages and Conditions of Employment in Agriculture*, Cmd. 24 (1919), para. 269.

25 Cmd. 24, para. 209.

26 See Appendix F.

27 *Census of Population*, 1911.

28 Cmd. 24, paras. 182–3.

29 Cmd. 25. On the other hand, the surviving WO census material should

be treated with care; the Essex results show almost all the labour loss as occurring amongst 'daymen', i.e., ordinary labourers; the total labour force (including farmers and relatives) had dropped by 17,000 between 1911 and the end of 1916, and almost 15,000 of this had been accounted for by the loss of ordinary labourers. This is implausible; what seems to have happened was that farmers had realised that skilled men were to be protected, and had classified their remaining ordinary labourers as being in charge of animals, and thus not eligible for military service; Essex RO, D/Z 45/1–14.

30 West Sussex, RO, WAEC, *Report of Land Survey*, 5 Feb. 1917, 4.
31 Board of Education, *Correspondence relating to school attendance between the Board of Education and certain Local Education Authorities since the outbreak of war*, PP 1914–16, L, Cd. 7803 (1915), 1–9.
32 Board of Education, *School attendance and employment in agriculture. Summary of returns supplied by Local Education Authorities*, Cd. 7881, PP 1914–16, L, 5–6; Cd. 7932, PP 1914–16, L, 4–5; Cd. 8202, PP 1916, XXII, 3–4; Cd. 8302, PP 1916, XXIII, 3–4; Cd. 8171, PP 1916, XXIII, 3–4.
33 Board of Agriculture, Cmd. 24, para. 149.
34 Oxford RO, CWAM I, 10 January 1916.
35 Wilts. RO, WAC minutes, 11 February 1916.
36 Montgomery, *Maintenance . . .*, 22–3; Middleton, *Food Production*, 140.
37 Montgomery, *Maintenance . . .*, 30–1.
38 PRO, NATS I/53, Board of Agriculture, 'Notice to farmers. Soldier Labour', A 178/L, 31 January 1916, para. 3.
39 Army Council Instruction 1056/1916; West Sussex WAC minutes, 6 June 1916.
40 Montgomery, *Maintenance . . .*, 23.
41 Middleton, *Food Production*, 144.
42 Wilts. WAC minutes, 11 August 1916, 8 September 1916.
43 PRO, NATS I/53, B/232/3, correspondence between the Board of Agriculture and Manpower Distribution Board, 29 Sept.–8 Nov. 1916.
44 Board of Trade, *Report on the State of Employment . . .* (July 1915), 6 (Yorkshire).
45 Cmd. 24, paras. 132–8.
46 *1908 Census of Production*, Cd. 6277, 62; *1911 Census of Population (England and Wales)*, X, Pt. 2, Table 13; *Census of Scotland*, II, 272–5.
47 Board of Agriculture, *Report of Sub-committee appointed to consider the employment of women in agriculture in England and Wales* (1919), 29.
48 These bases were not continuously adhered to in the reports, but the variations are minor.
49 See Appendix H.
50 MAF 59/1, Women's County Committees – organisation of women's labour, *Memorandum on training of women in practical farm work*.
51 MAF 59/1, L. 29047/1916; Imperial War Museum (IWM), LAND V, *Record of the Women's Land Army in Cornwall* (Truro, 1919).
52 PRO, MAF 59/1, L. 29047/1916, 12.

53 Ibid., circular A 259/C, 23 Feb. 1916.
54 Oxford WAC minutes, 10 Jan. 1916; W. Sussex WAC minutes, 22 Dec. 1915; Wilts. WAC minutes, 14 Jan. 1916.
55 PRO, MAF 59/1, L. 29369, *Work of the Women's War Agricultural Committees for the year ending August 1916*, and covering letter to F. C. Floud.
56 Salop WAC minutes, 13 May 1916; Oxford WAC minutes, 29 May 1916.
57 Wilts. EC, 15 Oct. 1916; MAF 59/1, L. 29369, *Work of the WWACs*.
58 Herts. WWAC minutes, 12 July 1916.
59 Montgomery, *Maintenance . . .*, 56–7; PRO, MAF 42/8, 13717/L. 3.
50 Andrews and Hobbs, *Economic Effects*, 71.
61 WWACs report to Aug. 1916.
62 Ibid.
63 Oxford EC minutes, 9 July 1917; Gloucs. WWAC minutes, 30 Oct. 1917.
64 IWM LAND IV, Women's Defence Relief Corps.
65 PRO, MAF 59/1, L. 29047, 20.
66 Andrews and Hobbs, *Economic Effects*, 73.
67 IWM, LAND IV (123), WNLSC (Land 5').
68 Interview with Viscountess Broome, 4 May 1972; Dewey, thesis, 264.
69 IWM, LAND IV (123); PRO, MAF 42/8, 12027/L. 3, *Report of Women's Legion Agricultural Section, 1916 and 1917*.
70 Andrews and Hobbs, *Economic Effects*, 73.
71 MAF 42/8, 12027/L. 3, note of 13 Dec. 1917 by 'A.D.H.'
72 PRO, MAF 59/1, L. 29369.
73 See Appendices F and G.
74 Board of Trade, *Report on the State of Employment . . .* (Jan. 1917), D/3.

Chapter Five

POWER AND MACHINERY

The main power source in pre-war farming was the horse. Much of the new field machinery introduced in the late nineteenth century had been horse-drawn, and the numbers of horses kept for farm work had been rising since records had first been kept in 1870. Including mares kept for breeding (which were put to work when not too near foaling), the average number of working horses on farms in 1909–13 was 1.07 million. Reckoning one horse as providing two-thirds of an HP unit, the horse stock provided about 707,000 HP for agricultural use. Most of the horse power was employed in field work, some in barn and yard work, and some in carting.[1]

The other major power source on the farm was steam. This had never lived up to the expectations of its protagonists as far as field work was concerned. In particular, steam engines usually had proved too heavy for direct ploughing and cultivating. But steam ploughing by the indirect method, using a plough attached to a cable, worked by either a single or a double engine, had some success. The double engine system was the more popular; about 600 sets were in use in 1910.[2] Most of these were hired to farmers by contractors, who also supplied steam engines for threshing, which was now almost wholly mechanised. Farmers also had engines of their own for threshing, and barn and yard work. These contributed about 213,000 HP in 1908; steam accounted for about half of this, the remainder being the more recent innovations of oil, petrol, and gas engines.[3]

The motor tractor was in its infancy in 1914. Even in 1925, when the first tractor census was taken, only 14,565 were employed in field work (and 2,116 in stationary work) in England and Wales.[4]

The number on farms before 1914 can only be guessed. The tractor industry was a small one in Britain; although more advanced in the USA, probably only a few hundred machines were exported from the US to Britain before the war.[5] Even at the end of 1917, when tractor usage had been stimulated by the war, the Food Production Department thought that there were only about 3,500 privately owned tractors in the UK.[6] At a maximum, the tractor stock was unlikely to have been above 1,000 before the war. Even assuming that they were of the larger type seen in the war (25+ HP), the tractor could not have contributed more than c. 25,000 HP to the total power supply.

The outbreak of war affected the farm power supply in several ways. There was a sharp fall in horse numbers in 1914–15, consequent on the impressment of horses from town and country by the Army. The number of horses used for agriculture fell from 926,820 in 1914 to 858,032 in 1915.[7] After mobilisation, the Army turned to other sources; out of a total of 886,000 subsequently purchased, 467,000 only were bought in the UK, the rest being imported.[8] Those bought in the UK were probably drawn from outside agriculture, since the number of farm horses recovered. However, even in 1916, farm horses (906,233) had not quite reached the 1914 level. While the shortage was not severe enough to curtail the tillage area, farmers were driven to other shifts to stretch their horse power, such as the increased use of breeding mares for field work.[9]

The power supply was also affected by wartime shortages of labour and materials. This was particularly apparent in the case of the steam ploughing sets. By 1917, it was thought that about half of them were lying idle for lack of skilled operatives, spare parts or coal.[10] The lack of labour had given concern even earlier; in March 1916, the drivers, attendants, and mechanics of steam ploughs and threshing machines had been given exemption from military service.[11]

The shortage of horses and of labour, coupled with high prices for agricultural produce, turned the more enterprising or wealthy farmers to thoughts of tractors. In January 1916, a trade journal commented on the machinery section at the Smithfield Show: 'Motor ploughs and milking machines were two outstanding classes of mechanism which received the closest attention, whilst agricultural motors were also keenly examined in view of the growing scarcity of horses.'[13]

Amongst the items advertised were nine motor cultivators of one sort or another; at least two were 'motor ploughs', behind which the operator walked (or sometimes sat). Six were motor tractors and one was a steam tractor (Mann & Co.). At least three of the motor tractors were imported from the USA.[14]

The Board of Agriculture helped to publicise the new machines. In November 1915 the Board's Journal carried an account of recent demonstrations of motor ploughs and tractors arranged by certain county councils in the eastern counties. Four types of motor plough and ten tractors were demonstrated, before audiences which totalled several thousand. Most of the tractors were petrol driven, although two were steam; three of the petrol tractors were USA models.[15]

The extent to which the tractor made headway in 1914–16 is difficult to ascertain. Manufacturers certainly made large claims; in February 1917, an advertisement for the Overtime tractor (a recent import from the USA) claimed that there were already 1,400 of them working in Britain, although two months later this was changed to the more modest 'over 1,000'.[16] The estimate by the Food Production Department was that there were 3,500 private tractors in the country at the end of 1917. At the same time, there were 1,550 government machines at work, so that the total then was about 5,000.[17] Home production in 1917 was estimated at about 1,500, so that the maximum national stock at the end of 1916 is not more than c. 3,500; taking the 1917 imports into account would reduce this even further.[18]

In spite of the number of manufacturers who by this time were catering for the home market, production per firm was low, and the bulk of the increase of 3,000 or so tractors in Britain between 1914 and 1917 was probably supplied from abroad. The trade statistics show that in 1915–16, 6,000 tons of 'prime movers' (i.e., engines of all sorts) were imported; if these were all tractors, this would amount to c. 3,000, since the average wartime tractor weighed about two tons. But in practice some of this tonnage would have been accounted for by static engines and spare parts. Even so, the dominance of USA models on the British market was assured by the end of 1916.[19]

In 1914, British farming was the most highly mechanised of all European agricultural systems.[20] This was particularly apparent in field operations; grass mowing, haymaking, and corn harvesting had long been performed by machine rather than by hand. Barn work had been partly mechanised; the threshing machine was almost universal, and much feed preparation was done by machines such as chaff cutters and cake crushers.[21] Dairying was the least mechanised. The manufacture of butter and cheese had by now largely moved into the factory; what remained on the farm used instruments which were, apart from the cream separator, of ancient design. Milking was still done mostly by hand; many experiments in mechanical milking had been made, but workable machines had only just come onto the market. It is doubtful if more than about 80,000 cows were mechanically milked on the eve of the war, and technically the milking machine had some way to go, so that its diffusion was to be slow even in the post-war period.[22]

The supply of machinery and implements came largely from the home machinery industry. This consisted of many firms, but most of them were small, and the industry was dominated by a few very large firms, mainly in the eastern counties of England. Industry sources estimated that the output of the industry in 1913 was worth some £6.5 million.[23] The industry was highly export-oriented, sending about 60 per cent of its output abroad. Export orientation was particularly marked in the case of steam engines; specialist firms such as Fowlers of Leeds sent about 80 per cent of their output abroad. To the £2.6 million of home sales should be added some £570,000 of retained imports, so that farmers in Britain were spending some £3.2 millions a year on machinery and implements.[24]

The home industry supplied the farmer with most of the heavier items – steam engines and tackle, other engines, and threshing boxes. Most ploughs were also home-produced. The chief foreign competition came from harvesting machinery, mainly from the USA. Of the £1 million or so of machinery imported (gross) annually before the war, the USA provided three-quarters. Some three-quarters of the American exports to the UK were mowers and reapers. There was also a small but growing influx of American ploughs and cultivators.[25]

During the first two years of the war, the supply of machinery to farmers was affected principally by the eagerness of the manufacturers to undertake government munitions contracts. The large machinery firms such as Ransomes were especially keen, but it is likely that the small firms also found this profitable. The history of the Ministry of Munitions records that by early 1917, when the Ministry took over responsibility for the industry, it was producing munitions 'to the virtual exclusion of normal output'.[26] This was something of an exaggeration, but what was not in doubt was the other great wartime change, the sharp fall in exports, due to the disappearance of foreign markets and shipping difficulties.

These trends may be traced through the records of two large firms, Ransomes of Ipswich, and Hornsby of Lincoln. While generalisation on the basis of two firms may seem dangerous, the industry was extremely concentrated; these two firms accounted for 19 per cent of the output of the industry before the war, and some 29 per cent of the home market. In addition, they made between them almost the whole range of farm equipment, although most prominent in ploughs, engines, threshers, and binders.[27]

Table 5.1: Ransomes' output (£'000), 1914–16

	1909–13	*1914*	*1915*	*1916*
Home	167	197[a]	487[b]	232
Export	391	340	105	115
War work	–	–	–	574
Totals	556	537	592	921

Notes: [a] Includes £26,000 of war work

[b] About £307,000 of this may have been war work

– Not separately accounted for

Source: Ransomes archive, Institute of Agricultural History, Reading University

While war work is not detailed as a separate category for 1915, it is clear that Ransomes was able to offset the decline in exports by war work to the extent of at least half its output in 1916 (Table 5.1). This process had begun early; faced with large order cancellations on the outbreak of war, the directors responded by obtaining the first war contract before the end of 1914.[28] A similar shift to war work is evident in Hornsby's records. Before the war, the firm already did some work for the Admiralty, to the extent of some 9 per cent of its sales. In 1914 this rose to 16 per cent, to 41 per cent in 1915, and 46 per cent in 1916.

The effect of the shift to war work on the production of machinery for the home market is uncertain. In the case of Ransomes, the actual numbers of machines and implements produced for the home market are unknown. However, bearing in mind that on average machinery prices had increased by about 50 per cent by the middle of the war, it seems fairly clear that home output was not maintained in real terms. In the case of the specialist export-oriented firm, like Fowlers of Lincoln, it seems that the sharp decline in wartime exports left some spare capacity which was not taken up by government orders, so that production for the home market actually increased; while Fowlers sold on average 9 steam ploughing sets on the home market annually in 1909–13, they sold 24 in 1914, 10 in 1915, and 20 in 1916.[29] Fowlers were, however, an exceptional case. Most firms were not quite so export-oriented, and it seems likely that for most of them any spare capacity released by the decline in exports was more than taken up by war work, so that the overall effect was a decline in output for the home market. Although their records are incomplete, this seems to have been the case for several other prominent firms such as Ruston, Garretts, Wm. Foster, and Clayton and Shuttleworth.[30]

The probable decline in production for the home market was not made good by a rise in imports. While the British import statistics seem to show a sharp rise in retained imports in the first two years of the war, they are unreliable, because they do not separately identify all types of agricultural machinery. More precision is possible using USA export data. Although these do not indicate how much of the exports were retained in Britain, they show that gross imports declined sharply; having been worth $1,065,000 in 1909–13, they fell to $757,000 in 1915. Although they had recovered to $1,274,000 in 1916, this was insufficient to make up for inflation, so that by the middle of the war, USA exports to Britain were still in real terms somewhat lower than pre-war.[31]

On balance, considering the probable course of home output and retained imports, there is a strong presumption that the supply of farm machinery and implements fell in the first two years of the war. However, manufacturers seem to have tried hard to maintain their home market, and the decline is unlikely to have been severe.

Apart from actual shortages of machinery and implements, farmers had other problems. Early in 1915, the *Implement and Machinery Review* commented on the dislocation to farm machinery deliveries caused by delays in rail transport. Shortages of skilled operatives and coal were alleged to be responsible for the fact that, by 1917, half of the steam tackle sets in the country were out of action. The West Sussex EC commented in January 1917 that 'there is tackle lying idle close to 100 acres of land in a fit state to plough, but it is impossible to get men for the work.'[32]

The decline in the supply of new machines and implements, and difficulties in getting them serviced and repaired (the supply of blacksmiths was also reduced, due to enlistment) led to a certain proportion of them falling into disrepair. The extent of this is indicated for Essex in a survey of machinery carried out in respect of all its 9,055 holdings in July 1917 (Table 5.2).

Table 5.2: Farm machinery stock in Essex, July 1917

	In good repair	*Capable of being repaired*
Binders	3,999	330
Corn & seed drills	3,918	83
Disc harrows	742	12
Portable engines	569	42
Horse cultivators	3,360	105
Ploughs	13,373	464
Potato sprayers	58	4
Rollers	8,054	171
Threshing machines	420	22
Traction engines	280	12
Toothed harrows	13,128	318

Source: J. Sheail, *AgHR* (1976), 118

While it is not known how this degree of ill-repair compared with peacetime, it does not seem particularly serious. The highest proportion was in binders. This reflects the fact that they were the most complex type of field machinery in use, whose moving parts were subject to much wear. The problem may also have been compounded by the fact that many of them had been imported, and spare parts were thus in short supply.

On the whole, the supply of both power and machinery was adversely affected by the first two years of the war. However, the most important power source, the horse, had recovered by the end of 1916, and was now supplemented by the tractor to some extent. Machinery supply suffered, but not seriously; manufacturers had some success in maintaining home sales, and the low depreciation rates of machinery and implements mitigated the impact of shortage.

NOTES

1 Board of Agriculture/Board of Agriculture (Scotland), *Agricultural Statistics, 1909–13*; P. McConnell, *Notebook of Agricultural Facts and Figures for Farmers and Farm Students* (1910), 59.

2 H. Bonnett, *Saga of the Steam Plough* (1965), 103; Middleton, *Food Production*, 226, finds 500 in 1917.

3 *Census of Agricultural Production* (1908), 62.

4 Ministry of Agriculture, *The Agricultural Output of England and Wales 1925* (Cmd. 2815, 1927), 108.

5 E. H. Whetham, 'The mechanisation of British agriculture 1910–45', *JAE* 21, 3 (1970), esp. 317–19; P. A. Wright, *Old Farm Tractors* (1962), 27; *Annual Statement of Trade*, 1909–13.

6 PRO, War Cabinet minutes, CAB 24/33, 297, 3.

7 War Office, *Statistics of the Military Effort of the British Empire during the Great War 1914–20* (1922), 394; *Agricultural Statistics*, 1914–15.

8 War Office, *Statistics . . .*, Pt. VI.

9 G. E. Evans, *Farm and Village* (1969), 117–20.

10 Ernle, *The Land and its People*, 130.

11 PRO, NATS I/53, R. 78, *List of Certified Occupations*.

12 Ransomes, Sims and Jeffries archive, Institute of Agricultural History, Reading University; P. McConnell, *The Agricultural Notebook* (1910), 59.

13 *Implement and Machinery Review*, 1 Jan. 1916, 1041.

14 Ibid., 1049–68.

15 *JBA*, November 1915, 760–2.

16 *FSB* (1917), 275, 616.

17 CAB 24/33, 297, 2.

18 J. Sheail, 'Changes in the use and management of farmland in England and Wales 1915–19', *Transactions of the Institute of British Geographers* (November 1973), 26.

19 *Annual Statement of Trade*; Wright, *Old Farm Tractors*, 12–13, 15–23.

20 G. E. Fussell, *The Farmer's Tools* (3rd edn, 1985), covers the history of mechanisation up to c. 1900.

21 P. McConnell, *The Complete Farmer* (1911), Pt. IV; J. R. Bond, 'Modern haymaking and haymaking machinery', *JRASE* 79 (1918), 44–67.

22 *Committee on the Production and Distribution of Milk* ('Astor Committee'), Final Report, Cmd. 483 (1919), 57–62.

23 Agricultural Engineers' Association, *Report on Trade Conditions in the Agricultural Machinery and Implement Industry* (1924), 5, 10.

24 Ibid., and *Annual Statement of Trade*, 1909–13.

25 *Annual Statement of Trade*, 1909–13.

26 Ministry of Munitions, *History of the Ministry of Munitions*, XII, Pt. VI, 1.

27 Ransomes archive, Institute of Agricultural History, Reading University; Lincolnshire RO, 'Hornsby; Sales, Stock and Wages, etc., 1905–21'.

28 Ipswich Engineering Society, *History of Engineering in Ipswich* (1950), 61.
29 IAH, Reading University, Fowler and Co. archive, 'Delivery Chart'.
30 Lincs. RO, 'Ruston Threshing Machine Registers 1905–31' and Rundle archive; R. A. Whitehead, *Garrett's of Leiston* (1964), Appendix 13; IAH, Clayton and Shuttleworth archive, 'Counties Book' (1880–c. 1927).
31 United States Department of Commerce and Labor. Bureau of Statistics. *The foreign commerce and navigation of the United States for the year ending June 30* . . . (Washington DC, 1910–16). Bureau of the Census, *Historical Statistics of the USA* (Washington, 1957), 361.
32 *Implement and Machinery Review*, 1 April 1915, 1487; Ernle, *The Land and its People*, 130; West Sussex RO, *Report of Land Survey*, 4.

Chapter Six

FERTILISERS AND FEEDS

FERTILISERS

Until the mid-nineteenth century, organic materials supplied the sole means of adding fertility to the soil. The principal fertiliser remained, as ever, farmyard manure, together with such items as town refuse, soot, rags, crushed bones and, latterly, imports of Peruvian guano. The beginnings of a new age were seen in 1843, when John Lawes first marketed his 'patent fertiliser'. This, the first artificial fertiliser, was superphosphate, produced by treating crushed bones or mineral phosphates with sulphuric acid. Farmers took eagerly to the product; by the late 1880s they were spending about £6 million annually on fertilisers, and about half of this was accounted for by superphosphate. Most of the remainder was spent on imports of naturally occurring sodium nitrate from Chile, known colloquially as 'Chile nitre'.[1]

In the ensuing quarter of a century before the outbreak of the First World War, superphosphate remained the artificial fertiliser most in demand, but it had been joined by two other products: ammonium sulphate and basic slag. Together with Chile nitrate, these three dominated the market.[2] The most important product apart from these was potash, imported from Germany, usually in the form of 'kainit', to the extent of some 180,000 tons a year.[3] By 1914, certain organic fertilisers were of less account. The trade in guano had shrunk considerably since the middle of the previous century; in 1909–13, the average import was only about 20,000 tons a year. Crushed bones were also less popular than formerly; their consumption was estimated at about 40,000 tons a year in 1913[4]

These products had various advantages in contributing to

farming the three most useful elements in soil fertility, nitrogen, phosphorus, and potassium. Nitrogenous fertilisers were of particular interest to the farmer, since under British conditions, and indeed in all areas where rainfall is high enough to cause any considerable amount of soil leaching, the supply of available soil nitrogen tends to be the main factor limiting plant growth. Nitrogen was supplied by sodium nitrate and ammonium sulphate. Sodium nitrate had the advantage of acting quickly on a growing crop, and of being effective in conditions too cold for sulphate of ammonia to operate. The latter was more suitable for application to land some time before the growing crop was ready to absorb it.[5]

The most popular fertiliser of all was superphosphate, which promoted root growth in young plants (particularly root crops) and early maturity and ripening of cereals. Prior to the war, about 41 per cent of superphosphate went on roots and potatoes, and 27 per cent on cereals, with a further 21 per cent on the production of hay.[6]

The other major phosphatic fertiliser was basic slag, a by-product of steel-making. As well as phosphoric acid, it contained a large amount of lime. This combination made it especially useful for the improvement of grassland, by encouraging the growth of clover and leading to an accumulation of nitrogen in the soil. Although small amounts of high quality slag were used on roots and wheat, most (about 70 per cent) was used on grassland prior to the war. Even so, British farmers had come late to the idea of applying fertiliser to grassland, and the amounts employed fell far short of the potential usage.[7]

The outbreak of war had most immediately serious consequences for the supply of sodium nitrate. Chile being the sole source of supply, shipping difficulties led to an immediate loss of imports, in spite of the ending of the modest pre-war re-export trade. Net imports, which in 1909–13 had been 112,000 tons a year on average, fell to 78,000 in 1916.[8] Not all the imported nitrate was destined for fertiliser; the assumption made here is that 80 per cent of net imports were used as such.[9] Applying this ratio to net imports, we can estimate the usage of nitrate as fertiliser (Table 6.1).

Shortage of nitrate, actual and potential, concerned the Board of Agriculture sufficiently for it to set up a Fertiliser Committee to rectify the situation. Known as the Acland Committee, after its chairman, T. D. Acland, MP (Parliamentary Secretary to the

Board), it began work in October 1915. Its early meetings indicated some of the difficulties. In the first month of its existence, it noted that the closure of the Panama Canal was affecting supplies. Also, although the Board had made some purchases, they could not be shipped, since the Admiralty could not provide the necessary shipping, and thus deliveries would not occur in time for the spring cultivations. In addition, nitrates were in great demand for the making of munitions.[10]

Table 6.1: Sodium nitrate consumption in UK agriculture, 1914–16
('ooo tons)

1909–13 av.	1914	1915	1916
90	122	62	17

Source: Appendix I

The situation was quite different in the case of the other nitrogenous fertiliser, ammonium sulphate. This was an entirely home-produced commodity, being a by-product largely derived from gasworks and coke ovens, with additional supplies from shale works and the iron and steel industry.[11] Chemically, it was a very acceptable substitute for sodium nitrate, and much of the work of the Acland Committee centred on the aim of using it to replace nitrate. There were three problems standing in the way of such a neat solution: there was a large export trade, which the manufacturers were keen to safeguard; farmers were reluctant to use it in larger quantities; and production fell during the war as the sulphuric acid used in its manufacture (and some of the sulphate itself) was diverted to the production of explosives. A further complication was the very large number of works (about 600) producing it.[12]

The Board's attempts to secure a greater supply of sulphate, and induce farmers to use it, centred on negotiations with the producers, in the form of the Sulphate of Ammonia Association. At a meeting with Acland in October 1915, the Association agreed to reserve a quarter of the next two months' output for farmers, and to deliver it at the low price of £14 10s (£14.50).[13] This was a noticeable cut on the existing market price, which had risen sharply (as had that of the other fertilisers), and now stood at £17 10s.[14]

If one of the motives of the Association was to forestall the imposition of export restrictions by the Board, they were temporarily disappointed. Fearing an incipient shortage, the government suspended export licences in January 1916. This fear cannot have been overriding, since the Board was circularising WACs in February to the effect that the suspension of export licences could only be prolonged if farmers would place large orders for sulphate. However, the expected shortage did not materialise, and export was again permitted on 31 March.[15]

In spite of the reduction in nitrate supply and the efforts of the Board, farmers were slow to increase their use of sulphate. Before the war, out of over 400,000 tons manufactured, farmers had only taken some 60,000 tons, and the rest was largely exported. In 1916 it is estimated that farm consumption rose to 80,000 tons. This may be a slight underestimate; in the period July 1916–April 1917, agricultural consumption was estimated as 110,000 tons, so that consumption in the calendar year 1916 may have been rather more than 80,000 tons.[16] On the other hand, exports continued at a high level, which suggests that agricultural usage was not rising particularly rapidly. In 1909–13, exports had been 289,000 tons on average. In 1914 and 1915 they were slightly higher, but fell in 1916 to 259,000 tons, presumably reflecting the ban on exports earlier in the year. In the absence of more reliable statistics, the best that can be done for estimating sulphate consumption is to intercalate 1914–15 figures (Table. 6.2).

Table 6.2: Ammonium sulphate: agricultural consumption, 1914–16
('000 tons)

1909–13	1914	1915	1916
60	(70)	(80)	80

Note: Bracketed figures are interpolations

Source: Appendix I

The supply of superphosphate was also curtailed by the war. This was because its raw materials, phosphatic rock and sulphuric acid, were in short supply. The former, being entirely imported before the war, was beset by shipping difficulties. The latter was in demand for making munitions. But the curtailment of superphosphate exports in wartime provided some relief. The fact that the rock was entirely imported, and that the superphosphate not used by agriculture was exported, makes it relatively easy to estimate

72

with some confidence the course of production, and hence consumption, during the war. On the basis that each ton of rock imported was converted into 1.73 tons of superphosphate, an estimate of consumption may be made (Table. 6.3).[17]

Table 6.3: Superphosphate consumption in agriculture, 1914–16
('000 tons)

	1909–13	*1914*	*1915*	*1916*
Production	843	865	648	572
LESS exports	−149	−66	−69	−14
Consumption	694	799	579	558

Source: Appendix I

These estimates are subject to two qualifications. The first is that there was before 1914 a rising import of manufactured superphosphate which was not separately identified in the trade returns, appearing under 'unenumerated' fertiliser. In 1909–13, this amounted to 156,000 tons p.a. Thus the pre-war consumption figure must be an underestimate. This qualification is less important during the war, an unenumerated imports fell sharply after 1914. Secondly, the increasing shortage of acid during the war meant that a certain proportion of rock, although imported, could not be converted into superphosphate. In January 1917, a memorandum to the Acland Committee considered that there were 50,000 tons of rock in the country lacking the acid for conversion to superphosphate. Thus the wartime estimates are likely to be too high. Middleton estimated that production in 1913 had been 820,000 tons, and that this had fallen to 504,000 tons in 1916. He also thought that pre-war agricultural consumption was 675,000 tons, which is close to the 694,000 tons estimated here for pre-war usage.[18]

The main influences on the supply of slag were the output of basic iron and steel (of which slag was a by-product), the balance of imports and exports, and the processing capacity of slag works. Basic iron and steel output rose steadily and substantially during the war, from 4.3 million tons in 1909–13 to 7.6 million tons in 1918. The raw material was thus not in short supply. Supply was also stimulated by trading changes. There had been a substantial net export of slag before the war, but this steadily decreased owing to hostilities and shipping difficulties. In 1909–13 the net export had been 150,000 tons p.a., and by 1916 it had fallen to 35,000 tons.[19]

Thus the supply of raw slag was not in doubt. In so far as there was a restriction on supply to farmers, it lay in the processing works. The process consisted of grinding the raw slag into a fine powder. There is some suggestion that the supply of grinding machinery was inadequate, but the greater problem was labour shortage. This was referred to by the Acland Committee early in 1917, as was a shortage of 'suitable' raw slag for grinding, and transport difficulties. The labour problem was solved by drafting into the factories Army Reserve Munition Workers; the committee reported in March 1917 that all except one of the 20 works producing slag now had their full complement of labour.[20]

On balance, it seems unlikely that there was any serious shortage of basic slag in the first two years of the war, although the Lancashire WAC noted that railway dislocation in 1915 was impeding the delivery of 'manures'. That delays occurred is also suggested by the unfilled orders of ten slag manufacturers in December 1916; amounting to 166,751 tons, they represented over six months' output.[21] The fragmentary evidence on output does not allow a reliable series to be constructed. Failing that, we have taken the pre-war agricultural usage estimated by Middleton (263,000 tons) and assumed that this varied in direct proportion to changes in the grassland area of the UK (since slag was essentially a grassland fertiliser). Having done this, consumption appears as unchanged in 1914 and 1915, and only falls by 1,000 tons in 1916.[22]

During the first two years of the war there were clearly shortages of some important fertilisers. Our estimate is that the consumption (by weight) of the four main products considered here had fallen to about 83 per cent of its pre-war level.[23] In addition, the supply of potash had been almost entirely cut off, since it had been largely a German export.[24] In terms of the two main fertilising agents, nitrogen and phosphoric oxide, the decline had been to 66 per cent and 74 per cent of the pre-war levels of application. In the case of nitrogen, most of the decline had been confined to 1916. The fall in phosphoric oxide extended over both 1915 and 1916. The effect of these shortages on crop yields will be considered later. For the moment, it may be noted that the decline of fertiliser input meant a saving on farmers' costs in real terms; at 1911–13 prices, the cost of the four fertilisers had fallen from £4,058,000 (in 1909–13) to £3,130,000 in 1916.[25]

FEEDSTUFFS

As in the case of fertilisers, so in that of animal feedstuffs, British agriculture had by the First World War passed to the stage of purchasing large quantities from outside the 'national farm'. Already in 1887–91, UK farmers were spending £12.8 million a year on purchased feeds. By 1907 expenditure had risen to £21.4 million in Britain alone (although this was practically synonymous with UK expenditure).[26]

There were two main types of feeds: those derived from cereals, and from oilseeds. The former were the product of both domestic and imported cereals. The latter were derived almost entirely from imports, either directly, in the form of oilseed cake, or as raw oilseed which was manufactured into cake in the UK. In terms of weight, cereal feeds were the more important; in 1907, the UK was thought to produce some 2.8 million tons, mainly in the form of wheat offals from flour mills. Production of cake was 807,000 tons, largely accounted for by cottonseed cake (485,000 tons). When account was taken of external trade, it was estimated that cereal feed consumption was worth £15.5 million, and cake consumption was worth £7.5 million.[27] Although the value of cake consumed in agriculture was much less than the value of cereal feed, cake had particular nutritional advantages, since it provided protein and oil which cereals lacked. This made it especially useful for feeding young animals, fattening older stock more quickly, and maintaining milk yields.[28]

It is only possible to give a rough estimate of the course of wartime cereal feed supply. The series presented here covers the three main products: wheat offals, barley meal and flour, and maize products. In the case of wheat, estimates of home grain supply have been made for this book, import figures are available from the trade statistics, and the calculation of offals yield can be made by reference to the flour milling percentages given by Beveridge. Barley supply figures are from the same sources. It has been assumed that the proportion of supply going to animal feed was the same during the first two years of the war as in 1909–13. The same assumption has been made for maize products; the supply being wholly imported, it can be obtained from the trade statistics (Table 6.4).[29]

Table 6.4: Cereal feed supply in Britain 1914–16 ('000 tons)

	1909–13 av.	*1914*	*1915*	*1916*
Totals	2,650	2,700	2,750	2,350

Source: Appendix J.

The variations in the supply of cake can be estimated more completely and accurately since, apart from rape cake, which was a minor product, it was either imported or derived from imported materials. Imports of prepared cake being available from the trade statistics, it remains to estimate the amount of cake which would have been manufactured from imported materials. This has been done by applying to seed imports the extraction rates given by F. M. L. Thompson (Table 6.5).[30]

Table 6.5: Feed cake consumption in Britain, 1914–16 ('000 tons)

	1909–13	*1914*	*1915*	*1916*
Cotton cake	528	514	470	364
Linseed cake	317	360	341	398
Rapeseed cake	54	77	33	49
Total cake	899	951	844	811

Source: Appendix J

The war brought an increasing degree of shortage. By 1916, cereal feed consumption was about 11 per cent below the pre-war level. This shortage was confined to 1916, being largely due to the poor harvest of that year, exacerbated by reductions in imports. The shortage of cake was similar, consumption in 1916 being about 10 per cent below pre-war. Here, the shortage was almost entirely due to a reduction in cotton seed imports, offset to some extent by a rise in linseed imports. However, the cake shortage was more serious, since it developed earlier, and consumption in 1916 was about 15 per cent below that of 1914.

Generally, the supply of both fertilisers and feeds fell in the first two years of the war. The decline in fertiliser was the larger, being of the order of one-fifth (by weight). Consumption of both cereal and cake feeds fell by about one-tenth.[31] Given that agriculture had come to rely heavily on these factors of production by 1914, this was a cause for concern. However, these shortages had as yet not had any serious effect on crop or livestock production.

NOTES

1. F. M. L. Thompson, 'The second agricultural revolution,' *EcHR*, 2nd ser., XXI (1968), 70, 77.
2. Dewey, thesis, 81.
3. Ibid.; Middleton, *Food Production*, 36; he adds also 130,000 tons of: 'bones, guano, shoddy, fish meal &c.' and 180,000 tons of 'potash manures, in terms of kainit'. The latter is confirmed by the Acland Committee's estimate of 23,000 tons of phosphoric oxide (= 184,000 tons kainit); PRO, MAF 36/80, 8 February 1917.
4. A. D. Hall, *Agriculture after the War* (1916), Appendix IV; Middleton, *Food Production*, 150.
5. J. A. S. Watson and J. A. More, *Agriculture: the science and practice of British farming* (8th edn, Edinburgh 1945), 65–7.
6. Watson and More, *Agriculture*, 70; *Departmental Committee on the Sulphuric Acid and Fertiliser Trades*, Cmd. 29, PP 1919, XXIX, 14.
7. Watson and More, *Agriculture*, 72–4; *Departmental Committee . . .* (Cmd. 29), 14; T. H. Middleton, 'The improvement of poor pastures', *Journal of Agricultural Science* I, Pt. I (Cambridge, 1906), 122–8.
8. *Annual Statement of Trade* (1909–16).
9. Thompson, *EcHR* (1968), 76.
10. MAF 36/58, Fertiliser Committee, minutes of proceedings, 8 and 30 Nov. 1915; Middleton, *Food Production*, 144.
11. MAF 36/62, Fertiliser Committee, 2 March 1917.
12. *Departmental Committee* (Cmd. 29), 4–5: Fertiliser Committee, MAF 36/60, 15 Jan. 1917; MAF 36/62, 27 March 1917, 1.
13. Fertiliser Committee, MAF 36/58, 1 Nov. 1915.
14. Lancashire WAC minutes, 31 Jan. 1916.
15. Ibid., 18 Feb. 1916; Middleton, *Food Production*, 148–9.
16. Middleton, *Food Production*, 149; Fertiliser Committee, MAF 36/62, 27 March 1917, 1.
17. Dewey, thesis, 74–5, 81.
18. Fertiliser Committee, MAF 36/60, 15 Jan. 1917, and memo of 8 Jan. 1917, 1–3.
19. Mitchell and Deane, *Abstract*, 134, 137; *Annual Statement of Trade* (1909–16).
20. Fertiliser Committee, MAF 36/60, 15 Jan. 1917, 4; MAF 36/62, 21 March 1917, 1; Middleton, *Food Production*, 187.

21. Fertiliser Committee, MAF 36/60, 15 Jan. 1917, 5; Lancashire WAC minutes, questionnaire of 15 Dec. 1915.
22. *Departmental Committee . . .* (Cmd. 29), 14; He later recorded pre-war usage as 280,000 tons, *Food Production*, 36.
23. See Appendix I.
24. Middleton, *Food Production*, 35–6, 152.
25. See Appendix I.
26. Thompson, *EcHR* (1968), 75–7; *Census of Agricultural Production*, Cd. 6277, 28–9.
27. Cd. 6277, 28–9.
28. Middleton, *Food Production*, 37.
29. See Appendix J; Beveridge, *Food Control*, 375; *Annual Statement of Trade*, (1909–16).
30. Thompson, *EcHR* (1968), 74.
31. See Appendix J for consumption at pre-war and current prices.

Chapter Seven

FARMING IN WARTIME

Agricultural history during the first two years of the war presents a large paradox; in spite of the increasing shortage of factors of production, comparatively little change can be discerned in the level or structure of production, or in farming methods. Thus the experience of the farming industry in the first half of the war was one of 'business as usual' rather than radical change to meet an emergency.[1]

The war broke out when the corn harvest was just beginning. The main concern of agriculturalists and the government was the adequacy of harvest labour. In this respect Britain may have been more fortunate than other European countries; the absence of conscription allowed the harvest to be gathered before the labour supply was much depleted. In addition, the weather was good, and extra effort was made by the labour force, so that the harvest was not appreciably affected.[2] The estimated yields of the three main corn crops, and of potatoes, compared well with the pre-war averages (Table 7.1).[3]

Table 7.1: British corn and potato yields, 1909–13 and 1914

	1909–13 av.	*1914*
Wheat (cwt/acre)	17.3	18.3
Barley (cwt/acre)	15.8	16.1
Oats (cwt/acre)	13.7	14.3
Potatoes (tons/acre)	6.2	6.6

Source: *Agricultural Statistics*

In so far as farmers had any official guidance on their future policy, this had been supplied by the Agricultural Consultative

Committee. The first item it recommended was that 'the area of wheat should be largely increased wherever possible'. Failing that, recourse might be had to winter oats, winter barley and rye, since these ripened early, and thus spread out the demand for harvest labour. To achieve this aim, it would be necessary to plough up a certain amount of grass (rotation and permanent); at the same time, the numbers of livestock should be maintained.[4]

In spite of the absence of a price guarantee, the markets worked in the government's favour. Relative product prices showed early on that cereals, especially wheat, were likely to be more profitable than livestock, and farmers followed the indications given by prices. The result was that the area under cereals was expanded for the harvest of 1915 (Table 7.2).[5]

Table 7.2: Cereal and potato area: increase in Britain, 1915 over 1914

	Acreage ('000)	Per cent
Wheat	379	20
Barley	−318	−19
Oats	222	8
Potatoes	− 6	− 1
Total	277	4

Source: *Agricultural Statistics*

While an overall increase in the area sown to these four major food crops of 4 per cent may not appear substantial, it was a considerable achievement under the circumstances. Since the prices of both wheat and oats rose in 1914–15 far more than that of barley and (especially) potatoes, farmers responded to the market in a rational way. The reduction in the area of barley accounted for about half of the increase in the area under wheat and oats. Of the remaining extra acres devoted to these four crops in 1915, almost half (123,000) was found by reducing the root break (turnips and swedes). The other sources were the breaking up of grass (27,000 acres of permanent and 38,000 of temporary grassland), and a reduction in the area under mangolds by 18,000 acres. The rest of the extra 1915 acreage was accounted for by the reduction in bare fallow (31,000 acres) and in minor crops.

Apart from the commercial attraction of wheat and oats, labour shortage dictated that labour-intensive root crops should be reduced as far as possible in the first year of the war. This was the line of least resistance, but it was also a short-term policy; the growing of corn after corn was at the time a ruinous practice, since before the days of herbicides farmers relied on labour to cultivate root crops to keep the land clean. The reduction in well-cultivated roots made it harder to keep the land clean subsequently, and contributed to the poor yields of corn in 1916. Such a policy might be justified for a time, but there was less justification for turning permanent grass into tillage, whose efficient cultivation could not be assured. Nor was it wise to reduce the area of temporary grass, which was essential for the well-being of the whole arable rotation. The same applied to the reduction in bare fallow, usually only resorted to in the first place to clean some particularly recalcitrant piece of land. The cropping of 1915 made commercial sense in the short term, but it was storing up trouble for the future.

On the livestock side, there was remarkably little change in the first year of the war. The milking herd was recorded as being 2,193,631 cows and heifers in 1909–13, and in 1914 was some 4 per cent above this level. In 1915 it fell to only 2 per cent above the pre-war level, and fell a further 1 per cent the following year. The task of maintaining numbers as far as possible was eased by reasonably adequate supplies of fodder. The 1914 hay crop had been as good as the average for 1909–13 (although the yield was poor in 1915). Although the production of turnips and swedes in 1914 and 1915 was lower than before the war, it was not a large drop (8 and 10 per cent respectively below that of 1909–13) for products whose yield usually varied sharply from year to year.[6] Also, the price of hay increased comparatively slowly, as did the price of cake.[7] While the shortage of manufactured feed was becoming apparent, this would affect milk yields and slaughter weights rather than herd numbers.

Apart from the milking herd, other cattle enterprises had to cope not only with wartime conditions but with the working out of pre-war trends. In particular, there had been a structural change in 1913 and 1914, when the calving herd increased substantially, and, in 1914, the number of cattle over two years had fallen sharply. For the next two years, farmers managed to maintain the size of the calving herd, and came near to restoring that of the two-year-olds. There were clearly commercial incentives for these actions. The maintenance of the calving herd could be seen as an investment for the future, made the more necessary on account of the reduction in

81

Irish exports of both store cattle and calves which occurred after 1914. The rebuilding of the two-year-old herd could be justified by the fact that fat cattle prices rose somewhat faster than veal prices. Also, once accomplished, it permitted a faster turnover of capital than did calf raising. The net result of these trends was to increase the total size of the cattle herd in the first two years of the war, from 7.03 million to 7.44 million.[8]

In the case of sheep, there was rather more change in the structure of the national flock. At the outbreak of war the breeding flock was recovering from a low point in its normal cycle, and continued to rise in 1915 and 1916, although it had not by then reached the pre-war average. A similar pattern was seen in the number of lambs (under one year) and of sheep over one year old. The overall result of these movements was that the total national flock had increased by 1916 by some 721,000, but was still, at about 25 million, 4 per cent below the pre-war level.

In preferring to maintain cattle rather than sheep, farmers may have had certain considerations in mind. These were not purely short-run commercial ones; prices of sheep and of cattle had risen since 1914 at about the same rate. Nor were they likely to have been particularly influenced by questions of fodder supply; sheep and cattle were both affected by the reduction in roots, and cattle were more affected than sheep by the increasing shortage of cereal and cake. But cattle represented a larger capital, which, if allowed to decline, would take longer to rebuild. They also had the advantage of producing a constant flow of income from milk. Thus in the short run sheep were more expendable than cattle. Even so, farmers must have made great efforts to maintain animal numbers, especially in view of the shortage of labour (even shepherds) consequent upon recruiting for the forces.[9]

If sheep were more expendable than cattle, pigs were more expendable than sheep, and the national herd was subject to a process of steady attrition. Numbers of both breeding sows and other pigs were reduced, so that in 1916 the national herd was 7 per cent below its pre-war level. However, these totals do not include the large (but uncertain) number kept on holdings of less than one acre. The main reason for the decline was probably the increasing shortage of feed, chiefly barley and brewers' grains; the former was affected both by the reduction of imports and the marked reduction in the British acreage in 1915; the supply of the latter was beginning to be affected by liquor control in 1916. In addition, since the cow and the sheep reproduced more slowly than the pig, it was realised that it was more important to maintain these in preference to pigs. But even in the case of pigs, the striking feature of the first two years of the war is the small extent to which farmers had had to give ground in the face of wartime difficulties.[10]

Whereas farmers were relatively successful in maintaining their herds and flocks in 1916 as well as in 1915, they were less successful in holding the pattern of cropping. Tillage took a step back in 1916, both in terms of area and of yield (Table 7.3).

Table 7.3: British cereal and potato acreage and yield: 1916 change over 1915

	Acreage		Yield per acre	
	'000 acres	%	cwt.	%
Wheat	−272	−12	15.8	−10
Barley	+121	+ 9	14.8	+ 3
Oats	+ 4	< 1	13.7	− 3
Potatoes	− 50	− 8	5.4 (tons)	−14
Total	−197	− 3		

Source: *Agricultural Statistics*

The overall reduction in tillage was 147,000 acres, that of the four main crops being partly counterbalanced by an increase in minor crops. Some permanent grass was ploughed, but overall, the total grass area increased by 162,000 acres, as the rotation grassland was increased to more than make up for the losses sustained in 1915. The net result was that the area under the four main crops was still 80,000 acres more than in 1909–13.

The behaviour of farmers in the 1915–16 crop year was governed by certain factors. In particular, labour shortage became a reality, there was a reaction to the excess wheat area of the previous year (spurred by the recovery of barley prices), and the weather at critical times was highly adverse. This affected the yields of wheat and oats, and especially of potatoes. The Scottish potato crop was very poor as a result of bad weather at lifting time (the per acre yield fell from 6.7 tons to 4.1 tons, the worst recorded). Perhaps surprisingly, crop yields seemed to be affected more by the weather than by shortage of fertiliser.[11]

The increasing shortage of labour affected farmers in various ways. In some cases, it led to changes in working practices. In south Wiltshire, the young A. G. Street, newly returned from working on a Canadian farm, and accustomed to economising on labour, found various ways to remedy the shortage on his father's farm. The military camps which sprang up locally having led to a shortage of ploughmen, he met the difficulty by using the three-horse double furrow plough in place of the two-horse single-furrow plough. He also promoted the use of sheaf-carrying appliances at harvest, to enable the binder to drop the sheaves in lots of four or five, rather than scatter them singly. Thus equipped, he gathered sixteen acres of oats in a day, compared with six acres by the old method. Apart from these innovations, the major wartime change on this corn-and-sheep farm was the selling off of the breeding flock, due to labour shortage. This was a drastic change, although mitigated by the fact that the farm still fattened sheep. But even for this large farm, dependent on hired labour, changes in cropping patterns seem to have been minimal. The overall effect of labour shortage was felt in a deterioration in the quality of work rather than its quantity:

> If the labour shortage made it impossible to do a certain job at a certain season, the fact of its being left undone was resented strongly. For instance, to have a good plant of rape and turnips, and to be unable to get them handhoed and singled out, rankled. Thinning them out by repeated harrowings was reckoned a poor job. To see banks untrimmed, ditches uncleaned, field corners not dug, and one's farm generally untidy, hurt one's proper pride. But there it was. There was only barely enough labour for essentials, and the frills had to be cut out. From 1916 the farms in the countryside were allowed to deteriorate or to 'go back', a local term which describes the situation admirably.[12]

Street may have been exceptional. In other areas, farmers seem not to have changed their methods in any noticeable way. In 1916 John Orr surveyed the agriculture of Berkshire, and had much critical comment to make on the standard of farming. Thus in Hampstead Marshall, in the Kennet Valley: 'The inferior equipment of farms seems to contribute largely to the poor condition of farming which prevails over the whole of this area.' This low standard had its origins in pre-war practice and antiquated capital. So far, wartime prosperity had been, he thought, too brief to lead to a material raising of standards. And, in spite of the fact that he considered labour shortage to be the most pressing problem facing farmers, old practices still survived, and they were not designed to save labour. He noted (approvingly) that hedging and ditching were still done in some areas, and even remarked on an example of broadcast sowing. In March 1917, when ploughing was in arrears, men still finished the day's work at 4.30 pm, even on a fine day.[13]

The labour shortage was the greatest problem in farmers' minds by this time, although they were exercised by others. At the third meeting of the Oxfordshire WAC, when substantive questions were raised for the first time, only three items were recorded: a decision to issue a leaflet urging women to undertake farm work, a resolution to remind the County Education Committee of the importance of getting children out of school 'at certain periods of agricultural activity', and arrangements for the shooting of wood pigeons.[14]

Similar concerns are apparent from the answers given in reply to a detailed questionnaire addressed to the 12 District Committees in Lancashire by the county WAC in January 1916. Complaint was made of a shortage of skilled labour (especially in arable farming), delays in the delivery of feed and fertiliser, shortage of traction engines and hay presses (due to requisitioning by the Army), and the depredations of animal and bird pests. Some of these concerns were still being voiced by the WAC four months later; the labour problem was still prominent, and farm pests were still considered a serious problem. However, the supply of feed and fertiliser was now satisfactory. An earlier problem, that of a disorganised and labour-wasteful system of milk delivery, was still very much in being.[15]

Concern over labour supply is also evident in the early deliberations of the Lindsey (Lincs.) WAC; in October 1915, the Derby recruiting scheme was criticised for failing to protect farm labour sufficiently, and complaint was made that many agricultural labourers 'starred' under the scheme were leaving farming and taking up better-paid urban occupations.[16] The committee also conducted a survey of farmers' opinions; the replies from the Brigg Rural District are worth quoting in full, as showing the range and nature of farmers' concerns at the time:

The returns from this District show that there is a scarcity of labour, also a shortage of railway sacks.

Exportation of Sulphate of Ammonia should be prohibited.

Tax foreign meat 10s cwt and foreign wheat 10s qr.

Stop malting barley to a specified quantity [?quality].

Reports of meetings [of the WAC] to be given to farmers not on Committee.

Artificial manures not to be exported.

Price of wheat guaranteed at 50s per qr.

Government aid in getting produce to market.

Help required from Committee in securing [railway] trucks and sheets.[17]

Labour shortage apart, the list reflects three concerns: insecurity in the face of foreign competition, concern about problems of distributing produce, and a fear of fertiliser shortage. The fear of foreign competition at this stage in the war is difficult to understand; the average 1915 wheat price had been 52s 10d a quarter (it had been 33s 4d in 1909–13), and farmers could not have been unaware of the high profits which were accruing to them. They may have had in mind the need for protection after the war, rather than even higher profits during it. Difficulties experienced in obtaining trucks, sacks and 'sheets' [tarpaulins?] appear to have been another aspect of the wartime shortage of items for which there was also military demand. The request that fertilisers (specifically sulphate of ammonia) should not be exported shows an awareness of the general fertiliser supply situation, and provides support for the Board's policy of prohibiting export and promoting the use of ammonium sulphate to repair the loss of sodium nitrate.

While the first two years of the war brought farmers many problems, none appeared insurmountable and, taken together, they did not cause the structure of production or methods of working to change appreciably. Such changes as did occur in the balance between tillage and grass, between cereal and other crops, and in the numbers of animals, were small in relation to the totals involved. To date, shortages of factors of production had had little effect on output.[18] At the end of two years of war farmers themselves may have been puzzled to realise that, in spite of the constraints which seemed very real to them, work went on much as usual. As an editorial in the *Farmer and Stockbreeder* put it in July 1916: 'That crops could not be sown and harvested has been prophesied over and over again, but somehow farmers have got through, though shortage of labour has been a serious problem.'[19]

NOTES

1 On the level and structure of production, see c. 14.
2 Middleton, *Food Production*, 103.
3 *Agricultural Statistics*, 1909–14.
4 See ch. 3.
5 *Agricultural Statistics*, 1914–15, and 1924, Pt. III for wartime prices.
6 *Agricultural Statistics*, 1909–16.
7 *Agricultural Statistics*, 1924.
8 *Agricultural Statistics*, 1914–15.
9 A. G. Street, *Farmer's Glory* (1932), 207.
10 See Guild, 'Numbers of live stock' on wartime reproduction rates.
11 Middleton, *Food Production*, 156.
12 Street, *Farmer's Glory*, 203–10.
13 J. Orr, *Agriculture in Berkshire* (1918), 49, 63, 100, 122, 133, 143.
14. Oxfordshire WAC minutes, CWAM I, 10 Jan. 1916.
15 Lancs. WAC minutes, WAM/I, 31 Jan., 29 May 1916.
16 Lincoln RO, Lindsey WAC minutes, vol. I, 29 Oct. 1915.
17 Ibid., 25 Feb. 1916.
18 On wartime output, see ch. 14.
19 *Farmer and Stockbreeder*, 10 July 1916, 45.

Part II

1917–18: FARMING AS A CONTROLLED INDUSTRY

Chapter Eight

POLICY: THE PEAK OF INTERVENTION

The appointment of Lloyd George as Prime Minister marked the watershed of wartime agricultural policy. Whereas opinion in 1915–16 had been moving towards some form of interventionist policy, the delays of the Asquith government had vitiated any action. Now, with the Prime Minister, Lord Milner (now a member of the War Cabinet), and Prothero, the new President of the Board of Agriculture, all in favour of some form of food production policy, the scales were decisively tipped.

Whether the new policy was the work of a single individual is more difficult to say. Prothero gave much credit to Lloyd George:

When . . . I accepted the Presidency of the Board, I had asked the Prime Minister whether he was in favour of a vigorous effort to maintain, and, if possible, to increase food production at home. 'Most certainly,' he replied; 'it is an essential plank in my platform.'[1]

But whether Lloyd George initially had a clear idea of the policy to pursue is uncertain. While his memorandum of 10 November to the War Commitee urging the appointment of a Food Controller envisaged the Controller as having wide powers over home food production, as well as over distribution and prices, this aspect was forgotten in the subsequent discussions on the appointment.[2]

The first decisions on policy were taken by the new administration on 13 December; as well as settling the spheres of responsibility of the Food Controller and the President of the Board of Agriculture 'through mutual discussion', it was at last decided to approve the principle of minimum prices, at least for the 1917 harvest; if it was thought desirable to extend the period of the guarantee, the War Cabinet would be consulted.[3]

Meanwhile, the government was reconsidering Lord Crawford's suggestion that funds should be provided for the stimulation of food production – in particular, that £350,000 should be provided for the purchase of 'machinery' (tractors) from the USA. As late as 16 December, the Treasury had rejected this proposal, but reversed its decision on 23 December, following intervention by Bonar Law.[4]

The wider campaign for increased food production had already opened, with a speech by Prothero on 20 December at a meeting of the Federation of War Agricultural Committees, followed up by circulars from the Board on 28 and 29 December. Dubbed the 'plough policy', it rested on three principles: an extension of the arable acreage, compulsory powers, and decentralisation. The first, as Prothero recognised, was inspired by the Milner Committee report of 1915. The scientific basis for this was that land growing crops directly for human food could support many more people per acre than if devoted to animals. The reason was that most of the energy in the crops grown for animals went to maintain them rather than to produce meat and milk. Thus, for example, Middleton estimated that 100 acres devoted to wheat could support 208 persons for a year on the bread thereby produced, whilst 100 acres of the finest pastures would only support 40 persons on the beef and mutton which they yielded.[5]

The second principle had already been partly supplied, in the form of Regulation 2L of the Defence of the Realm Act, which gave the authorities access to unoccupied land. It was followed up on 10 January 1917 by Regulation 2M, which gave them powers to inspect land, enforce cultivation orders, and take over the running of the property if it was felt that the occupier was unable or unlikely to comply.[6]

The third principle was due to the impossibility of running 500,000 holdings (or 300,000 farms) directly from Whitehall, and the probable resistance of farmers to any form of direct control. Instead, it was proposed to reconstruct the existing County War Agricultural Committees so as to form County Agricultural Executive Committees (ECs) of between four and seven persons, on whom would be placed the responsibility of seeing that the Board's policy was carried out. To assist them, the powers of the Board under Regulation 2M were delegated to the ECs.[7] At the head of this structure would be a newly created sub-department of the Board of Agriculture, the Food Production Department (FPD), which was constituted on 1 January 1917, with T. H. Middleton as its first Director.[8]

The food production policy thus began as an attempt to stimulate arable cultivation, with an early commitment to guaranteed prices for farmers, backed up by compulsory powers to enforce cultivation. This in itself was revolutionary enough. As time went on, however, the government added other elements to the policy. On 21 February 1917, the War Cabinet decided that, as a counterpart to the guaranteed prices, a minimum wage of 25s (£1.25) a week should be offered to farm workers, and that the Board of Agriculture should take powers to prevent rents being raised during the period of guaranteed prices.[9] It was also decided to extend the period of guaranteed prices to six years.

The provisions of the new policy were enshrined in the Corn Production Act, which was introduced into the House of Commons in April, and, after having been keenly debated in the House of Lords, passed into law on 21 August. It consisted of four parts. Part I concerned the guaranteed prices. In 1917 these were 60s per quarter for wheat and 38s for oats; barley prices, in deference to the anti-drink lobby, were not guaranteed. After 1917, prices were guaranteed at a lower level; 55s and 32s for 1918 and 1919, and 45s and 24s in 1920, 1921 and 1922. The mechanism of support was that, should the average market price fall below the minimum price, compensation would be paid equivalent to the difference between the two, on the assumption that the average yield per acre was four quarters of wheat and five quarters of oats. The compensation would be paid in respect of cereals grown; it would not be necessary to prove that they had been sold.[10]

Part I aroused much hostility in Parliament, especially among Liberal and Labour members, who felt that it amounted to enriching one section of the community at the expense of the rest. Nor were they mollified by the government's assurance that current grain prices were so high that the guarantee was unlikely to come into operation.[11] In fact this was the case; the average prices for wheat and oats in 1917 were 75s 9d and 49s 10d per quarter, and remained at roughly that level for the rest of the war.[12] The guaranteed prices should perhaps be seen as a gesture to farming opinion, to obviate apprehension over future prices, and thus gain cooperation in the new policy.

Part II of the Act concerned the minimum wage of 25s a week, to be enforced by fines on employers. It was also provided that the minimum wage should be thereafter decided by a central Agricultural Wages Board. This was another innovation for which there was no precedent, and which had not originally been envisaged. When it was put forward, the War Cabinet view (as late as 4 April 1917) was that its operation would be best postponed until after the war, apparently for fear of alienating farmers. However, the Board of Agriculture seems to have decided that it was best proceeded with during the war.[13]

The AWB took a long time to become effective, spending its first few months in setting up county wages boards. The first minimum wage order (for Norfolk) was not effective until May 1918. However, it was a revolutionary development for agriculture, not least because it led to the specification, for the first time, of a standard working week and overtime payments. In the interim, the 25s minimum of the CPA was enforced. This may be criticised as on the niggardly side. The level of wages for ordinary labourers in 1914 was estimated at 16s 9d (84p). Since retail prices by August 1917 were some 80 per cent above the July 1914 level, the wage would have had to be about 30s (£1.50) to have kept up with inflation.[14] However, the CPA wage seems to have been based on the current rate for ordinary labourers, which was about 24s.[15]

Part III of the Act concerned rent restriction. Here, the provision was that any rents arranged after the passing of the Act should: ' . . . not exceed such rent as could have been obtained if Part I of this Act had not been in force.'[16] Any question as to whether a particular rent was permitted under this provision was to be referred to an independent arbitrator. Requests for reference to arbitration had to be made within one year from the commencement or variation of the tenancy. The arbitrator's award was to be final.[17]

The provisions of Part III were in principle inequitable, in that the previous two sections had at least purported to benefit the two other main agricultural interests, whilst landowners were denied the right to profit from the situation. The section was probably also unworkable, in that it would have been impossible to determine what the hypothetical rent would have been, on the assumption that Part I of the Act did not exist. The section was further undermined by the inoperation of the price guarantees.[18]

Part IV of the Act concerned the control of cultivation. Here, the Board was empowered to direct that land should be cultivated according to the rules of good husbandry, or that the mode of cultivation or the use of land should be changed 'for the purpose of increasing in the national interest the production of food'.[19] If carrying out the Board's directions should involve a tenant in the breach of a tenancy covenant or condition, the covenant or condition should be regarded as suspended in relation to the Board's direction. In making this stipulation, the Board particularly had in mind the not uncommon covenant forbidding tenants to plough up permanent pasture. If the tenant should profit from the suspension of such a condition, the Board could make provision for passing on to the landlord such benefit. Persons aggrieved by the Board's direction had the right of appeal by the same procedure as in Part III. In case of non-compliance with the Board's orders, the landlord could be directed to terminate the tenancy, or, if the occupier was not a tenant, the Board could enter and cultivate the holding. Finally, in cases where damage was being caused by vermin, the Board could authorise entry on to the offending land, the destruction of the vermin, and the recovery of costs from the occupier.

The enormous and unprecedented powers conferred on the government by Part IV of the CPA have often been seen as revolutionary.[20] Yet it must not be overlooked that the operation of Part IV was to be suspended for one year after the passing of the Act; meanwhile, the food production policy was carried out under the amendments to the Defence of the Realm Act, which would themselves lapse when Part IV came into effect. The reason for the suspension of Part IV can only be conjectured; one suggestion is that it would have been politically inadvisable to put into effect a law which in effect threatened large numbers of tenant farmers with eviction.[21] However, this was also implied by the DORA amendments. It seems more likely that Part IV was postponed because it gave the right of appeal against the Board's directives to an independent arbitrator. This right was not enjoyed under Regulation 2M of DORA,[22] and, as events in 1918 were to show, the plough policy would have been unenforceable if farmers had had such a right.

In the interval before Part IV of the CPA became effective, the Board could rely on Regulation 2M, which, as well as giving the

Board power to prescribe the method of cultivation, allowed it to enter on and take possession of land which in the Board's opinion was not being cultivated so as to increase, as far as possible, the food supply of the country.[23] Thus equipped, the sub-department of the Board formed for the implementation of the plough policy, the Food Production Department, began work on 1 January 1917 under its first Director-General, T. H. Middleton. The powers of the Board under Regulation 2M were delegated to the WACs, and via them to the newly formed ECs, beginning with the first Cultivation of Lands Order of 18 January.[24]

Whilst this activity seemed impressive, it was seriously flawed in practice. While farmers on the whole were willing in principle to agree to the directives which the Committees were beginning to issue,[25] they were powerless to give effect to these unless the necessary supplies of labour, horses, machinery, and fertilisers were forthcoming. The early organisation of the FPD did not provide for this. Supply of labour was effectively in the hands of the War Office, although the War Cabinet had already taken a decision to replace the 30,000 agricultural recruits recently asked for with the same number of soldiers.[26] The supply of horses was subject to the continuing demands of the War Office, either directly, or indirectly, via the towns. The supply of machinery was under the control of the Ministry of Munitions, which had recently been given permission to recommence manufacture; in addition, there was the prospect of tractor imports from the USA. The supply of fertilisers was likewise in the hands of the Ministry of Munitions; the supply of feeds was controlled by the newly formed Ministry of Food.[27]

These weaknesses were offset by a substantial reorganisation of the FPD from 19 February 1917. The Department was made into a separate department of the Board of Agriculture. Although its Director-General was nominally responsible to the President of the Board, this was the only link between the two organisations. Whether the President became involved to any great extent in the running of the FPD would depend to a large extent on the personalities involved. That the two would not overlap to any great extent was ensured by appointing a new Director-General of the FPD, Sir Arthur Lee, a Conservative MP. The appointment of Lee, who, it was felt, would give the Department 'push', virtually ensured the independent day-to-day working of the FPD. While the President of the Board of Agriculture, Prothero, was rather gentle, scholarly and not very astute politically, Lee was dynamic, abrasive, and ruthless. While not himself particularly able in a political sense, he was a devoted adherent of Lloyd George, and keen to do a good job for his political mentor. It is hardly surprising that Prothero left him alone to get on with the work of the FPD.[28]

At the same time, the FPD was made responsible for supplying labour, fertiliser, and machinery to farmers. While the Ministry of Munitions still had responsibility for the manufacture of both ferti-lisers and machinery, this was now done to the orders of the FPD, which was made responsible for their distribution. As regards labour, the ability of the FPD to guarantee supply was ultimately dependent on decisions of the War Cabinet, in which the War Office and National Service Department also had a say. Other supplies remained with other bodies; petrol and paraffin were controlled by the Petrol Committee; feeding-stuffs remained under the Ministry of Food. While the changes of February 1917 undoubtedly strength-ened the FPD's ability to effect the plough policy, it was, according to Prothero, ' . . . never able to give to farmer those absolute assur-ances of supply that they not unreasonably demanded'.[29]

The hallmark of the FPD was decentralisation; its powers were delegated to the County Agricultural Executive Committees (ECs) formed from the pre-existing War Agricultural Committees. The ECs were speedily formed, mostly being constituted in late December 1916 or early January 1917. In some cases, the formation of ECs preceded the formation of the FPD; the Lindsey (Lincs.) EC had been formed in June 1916 to cope with the increased work of the WAC.[30] Apart from the weekly reports which the Board demanded from the ECs, communications were maintained via a system of 17 District Commissioners, in charge of small groups of two or three counties. In addition, the FPD nominated to each EC a local representative of its own.

Decentralisation was likewise the hallmark of the county ECs. They were encouraged in this by the need to act speedily in order to make any significant extension of tillage in 1917. Thus the Lanca-shire EC, holding its first meeting on 5 February 1917, found in existence 16 District Sub-committees covering the whole county, which were 'admirably adapted' for the purpose of decentralisation. Accordingly, it was resolved that the DCs be appointed as Sub-committees of the EC for the purposes of the Cultivation of Lands Order (1917), and the powers of the EC under Regulation 2M were delegated to the DCs. The DCs were requested to appoint Inspecting Sub-committees for each township, with the functions of going over the farms in their area, marking down grassland to be ploughed and arable land requiring improved cultivation. Having done so, they were instructed to form district Executive Committees, which could meet frequently to consider the reports of the Inspecting Sub-committees and to issue notices to owners and tenants concerning the cultivation to be carried out. Where farmers disagreed with the decision of the DC, there was a right of appeal to the county EC.[31] The DCs therefore played a crucial role; for most farmers, they were the government agency responsible for implementing the policy, and not, as the 1917 War Cabinet Report suggested, merely advisory bodies to the county ECs.[32]

The plough policy for 1917 had amounted to nothing more than a general request to the ECs to try to schedule for ploughing as much land as possible. Once the work of the ECs was in progress, attention in the War Cabinet turned to the larger problem of the 1918 harvest. A conference of the three agricultural departments in the UK was held, and it was decided that the increase of tillage in 1918, over and above the 1916 area, should be 4.85 million acres in the UK, of which Ireland should account for 1.5 million. The target for England and Wales was 3.0 million, and for Scotland 0.35 million acres.[33]

The War Cabinet accepted these targets, while recognising that their achievement depended upon adequate supplies of labour, fertiliser, machinery, and horses. The requirements would be large: an extra 80,000 men (in addition to the 40,000 or so soldiers already employed in farming) in England and Wales, and 10,000 in Scotland; 25,000 women; 66,000 horses; 6,000 tractors with ploughs, other machinery, 60 steam ploughs, and about two million tons of fertilisers or their raw materials. It was hoped to manufacture Fordson tractors in the UK, with the advice and assistance of Henry Ford. The bulk of the extra labour, it was realised, would have to come from the Army; to this end, Lord Milner was given authority to arrange the necessary labour for the 1918 programme; a duty which he performed energetically and to the dismay of the War Office.[34] He was also asked to report on the position regarding horses and the import of fertiliser; for the latter, his recommendation that an extra 50,000 tons a month of phosphatic rock should be imported was accepted by the War Cabinet.[35] The use made of

Lord Milner at this time, given the high opinion that Lloyd George had of his value, coupled with the fact that he had already made his mark on the Corn Production Bill, is a testimony to the high priority attached to the food production policy in these months.[36]

Almost at the same moment as the 1918 programme was accepted it had to be modified, since the labour position deteriorated and it was realised that the spring ploughing currently being carried out was not enough. It had been hoped that in 1917 some 0.8 million acres would be added to the tilled area in England and Wales, leaving 2.2 million for 1918. However, the total extra tilled in 1917 was only 0.9 million acres for the entire UK, and 0.6 million of this was contributed by Ireland. In Britain, the increase was only 339,000 acres. The target for 1918 for England and Wales was therefore scaled down to 2.6 million acres above that of 1916. It was hoped that the necessary ploughing would be done by April 1918, and would be achieved by breaking up 2.05 million acres of permanent grass and 0.645 million acres of temporary grassland.[37]

The new programme, with quotas for each county, was communicated to the ECs on 14 June. Overall, for England and Wales, the target was some 31 per cent above the 1916 tillage area; an enormously ambitious project to accomplish in one year, and one which, if achieved, would have taken the tillage area back to what it had been in 1882–3. Of the few county quotas which have survived, most are about a third above the 1916 tillage area (Cheshire 33 per cent; Lancashire 35 per cent; Salop 32 per cent; although Lindsey was 15 per cent).[38]

Prior to this, the local organisation had been elaborated. The FPD itself had already been divided into various sections: local organisation, labour, cultivation (mainly concerned with tractors and machinery), supplies (mainly fertilisers), and horticulture. These were to some extent replicated at county level. Prior to the formation of the ECs, the only usual sub-committee of the WACs was a women's labour committee (WWAC). In the spring, the FPD requested ECs to form sub-committees to deal also with labour generally, machinery and supplies (and perhaps also land surveys and finance), and to set up District Committees where they did not yet exist. Thus strengthened, the ECs prepared for the 1918 programme.[39]

The summer of 1917 saw the high-water mark of government commitment to the plough policy. This is clearly brought out by the

War Cabinet decision of 27 June that no more full-time agricultural employees should be taken for military service without the consent of the county EC.[40] Thus agriculture became for the first time a completely protected occupation, on a level with other industries which had earlier gained protection, such as munitions and mining. In addition, the importance of the ECs was greatly enhanced; the Salop EC issued 1,104 exemption vouchers between June 1917 and January 1918.[41] At the same meeting, the War Cabinet began to make good its commitment to find extra labour for the plough policy; overruling Lord Derby, it directed that all soldiers at present in agriculture should remain there unless replaced by men of equal quality, and that a further 50,000 should be supplied. The future labour supply thus underwritten, farmers could cooperate with the authorities with an easier mind. Middleton considered that such progress as the plough policy made in the winter of 1917 and the spring of 1918 was largely due to the sense of security thus engendered.[42]

In these conditions, the plough policy made much headway, 1.86 million acres being added to the tillage area in England and Wales, and 0.28 million in Scotland, as compared with 1916. While this fell short of the revised 1918 programme, it was a considerable advance. Plans were being laid in early 1918 for a further 1.0 million acres in 1919. However, two problems emerged which spelt the end of the brief ascendancy of food production as a national policy. The first originated in the realisation by the FPD that, since the campaign so far had led to the breaking up of land which was most suited for crops, further progress would only be made by encroaching on land that was in principle more suited for grass, and that farmers would be more reluctant to break it up. Thus it was felt that an even greater degree of compulsion would be needed. In these circumstances, the powers conferred on the FPD under the DORA regulations would still be needed. The corollary was that, contrary to expectations, Part IV of the Corn Production Act, with its provision for farmers and landowners to refer cultivation orders to independent arbitration, could not be allowed to come into effect in August 1918 as scheduled.[43]

In the light of these considerations, the government introduced into Parliament the Corn Production (Amendment) Act 1918, which proposed that operation of Part IV of the Corn Production Act should not come into effect until the end of the war, and that meanwhile the DORA powers should continue to be exercised.[44] However, the bill was much amended in the House of Lords, where some influential peers had opposed the plough policy from the start, and it emerged much altered.[45] While it was agreed that the implementation of Part IV should not occur until after the war, its provisions were effectively reinstated. Any tenant or landowner would have the right to apply for arbitration in respect of any cultivation order, or order determining a tenancy, unless the order was solely for the purpose of ensuring cultivation 'according to the rules of good husbandry'.[46] The arbitration envisaged, unlike the appeals previously made by farmers to the ECs, was to be independent. Thus the FPD was faced with the prospect of potentially unlimited arbitration appeals against cultivation orders after 21 August, when the Act came into force. In these circumstances, there was no prospect of continuing the food production policy.

Even before this, however, the policy had been effectively abandoned due to military exigencies. The German spring offensives in 1918, beginning with the Somme attack on 21 March, led to pressure for increased recruiting from many industries. On 20 April the Ministry of National Service withdrew the exemptions granted to agriculturalists aged 18–23. The Cabinet confirmed this decision, and fixed the quota of recruits from agriculture in England and Wales at 30,000. Taking into account 15,588 men yielded under the proclamation of 20 April, this left 14,412 men to find (aged 23–31). In spite of a fresh effort by the labour sub-committees of the ECs, which involved sending out (via the police) census forms to every farmer and occupier of land, and then deciding which individuals should be called up,[47] only a further 7,066 men were found.[48]

The action of the Ministry of National Service and the War Cabinet had a disastrous effect on agricultural attitudes to the plough policy, made more acute by Prothero's defence of the Ministry's action in the House of Lords. He himself was now convinced that it was impossible to persevere with the 1919 programme. He wrote later:

> The President [of the Board of Agriculture] . . . came to the conclusion that neither the military position, nor the transport difficulties, nor the food prospects justified the risks of a compulsory extension of tillage, which was certain to be strongly

opposed, and, at the best, would not increase supplies until September, 1919.[49]

There is an air of self-justification about this memorandum; in particular, was the fact that a successful 1919 programme would not be effective until September a justification for dropping it? If so, the same could be said of the 1917 and 1918 programmes. It seems more likely that the decision to drop the 1919 programme was largely taken on the grounds of the need for military manpower and its effects on farmer opinion, and other decisions flowed from it. Thus Prothero did not seek to overturn the Lords' amendments to the Corn Production (Amendment) Act. These, and the virtual abandonment of the 1919 programme, led to the resignation of Sir Arthur (now Lord) Lee on 22 July 1918. Lee seems to have hoped that his threat of resignation would compel a readoption of the plough policy, and was surprised when Lloyd George accepted his departure; another view is that Lloyd George forced him out of office. What seems certain is that Lee was obnoxious to leading Conservatives in the Lords, who resented his interventionist policies.[50] The sacrifice of Lee offered an expedient way of mollifying the Conservative wing of the Coalition, and the FPD programme had in any case been running long enough to provide some impressive statistics in the House of Commons.

Whilst the calling up of 30,000 agricultural workers was probably necessary, given the need for fit men, it is surprising that this had to spell the end of the 1919 programme. The estimated labour requirement for Prothero's plan for extra tillage in 1919 is shown in Table 8.1.

Table 8.1: Labour requirements for the 1919 tillage programme

Replacement of the 30,000 recruits.
3,000 PoWs for drainage schemes.
3,400 skilled men in autumn 1918.
5,600 skilled men in spring 1919.
15,000 unskilled in spring/summer 1919.

Source: CAB 24/52, 422(1), GT 4658, 30 May 1918.

Including the replacement of the recruits, but omitting the PoWs, whose employment in agriculture was already rapidly increasing, the labour needs of the programme came to 54,000 men. These would have to be found largely from the Army, although surprisingly Prothero made no mention of the use of female labour which, in the form of the Women's Land Army, was also increasing rapidly. Even assuming that the Army was the sole source of labour, this should not have been insurmountable, in view of the large numbers of troops in the UK. Even earlier, in August 1917, the number of troops in training or doing garrison duty at home amounted to 1.5 million.[51] At the Armistice there were still 1,514,993 on the UK ration strength.[52] The large number of troops at home seems to have been an aspect of Lloyd George's military manpower policy; he was reluctant to accede fully to the generals' demands for troops abroad, since he feared that they would then indulge in reckless and wasteful assaults.[53] Even given that there were by spring 1918 some 60,000 soldiers already at work in agriculture, it should not have been beyond the powers of the government to find an extra 54,000 – especially since all that would be required for the first six months would have been to replace the 30,000 recruits.

In all, it is difficult to believe that labour alone was the barrier to the implementation of the 1919 programme. Nor did it fail due to excessive demands for other factors of production. Lee's requirements for machinery and fertilisers were very modest, amounting to machinery worth £1.4 million, and 90,000 tons more fertilisers.[54] Nor could it be safely said that the problems which engendered the plough policy had been overcome; rationing was now in force, there were predictions of a world cereal shortage in 1919, and shipping still had to be economised to bring over the US Army and its equipment. The problems were still potentially acute, but the plough policy, having gone some way to overcome immediate worries, was proving a political liability, and so it was jettisoned.

Having abandoned the 1919 programme, the efforts of the FPD until the Armistice were concentrated on maintaining the existing tillage area, and persuading ECs to work towards the upgrading of existing arable practice. Lee's successor, Sir Charles Fielding, although a strong adherent of a plough policy, had to work within this framework. In fact, given continuing high prices for cereals and potatoes, farmers tried to maintain tillage more or less intact, and the 1919 tillage area was 12.02 million acres, compared with its high point of 12.36 million in 1918 – the highest figure reached between 1886 and 1942.[55]

NOTES

1 Ernle, *Whippingham to Westminster* (1938), 285, 289.
2 CAB 42/24, 13 Nov. 1916, memo G. 95 of 10 Nov. 1916.
3 D. Lloyd George, *War Memoirs* (1938), I, 761.
4 MAF 42/11, L. 34106/1916.
5 Middleton, *Food Production*, 83.
6 Ernle, *The Land and its People*, 106–10; Middleton, *Food Production*, 163–7 and Appendix I.
7 Ibid. and Barnett, *Food Policy*, 197–8.
8 The FPD did not have responsibility for Scotland, where the programme was supervised by the Scottish Board of Agriculture, but ECs were formed in Scotland from the WACs, which had been established in Scotland also; H. M. Conacher, 'Agriculture, with special reference to food production', in D. T Jones et al., *Rural Scotland during the War* (1926), 166.
9 CAB 23/1, 76(8–10).
10 Corn Production Act 1917, 7 & 8 Geo. 5, ch. 46, Pt. I.
11 Barnett, *Food Policy*, 197–8.
12 *Statistical Abstract* (1921), 311.
13 Corn Production Act, Pt. II and CAB 23/1, 76(8–10), CAB 23/2, 112(7).
14 Corn Production Act, Pt. II; A. W. Ashby, 'The work of the Agricultural Wages Board in 1918', *JRASE* 79 (1918), 139–40; Cmd. 24, 275–6; A. L. Bowley, *Prices and Wages in the United Kingdom 1914–1920* (Oxford, 1921), 70.
15 Cmd. 24, 275–6.
16 Corn Production Act, Pt. III, 8(1).
17 Second Schedule, Agricultural Holdings Act 1908, 8. Edw. 7, ch. 28.
18 K. A. H. Murray, *Agriculture*, 14; rent control was widely resented by landowners, who felt that unfair advantage was being taken of wartime conditions to impose an anti-landlord policy; A. F. Cooper, 'The transformation of agricultural policy 1912–1936; a study in conservative politics', unpublished D.Phil., Oxford 1979, 45–6.
19 Corn Production Act, Pt. IV, 9(1).
20 A. M. Gollin, *Proconsul in Politics* (1964), 417–19.
21 Barnett, *Food Policy*, 197.
22 Ernle, *Land*, 110.
23 Regulation 2M (1)(a) in Middleton, *Food Production*, 352.
24 Ernle, *Land*, 110.
25 See opinion in *Farmer and Stockbreeder*, 5 March 1917, 371.
26 CAB 23/1, 32(12), 12 Jan. 1917; CAB 23/1, 42(1–4), 23 Jan. 1917.
27 Middleton, *Food Production*, 174 fol.
28 Ibid., 175–6; Alan Clark (ed.), '*A Good Innings'; the private papers of Viscount Lee of Fareham* (1974), Introduction and 165–7; H. E. Dale, *Daniel Hall; pioneer in scientific agriculture* (1956), 109, 130–1; Cooper, thesis, 46.
29 Ernle, *Land*, 119.

30 Lindsey WAEC, *Report of the Proceedings of the Committee for the Period ended 31 March, 1918*, 1.
31 Lancashire EC Report, May 1917, 1.
32 *War Cabinet Report, 1917*, 157. Middleton wrote (*Food Production*, 214) that ECs could not delegate their DORA powers to the DCs, although this county clearly did. The FPD advised ECs in May 1917 to set up DCs.
33 CAB 23/2, 135 (10, Appendix), 9 May 1917.
34 Ibid., and CAB 23/2, 145(9), 24 May 1917; Gollin, *Proconsul*, 417.
35 CAB 23/2, 153(1).
36 Gollin, *Proconsul*, 418–19.
37 Middleton, *Food Production*, 191, 210–11. The Scottish and Irish targets were apparently retained unaltered.
38 Cheshire EC, Review of work of the EC . . . to 30th June 1918, 5–6; Lancs. EC, Report of EC, May 1917, 2; Salop, Report of EC to 12 Jan. 1918, 2–3; Lindsey, Report of WAEC to 31 March 1918, 4.
39 Middleton, *Food Production*, 212. On DCs, see n. 32 above.
40 Cheshire EC, Review of work . . . to 30th June 1918, 5–6.
41 Lindsey, Report . . . to 31st March 1918, 4–8.
42 CAB 23/3, 170(1).
43 Salop EC, Report to 12th January 1918, 5.
44 Middleton, *Food Production*, 221.
45 Ibid., 262–3.
46 Ernle, *Land*, 163.
47 E.g., the procedure in the Lancs. EC report for July 1918, 3.
48 Middleton, *Food Production*, 267.
49 Ernle, *Land*, 164–6, from a memorandum by him of 20 July 1918.
50 Clark, *Innings*, 177–81; Cooper, thesis, 46–8.
51 CAB 23/3, 225(13), 28 August 1917.
52 War Office, *Statistics of the Military Effort*, 877.
53 C. Barnett, *Britain and her Army 1509–1970* (1970), 405.
54 CAB 23/7, 422(1), GT 4409, 30 May 1918.
55 Ministry of Agriculture, *A Century of Agricultural Statistics 1866–1966* (1968), 95.

Chapter Nine

LABOURERS, SOLDIERS, PRISONERS, AND WOMEN

THE CONVENTIONAL LABOUR SUPPLY

The adoption of a food production policy was accompanied by a growing realisation that the retention of labour on the land was a prerequisite for its success. However, this realisation took effect slowly, and the early months of 1917 saw fresh recruiting of agricultural labour. This can be taken as evidence that agriculture still did not command the highest political priority.

The government began to consider the labour implications of the new policy at the end of 1916. The question of exemption of agricultural workers came up in the War Cabinet on 31 December, when it was decided that the matter should be discussed by the Secretary of State for War and the President of the Board of Agriculture. In particular, they would consider increasing exemptions for men aged over 25.[1] Nothing seems to have come of this. Indeed, the government was not yet prepared to afford protected status to the farm labour force as a whole, since it decided in mid-January 1917 to take for military service a further 30,000 men. The blow was softened by promising to supply an equivalent number of soldiers for farm work.[2] In May, a further slight concession was made; if a potential recruit was considered essential for farm work by the EC, the call-up would be delayed by up to 3 weeks, while the EC tried to find a substitute (military or civilian).

The final stage of protection came on 27 June, when it was accepted that no man who had been employed full-time on work of national importance on 1 June would be called up for military service, or even medically examined, without the consent of the EC – even if a substitute could be provided.[3] This decision was an effective barrier against further losses, and for the next nine months the ECs were at the height of their influence, and had to cope with a large volume of work.

The new arrangements effectively preserved the existing 'conventional' labour force for the next nine months, according to the Z8 surveys (Table 9.1).

Table 9.1: British permanent male labour force, Jan. 1917–April 1918 ('000)

Jan. 1917	April 1917	July 1917	Oct. 1917	Jan. 1918	April 1918
562	569	597[a]	589	586	589

Note: [a] See note 4
Source: Board of Trade, *Report on the State of Employment in the United Kingdom . . . (1917–18)*

Since, whatever the deficiencies of these surveys in yielding absolute numbers, they seem to be reliable in indicating trends or changes of trend, they may be accepted as showing the near-stasis of the regular labour force in this period. There is even a slight rise in the first half of 1917; assuming that this is real, it seems to be the normal seasonal rise, kept in being for the next nine months by the operation of the new policy.

This comparatively brief period of security was broken by the German offensive which began on 21 March 1918. The government was forced to issue a fresh call for soldiers. The upper age limit was raised to 51 by the Military Service Act (No. 2), which became law on 18 April. On 20 April a proclamation of the Ministry of National Service cancelled exemption certificates held by men aged 18–23 (in medical Grade 1 or Category A). It was also made clear that further calls on manpower would be made. The ECs protested vigorously. Prolonged negotiation followed, the result of which was that the demands were made precise. It was agreed on 8 May that agriculture in England and Wales should yield up 30,000 men aged 19–31. Scotland was asked for 5,500 men. Quotas for each county were agreed, and the ECs given the task of filling them.[5]

The ECs resented this new policy deeply. From being engaged to preserve the labour force they were now directed to curtail it. Their invidious position, and the extra work, were deeply resented. Under the 'clean cut' of the April proclamation, 15,588 men had been taken; a further 14,412 therefore had to be found to make up the 30,000 and it was these that caused the most difficulty.[6] The Cheshire EC, having been faced with a demand for 1,000 men, investigated 2,600 cases before being able to fulfil the quota: ' . . . not, however, that they were satisfied from an agricultural point of view that the men could be spared, but in deference to the urgent requirements of the Nation'.[7] Lindsey, faced with a quota of 1,000 men, had recruited 597 before reporting to the Board of Agriculture that: ' . . . The Committee could not be responsible for the non working of the farms if more men were taken from Agriculture for the Army.'[8]

The Ministry of National Service noted the great difficulty in obtaining labourers from Wales; in Cardigan, feeling was running so high that farmers were threatening to turn cattle into the crop fields.[9] In Lancashire, the work involved the labour sub-committee sitting continuously for 10 days to examine 1,365 applications for leave to appeal against the withdrawal of exemptions; leave was granted in 772 cases, so that 593 recruits (at a minimum) were produced. Subsequently, after quotas had been arranged, the county's quota was fixed at 1,200. To obtain the remainder, the sub-committee issued census forms (over 20,000) to every farmer and occupier of land in the county, and sat for a further 12 days examining them before finding the quota.[10] Some areas got off more lightly. Hertfordshire had a quota of only 300, since it had allowed recruiting fairly freely in the past.[11]

In the country as a whole, the ECs failed to meet the target. By 27 June only 22,654 men had been recruited. Leaving aside the 15,588 of the 'clean cut' of 20 April, about whom there could be no argument, the national quota was still 14,412, and enormous effort by the ECs had yielded only 7,066.[12] The Cabinet agreed on 27 June that no more men would be called up until after the harvest. Thereafter, the military position so improved that no more demands were made for agricultural labour, and the ECs reverted to their former position as protectors of labour.[13]

In spite of the demands of military service in the spring and early summer of 1918, few inroads seem to have been made into the 'conventional' farm labour force. Having fluctuated, according to the Board of Trade reports, at around 590,000 from October 1917 to April 1918, it was still recorded at 588,000 at the end of July 1918, and only fell to 578,000 at the end of November, after the Armistice.[14] To a large extent, the losses to the forces seem to have been offset by inflows of fresh labour; the Z8 reports indicate that the loss of 25,000 men to the forces between April and July was reduced to a net loss of only 6,000 by this means.[15]

Although checked after the summer of 1917, recruiting of farm labour had implications for the age-structure of the civilian labour force, and its working arrangements. Prior to the war, the 1911 population census had shown that there were 398,000 employees in British agriculture aged 20–44 (49.8 per cent of the total). By January 1917, the Board of Trade reports (the only extant source on the subject) recorded that only 177,000 (31.5 per cent) were of military age (18–41), and this ratio remained almost constant for the next year; in January 1918 it was 32.6 per cent. Thereafter it rose, to a maximum of 48.0 per cent in July 1918, but this was due to the raising of the military age limit to 51.[16]

The loss of men of military age could naturally be expected to affect more seriously the occupational groups with a high proportion of men of military age. Thus horsemen, and to a lesser extent cattlemen, were more vulnerable to recruitment than were ordinary labourers, a higher proportion of whom had been, at the last population census, above military age. Thus a redistribution of function might be expected to occur, as ordinary labourers took over tasks formerly performed by the more specialised men in charge of animals. That this was happening by 1917 is indicated by the 1918 Agricultural Wages Board enquiry into agricultural labour.[17] Horsemen, it was said, had been the class of labour most recruited, so that ordinary labourers had been upgraded to look after animals. However, they were reluctant to do horse work or milking, because of the long hours and the constant Sunday work. Recourse was thus had to other forms of labour. In Lincolnshire, 'mere lads' were given the job of carting 5-ton loads, in waggons drawn by 4-horse teams, along the roads, the principal horsemen being confined to field work. In northern counties, women had been brought in to replace 'hinds' in field work (there being few 'ordinary' labourers to replace the missing hinds). Part-time labour was also resorted to; beechwood and chair factory workers in Buckinghamshire, dockers in Gloucestershire, fishermen in Norfolk, and quarrymen in Kesteven. Female labour, it was thought, was, apart from the Women's Land Army, still mainly part-time or seasonal, and largely confined to arable or market gardening districts.[18]

The quality of the labour force therefore declined as a result of recruiting. The labour force also suffered indirectly from wartime conditions, in that real wages fell, and the supply of food deteriorated slightly. These constraints raise the possibility that the supply of effort per worker also fell, so that the decline in labour force quality was not made good by greater effort per head.

Information on wartime wage-rates is scanty. The enquiry by the Agricultural Wages Board early in 1918 suggested that between July 1914 and early 1918 English labourers' weekly wage-rates rose by 56–61 per cent.[19] The rises in rates would not be substantially altered by the value of extras and allowances.[20] The significance of this is that earnings did not keep pace with inflation. The official index of retail prices had risen by February 1918 to 190; taking food alone, the index was 208 (July 1914 = 100). To some extent, the official index of food prices had become by this time misleading, since certain foods consumed in 1914 were no longer available in the same quantity. A. L. Bowley made an adjustment for this, by which the index number for food in February 1918 was reduced to 198. However, even allowing for this, the general index of retail prices would still be above that of agricultural wage-rates. In the case of agricultural labourers' families, who devoted about two-thirds of their pre-war expenditure to food, Bowley's modification would imply a general price index for February 1918 of about 183.[21]

The outstripping of wage-rate increases by inflation was a general feature of wartime labour history. From this it has often been concluded that the British labour force suffered a decline of real wages during the war. However, for the national labour force as a whole, wage-rates were not synonymous with earnings; there is good reason to think that overtime working and full employment meant that the real earnings of urban working-class families were maintained at or near the pre-war level.[22]

For the agricultural labourer, however, these palliatives did not operate. There is no evidence that unemployment in wartime differed markedly from that of pre-war; fluctuations in the labour force still followed the seasonal patterns (except in 1918). Nor was the labourer able to take advantage of overtime; until the Agricultural Wages Board began work in 1918, hours worked were customary ones, and institutionalised overtime payments were rare.[23] Thus the rises in earnings must have been very close to rises in wage-rates, so that a decline in real wages could not be avoided.

The decline in real wages is confirmed by an enquiry by the

Agricultural Wages Board into the cost of living of the families of agricultural labourers. Comparison with the pattern of expenditure in 1914 revealed that the expenditure of the average family had risen by about 86 per cent by the spring of 1918 (Table 9.2).

Table 9.2: Household expenditure of farm labourers' families, 1914–18

	Estimated pre-war expenditure		Expenditure of 396 families March–June 1918		% rise
	s.	d.	s.	d.	
Main foods	15	10	28	11	83.1
Other food	1	0	2	1	108.3
Rent	1	11	2	1	8.7
Fuel, light	1	9	4	1	134.5
Clothes	3	6	6	8	90.3
Insurance		9	1	6	100.0
Cleaning materials		6	1	0	100.0
Totals	25	3	46	5	85.6

Source: Cmd. 76, 37

This list is not exhaustive; in particular, it omits household durables, and the clothing estimate for 1918 is largely guesswork. However, the investigation of food expenditure was a careful one. From this estimate it can be seen that the official index of retail prices was a fairly good proxy for the rise in family expenditure during the war, so that the reduction in real wages can be confirmed. Taking the rise in expenditure as the 86 per cent shown above, and taking wages as having risen by 59 per cent (the average of the rates above), the reduction in real wages would be 14.5 per cent [100 − (159/185 × 100)]. However, it must be remembered that the wage-rates used in the calculation are for winter 1918, and would have been slightly higher by March–June, when the family budgets were collected.

For the agricultural labourer, as for all classes, there was a slight deterioration in the quality of the diet consumed during the war. By 1918, sugar had become scarce, as had the better qualities of meats; margarine had been partially substituted for butter; and the quality of bread had fallen, as the extraction rate rose. In addition, a higher proportion of protein was now of the second class sort, derived from potatoes and cereals rather than meat and dairy products. Some of these deficiencies are referred to in the AWB report on living costs (Table 9.3).

111

Table 9.3: Rural labourers' families: protein and calorie supply, 1912–18

		Supplied per day (per average 'man'):		
	Protein (grammes)		Calories	
1912	*1918*		*1912*	*1918*
101.5	101.0		3,575	3,445

Source: Cmd. 76, Appx XII, 69

There had thus been a negligible fall in protein supply, as reductions in one type were offset by increases in others. The decline in calorie supply is larger, at 3.7 per cent. However, it is in itself slight, and similar to the national decline of 3 per cent found in Beveridge's investigations.[24]

The decline in real wages was to some extent repaired in 1918, with the introduction of the minimum wage. This, agreed in Cabinet as long ago as February 1917, and forming a section of the Corn Production Act, did not begin to compensate for inflation until the first AWB wage order was made, for Norfolk, in May 1918. By October, orders had been made for each district in England and Wales (Table 9.4);

Table 9.4: Minimum wages in 27 English counties, May–October 1918

	s.	d.	% rise from July 1914
Shepherds	38	2	110
Cattlemen	37	10	110
Horsemen	37	10	109
Ordinary labourers	33	7	100

Source: A. W. Ashby, *JRASE*, 1918, 151–2

Since by the summer of 1918 price control and rationing had reduced the rate of inflation (especially of food), the gap between wages and prices had also been reduced. Taking July–August 1918, as falling halfway through the AWB wage-raising operation, the general index of retail prices was about 205 (the level is not precise),[25] and food prices were about 214 (average of July and August in both cases). Bowley's modification of the official index for July 1918 gives a figure for food of 198.[26] It could thus be said that agricultural labourers had made up the fall in real wages suffered in the first three years of the war, although the quality of food and other purchases was not as good as pre-war.

There were other benefits from the AWB; as well as the fixing of hours of work, and the introduction of overtime payments on a regular basis, there was the introduction of a weekly half-holiday. This did not necessarily amount to time off, but if hours were not reduced, overtime would become payable after 6.5 hours work on one non-Sunday day. This was not implemented until March 1919. However, these were all novel reforms, which eased the life of the labourer, as well as restoring his real wage.[27]

While the quality of the labour force had declined in the first two years of the war, and was not subsequently made good, it can also be said that the supply of effective effort per man may have fallen, since real wages had fallen by 1917, and were only restored towards the end of 1918. In this situation, the morale of the labour force may have declined. In addition, the diet of the labourers' families declined slightly in quantity (measured in calories), and in quality (although this is not easily measurable). Taking all these factors together, it may be said that the civilian labour force was of lower quality than pre-war, and the individual members of it were unlikely to have expanded their efforts so as to compensate for this decline.

SOLDIERS

Before the introduction of the food production policy, soldier labour was not used in large amounts, or on a permanent basis. But the introduction of the new policy implied a large rise in the labour force, and soldiers were the most convenient replacement. The labour problem was exacerbated by the unexpected call for a further 30,000 farm labourers for military service made in January 1917. The initial reaction of the War Cabinet was to say that they should be entirely replaced by soldiers from the Home Defence Force.[28] A novel start was made with the formation of Agricultural Companies, composed of soldiers of medical category CIII, 'unaccustomed to agricultural work, and physically unfitted for service in the Army'.[29] However physically inadequate, the novelty lay in their permanence; they were to be made available for the duration of the war. The initial number in Agricultural Companies was to be 11,500. However, they took some time to reach full strength; even at the end of June, they only numbered 9,800.[30] Further temporary help was to be given by the Army, in the form of 12,500 Home Defence Force men on agricultural furlough until 30 April. The intention had been to help with the spring ploughing, but it was found that not more than 3,000 out of all the Agricultural Company and Home Defence men could plough.[31] The mixed nature of the soldiery can be judged from the experience of the Somerset EC; 40 soldiers professing to be ploughmen had been sent to the depot at Taunton in February. Of these, only 18 proved to be ploughmen, 2 had a little ploughing experience, 4 were general farm workers, and the rest (including a dustman) had merely some experience with horses.[32]

This failure was rapidly made good. On 12 March all skilled ploughmen in the UK were ordered to return to their depots on agricultural furlough until 30 April. This yielded 18,000 men, who were not only skilled ploughmen, but physically of a higher grade than men in Agricultural Companies. Furlough for both the HDF men and the skilled ploughmen was extended until 10 May, in view of the lateness of the ploughing season.[33] Thus reinforced, the military contingent grew rapidly; by 10 April, 36,295 soldiers were working in agriculture.[34] However, most of the assistance was still temporary. Shropshire EC had by late April the use of 951 soldiers, but 731 of them were due for recall in May. The remainder were Agricultural Company men, who had proved already 'most satisfactory'.[35] In Lindsey, while 'a considerable number' of soldiers had been furloughed in the spring, an Agricultural Company was not established until August.[36] In Oxfordshire, an Agricultural Company was not established until January 1918.[37]

The temporary nature of the military assistance was revealed in May, when 18,000 ploughmen were recalled to the Army before the tillage work had been completed. As a concession, furlough for the rest was extended to 25 July. In addition, faced with the need for assistance with the coming hay and corn harvest, a further 17,000 soldiers were supplied; they began to arrive in June.[38]

By June 1917, the long deliberations by the government over the 1918 agricultural programme were over. The decision to substantially extend tillage having been taken, fresh efforts had to be made to increase the labour supply. At the same War Cabinet meeting at which the decision was made to take no more agricultural workers from the land without the consent of the ECs, a fresh supply of military labour for the coming year was agreed. The men now loaned until 25 July were to be retained. In addition, a further 50,000 were to be supplied (of whom half were to be men with agricultural experience) at the rate of 5,000 per week for 10 weeks, from the first week in July. Existing soldier labour, and the 50,000 to come, was to be retained indefinitely, unless replaced by soldiers of the same quality. The only drawback to these arrangements was that the 17,000 already lent for the harvest were to be regarded as part of the 50,000, so that the Army commitment was in reality only a further 33,000.[39]

This decision was a turning-point in agricultural policy, and laid the foundation for the permanent assistance of military labour for the rest of the war. While the extra quotas agreed in June fell behind schedule, the net effect was that the labour force by the end of the year was larger than it had been in the spring. More importantly, perhaps, it was in effect permanent. Thus, while the numbers in April had been 36,295, the withdrawal of the 18,000 ploughmen had been offset by the further 17,000 added in June for the harvests. Thus total numbers must have still been about the April level by June, when the extra detachments were agreed. There is some dispute about the size of this proposed extra labour force. Ernle seems to have envisaged a net gain to agriculture of the whole 50,000. A War Cabinet minute in December thought it was 43,000. The original agreement was, though, clearly for only 33,000. Given that, Ernle's strictures on the non-fulfilment of the programme lose much of their force. He complained that 50,000 should have arrived by September, but by December only 30,000 had arrived. If that is so, then the programme can be convicted of delay, but not serious non-fulfilment. Even so, the problem exercised the War Cabinet in the autumn, to the extent of suggesting in October that the Army should release soldier ploughmen serving at the front, even if they could only be spared for two or three months. In November it was noted that the shortage of ploughmen meant that there were 2,000–3,000 sets of ploughing equipment idle.[40] By late December the War Cabinet recorded that 26,000 of the extra soldiers had arrived, so that only 7,000 still remained to fulfil the quota. Given that 22,000 soldiers (from Agricultural Companies and others) remained on the land from the spring, there were now 48,000 permanent soldier workers in agriculture. This may be an overestimate; the War Cabinet report for 1918 recorded 41,361 'on

115

farms' on 1 January 1918, but the discrepancy may be due to the slack season, some soldiers being in depots rather than on farms.[41]

More worrying, perhaps, was the lack of skill. It had been hoped that 25,000 would have agricultural experience, or at least be used to handling horses, but complaints were still made. In Worcestershire, soldiers who were supposed to be skilled failed to use reaping hooks efficiently on 150 acres of laid corn, and the EC complained to the FPD.[42] Even as late as September, *soi-disant* ploughmen were still being unmasked by the ECs; in Hereford, out of 47 'ploughmen' soldiers, only one proved to be genuine, and 21 had no previous connection with agriculture.[43] Ultimately, only 2,500 of the soldiers were found to be skilled.[44]

In 1917 also, the payment arrangements for soldiers were altered. In the spring, wages were not laid down officially, but were to be those of the district. While pay scales were still promulgated for the harvest, they were only slightly above those of the previous year; if the men could not be found harvest work, they were to be paid at the rate of 4s 2d a day; only 2d more than in 1916. Since labourers' wages had risen more rapidly, the gap between military and civilian pay scales was now small or non-existent. If local rates were higher, they were to be applied. Apart from wages, the only significant change in conditions of service was that the period of notice was now two weeks on either side. After the 1917 harvest, the general rule was adopted that local rates of pay were to be applied, so that soldier labour lost its financial disincentive for farmers.[45]

Apart from harvest work, for which no special training was required, soldier labour was mainly intended to help with ploughing and cultivating work consequent on the tillage programme. It was to this end that the extra contingents of June 1917 had been granted. However, the lack of skill amongst the soldiers made necessary the establishment of training centres for horse-ploughmen. These were set up from September 1917. Two weeks' training was provided, at a wage of 21s a week, rising to 31s when trained. Thereafter the ploughmen would be employed at the local rate. In addition, on-farm training centres were also established. Eventually, about 30 schools were established near military Distribution Centres, and they trained about 4,000 horse-ploughmen.

In addition, from early in 1917, men were being trained in tractor work. They were initially given a fortnight's training by the FPD. Later it was found more satisfactory to send them direct to the

Tractor Representative of each EC for training; they were asked to undertake training at the rate of one man for each tractor operated by the county. After training, the men would receive 30s a week, and a bonus of 1s for each acre ploughed. In all, 4,093 men were trained in tractor operation. Finally, about 200 soldiers were sent out for training with the crews of steam-ploughs and threshing sets.[46]

The lack of trained ploughmen proved a continual problem; the late arrival of the June contingent, its unskilled nature, and the necessarily slowly rising output of ploughing schools meant a continual shortage. In the autumn of 1917, the supply had to be augmented by three months' furlough for 1,500 ploughmen from the Army in France.[47] It is in fact unlikely that the number of soldier ploughmen present in early 1917 was again reached until well into 1918. The Lancashire EC had the services of 1,301 Army ploughmen in the spring of 1917, but these were recalled. By the end of the year, a ploughing school had been established at Fulwood, and the EC hoped that its work, and the use of Army ploughmen, would enable it to have the services of at least 250 ploughmen. Whether it reached this figure is not clear, although it was thought worth recording that 150 skilled ploughmen from overseas were recalled to the Army following the German spring offensive in March. The shortage of ploughmen provoked the Gloucester EC to protest acerbically to the Board of Agriculture in February 1918.[48]

During 1918, the supply of soldier labour was greatly increased. At the end of 1917, our estimate is that there were 48,000 men in agriculture in England and Wales. By March 1918, there were 63,000, mostly in Agricultural Companies.[49] The companies reached a peak in November 1918 of 79,000. In the harvest month of August they had already reached 70,000, to which were temporarily added 10,000 for the harvest.[50] Added to this was Scottish soldier labour; in late 1918, the Scottish Agricultural Companies numbered 9,000 men, and 10,000 were added temporarily for the harvest.[51] It was noteworthy that the German spring offensives had been met by recruiting fresh civilians from agriculture, rather than depleting the companies, even though at least 45,000 of their men were thought to be fit for service on the Western Front.[52]

Since soldiers formed the largest single category of replacement labour, their level of efficiency is of particular interest. The AWB report of early 1918, having instanced several examples of soldiers' inefficiency, shied away from drawing a distinction between soldiers and the civilian labour they replaced, and concluded that each soldier was as efficient as each civilian worker.[53] Since the quality of the remaining civilians had deteriorated, the gap between the two may not have been large, but there are several reasons for considering that soldiers initially were not as efficient as the labour they replaced. Firstly, there was the poor physical condition of the men in the Agricultural Companies. Farmers, wrote Lord Ernle, grumbled that they were being asked to keep infirmaries.[54] Little could be done about that. But there were two further problems which could to some extent be overcome: selection and training.

The question of selection greatly exercised farmers, who were only really satisfied when they could obtain a soldier whom they could specify by name. During the early part of the war this was to some extent possible; of the 16,690 soldiers supplied to farmers between 12 August and 13 October 1916, 7,679 had been asked for by name. With the growth of the soldier labour force, this practice was less marked; in Norfolk by September 1917, applications for 800 named men on temporary leave were made, but only 10 per cent of these were granted.[55] The next best alternative for farmers would be to obtain a man who knew the district. This was rarely possible. Thus in early 1918 there were complaints from northern farmers who could not obtain northmen, and Cornish farmers who could not obtain Cornishmen. Failing this, farmers thought that at least the soldiers should have some experience, but the early selection of men left much to be desired. In Somerset, 784 men had arrived at the Taunton depot by 25 March 1917, but 200 of these had to be returned to their units as unsuitable.[56] In south-east and east midland counties, the 1918 AWB report on farm labour thought that selection had been very poor at first, although improved since mid-1917. In Loughborough, it was found that few were used to horses or knew how to milk.[57] However, selection improved by 1918; the AWB report thought that the lack of care in selection had by then been diminished if not entirely swept away.[58] Hertfordshire EC in January 1918 thought soldiers were by then usually well chosen.[59]

As regards training, most soldier ploughmen seem to have either been already trained, or were trained by farmers. The evidence for this is fragmentary, and rests on the fact that there must have been many more soldier ploughmen at work than were ever produced by the training schools. The output of ploughmen from the latter was c. 8,000, yet in Shropshire alone there were in December 1917 414 ploughmen, and in December 1918, 534. In Lindsey, the output of the ploughing school to the end of March 1918 had been only 85 men, to which were added 40 ploughmen from overseas, recalled in February. But there were at the time 746 'skilled' soldiers working on farms, and the likelihood is that a high proportion of these were in fact ploughmen.[60]

For other sorts of work, formal training was not available, but even so, a fairly high proportion of soldiers were already skilled, or acquired skill as time went on. In the Kesteven district of Lincolnshire early in 1918, 957 soldiers were on farms, but only 109 of them were classified as unskilled, while 468 were described as 'Old Company, semi-skilled' (presumably the original Agricultural Company men), and 275 were classed as skilled.[61] In Shropshire, less than half of the soldiers at work in December 1917 (43 per cent) and December 1918 (45 per cent) were classed as 'carters/ general farm workers'; it hardly needs saying that general farm work often required a high degree of particular skill.[62] The bulk of training must have been done (or not done) on the farm. It was noted that, although unskilled, the soldiers were mostly very willing to learn,[63] and when farmers were prepared to take pains in instructing the men, the result was pleasing; Lindsey EC noted that, as well as the 746 skilled men at work in March 1918, there were 226 unskilled men, of whom it was said: '. . . the majority are becoming more useful as time progresses – the efforts of certain farmers in training these men having been most praiseworthy'.[64] It may be presumed that the average level of skill rose over time regardless of the soldiers' previous occupations, although there must have been difficult cases; the pinnacle of frustration was probably that of the Shropshire farmer who said: 'One of the men I got was a piano-tuner; I could knock nothing into him'.[65]

Physique, selection, and training were the main problems attending the use of soldier labour in 1917–18, and they were not entirely overcome even by the end of the war. Two minor problems were also mentioned during the war: pay and hours. Pay has been discussed above; while it seems that the high rates of soldiers' pay were a disincentive to their employment in 1915–16, this situation had been rectified by 1917, since labourers' rates had by then caught up with those of soldiers. As regards hours, farmers were wont to complain even as late as 1918 that the shorter hours specified for soldier labour were causing dissatisfaction amongst civilian workers.[66] However, the complaint was unjustified; from the start, it was laid down by the War Office that hours were to be those of the district. While hours were specified (10 a day) for the harvest, this was with a view to determining overtime rather than actually limiting the working day.

That the cost-efficiency of the soldiers fell below that of the men they replaced is most probable, although the gap between soldiers and the remaining civilians is unlikely to have been large by the end of the war. In all, the comment of the Buckinghamshire reporter in the 1918 AWB report is not unreasonable: 'Soldiers have not always a capacity equal to that of the trained farm worker, but they must be in general be reckoned in terms of men.'[67]

PRISONERS OF WAR

The use of prisoners of war in agriculture came belatedly, but when it did so it rapidly expanded. Negligible before the spring of 1917, by the end of the war the contingent of prisoners working in agriculture was almost twice the size of the Women's Land Army, and almost half the number of soldiers. Their employment must be accounted one of the more successful operations of the food production campaign.

Attempts to use prisoners were first made by the Board of Agriculture in February 1916, when WACs were asked for their views. Since this was still a sensitive subject, the letter was confidential.[68] The response was not encouraging; Lancashire decided to take no action, as did Oxfordshire.[69] West Sussex thought that their use would not be allowed, the county being a prohibited area.[70] The scheme was not implemented. There seems no doubt that it was premature; public feeling was not favourably disposed to prisoners, and antagonism died slowly, as Cheshire EC reported in June 1918.[71]

In January 1917 the Board tried again to interest the WACs in using prisoners. It was proposed to send them out in batches of 75, with a guard of 35 soldiers.[72] This fresh approach, coming as it did soon after the proclamation of the food production policy and the formation of the ECs, was favourably received. The ECs of Cheshire, Hertfordshire, and West Sussex applied for batches.

Oxford thought that batches of 75 were too large to be useful in agriculture; Wiltshire had already made this suggestion in December.[73]

The Board soon tackled the problem of large batches. In February, Prothero wrote to the ECs saying that the War Office had agreed to reduce the batch size to 40 if required. Somerset promptly put in for four batches. Norfolk noted that it was expecting 150 prisoners.[74] But the early establishment of camps proceeded slowly. Generally, this was due to the failure of the authorities to provide the numbers of men at first envisaged. The original plan had been to provide 2,300 for agriculture. Large demands were then made on prisoner labour by other government departments, so that all that survived was permission given to the Board to use 'a few' who had been allocated to other forms of work, but could not for the moment be employed on them.[75] As a result, agriculture lagged behind. By the end of July, only 15 camps had been provided, housing 1,476 prisoners.[76]

There were other problems also, chiefly the finding of suitable accommodation. Somerset proposed to house its first four batches in the Bridgewater skating rink, the Shepton Mallet Union work-house ('or, failing this, the disused brewery at Holcombe'), Lang-port Union workhouse, and the school buildings at Long Ashton Union workhouse. These may have been acceptable, but they had to pass inspection by the military authorities, and this took time. In Norfolk, the first camp was not ready until August, since the War Office declined to take over the furniture in the selected house, and arrangements to move it had to be made. The West Sussex scheme was abandoned by the War Office in March 1917; the reason is unstated, but it may have been that the area was prohibited – although camps were later established in the county.[77]

The scheme was boosted in June by being allotted 'a considerable number' of prisoners, either for farm work or for the new land drainage schemes which the Board was undertaking in the eastern counties.[78] The early work in establishing camps was now bearing fruit. Hereford's first camp (at Ross, for Austro-Hungarians) was almost ready by the end of June. Bedford had three camps operating by July. In August, 380 prisoners were at work in Worcestershire.[79] But the idea was not universally popular. Cheshire farmers, as noted, were still resistant to prisoner labour in 1917. In Lindsey, as late as October, the EC thought that high feelings made it impossible for prisoners to work on farms, so that they were better confined to drainage work, on which 20 were employed in May.[80] But the use of prisoners was now well established, and their number had grown substantially. The War Cabinet records 5,934 on farms on 1 January 1918, although the numbers at work were probably less. The first recorded survey, for 9 February 1918, shows that there were 4,279 agriculturally employed prisoners. Strictly, there were less in 'general' farming, since 692 of them were being used in land reclamation, market gardening, or drainage work.[81]

In 1918, the use of prisoners expanded dramatically. Shortly before the Armistice, there were over 30,000 at work in agriculture. This reflected several developments. With the German offensives of the spring came a rapid rise in the number of prisoners. The government also took the decision to make more of them available for work in the UK, instead of confining them to France or the Dominions as formerly. Given the importance of the food production policy, a decline in hostility to the use of prisoners, and the fresh calls for agricultural recruits made in the spring, the decision was taken to give agriculture a dominant role in prisoner employment (Table 9.5).

Table 9.5: Use of prisoners of war in agriculture, 1918

| | Prisoners in UK: | | % in agriculture |
	Available for work	Working in agriculture	
9 Feb. 1918	25,497	4,279	16.7
23 May 1918	33,200	9,783	29.5
10 Oct. 1918	40,410	25,213	62.4
3 Nov. 1918	50,179	30,405	60.5

Source: PRO, NATS 1/132, L. 1/626, *Reports on Prisoner of War Camps*, Item 28 (Appendix IV), Report by Ben. H. Morgan (Dilution & Technical Branch, Ministry of National Service); CAB 23/6, 409(7), 11 May 1918

Late in 1917, the expansion of prisoner labour was seen as a way of overcoming the shortage of ploughmen, which by this time had become serious. The War Cabinet decided in December to prepare a trade index of all prisoners, and to release for farm work any ploughmen as soon as they had been identified. The corollary of this scheme was that the guard system would have to be relaxed; there were not enough guards to send out with tiny ploughing groups. Sir Arthur Lee's proposal to relax the guard restrictions was accepted by the War Cabinet in December.[82] In January 1918 the decision was taken to establish ploughing camps of 30–40 prisoners, 4 or 5 camps in each county. The prisoners would be guarded in camp, going out to work unaccompanied by guards, but by a soldier (or policeman) ploughman, who would work with them and presumably act as a foreman. Importantly, they would be permitted to perform other tasks if ploughing was not required.[83]

The final, and most useful concession, came at the same time; prisoners were now allowed to be boarded out on farms. Up to three per farm were allowed. The conditions were not onerous. They were to be kept in safe custody, protected from interference by local people, housed in healthy, comfortable and warm premises, and be given three meals a day, of no worse quality than would be given to an English labourer; the government would supply clothing and bedding.[84]

The concessions on guarding were important as showing the changed attitude of the authorities. Formerly, they were greatly exercised by the possibility of escape, and by civilian hostility. However, by this time it was becoming apparent that few prisoners were going to attempt escape or succeed in the attempt. In September 1917, only 18 prisoners were at large in England, and only one officer and two men had succeeded in getting back to Germany by October.[85] It seemed also that civilian hostility was diminishing. Thus the authorities could relax conditions which had already delayed the setting up of camps.

The expansion in the prisoner supply, the setting up of special ploughing camps, and the relaxation of guard restrictions permitted the use of prisoners to rise rapidly. Counties which had shown resistance to their use in 1917 now established camps. Cheshire acquired two, and would have had more had the EC been able to satisfy the accommodation requirements of the Army. Hereford had three (possibly four) in May, and had premises approved for a further seven by late June, although prisoners to fill them were not yet available. Hertfordshire was already to the fore, with six camps working (one was a ploughing camp), and four more in the course of formation in February; when complete, the scheme envisaged twelve camps, with about 600 prisoners. Even in Lindsey, which did not regard prisoners with favour, six depots were established in the spring, with a complement of 175 prisoners. Salop, which had not been allocated prisoners in 1917, acquired enough in 1918 to operate five camps.[86]

For the 1918 hay and corn harvests, the use of prisoners was eased by the establishment of migratory gangs. These consisted of 10 prisoners, with two guards, living under canvas. The final administrative development, in October 1918, was that prisoners were to be allowed to operate as threshing teams in the vicinity of their permanent camps.[87]

Most prisoners were supplied to farmers by such special agricultural camps, principally in the summer and early autumn of 1918; the peak was reached in October 1918, with 330 camps.[88] However, another system existed. This was the system of general camps. These were not usually situated in rural areas, and were also much larger than the purely agricultural camps. However, they did supply some prisoners to agriculture. They were inspected in autumn 1918, when it was found that out of some 15,000 prisoners (in 24 camps) about 3,350 were engaged in agriculture. Most of these came from only two camps: from the Beachley (Gloucs.) camp, 1,000 had been distributed elsewhere to work in agriculture, and 1,031 from the Brocton (Staffs.) camp were in agriculture, mainly in migratory gangs. These apart, the largest contingent came from seven camps in the Southern Command area, employing 462 men.[89]

Unlike soldiers, prisoners remained in agriculture in large numbers after the Armistice. Repatriation was slow, and the 1919 railway strike slowed it further. Farmers and ECs were also reluctant by this time to lose prisoner labour, especially since the ECs were still issuing ploughing orders (although these had by now lost their legal force). Thus they remained to help with the harvest, and even with the autumn ploughing of 1919. In January 1919 there were still 30,679 prisoners working in agriculture, and this had fallen only to 25,103 as late as September. Most of these (19,319) were going out to work daily from the 321 agricultural camps still operating; 1,735 were boarded out on farms, 1,008 were in 'parent' camps (presumably general camps), and 3,041 were in migratory gangs.[90]

By the end of the war, prisoners had been set to work on most types of farm work. It must be presumed that the 1917 contingents were used in a variety of more or less unskilled tasks, since there is no evidence that they were particularly skilled. This situation altered with the setting up of ploughmen's camps in January 1918. The

4,279 prisoners already in agriculture were shortly to be joined by an allotment of 4,713, of whom 3,771 were ploughmen.[91] Since there were still less than 10,000 prisoners in agriculture towards the end of May, most of the expansion in the first half of 1918 must have been due to the utilisation of ploughmen. Rather remarkably, these seem to have been genuinely skilled men – unlike many of the soldier 'ploughmen' who had plagued the ECs in late 1917 – if one may judge by the fact that no system of training them was established, and only one complaint as to their ability has been found in the minutes and reports of the ECs. Even the Lindsey EC, which was not noted for a predisposition in favour of prisoner labour, recorded that, to the end of March 1918: 'The prisoners are specially selected agriculturalists, and are engaged in farm work, and in ditching, hedging, &c. They are reported in all cases to be working satisfactorily, and giving no trouble.'[92] The wide variety of work done by prisoners was also apparent in Bedford at Armistice time. About 235 men were at work; their duties comprised 'general farm work', potato picking, ploughing, drilling, threshing, mangold pulling, and mowing.[93]

The attitude of the prisoners to their enforced employment seems to have been one of acceptance. There were 'comparatively few' cases of idling reported to the central committee (the Prisoners of War Employment Committee) which allocated prisoners, although the Worcs. EC noted a case of prisoners leaving their work at midday without notice.[94] The only case reported to an EC of prisoners refusing to work occurred after the end of the war; in May 1919, it was reported indirectly that prisoners at Eardiston camp (Worcs.) had refused to work; the reason alleged was the prisoners' fear that, when repatriated, they would not be permitted to take with them the money that they had earned. It was alleged in an FPD report that 'in a few instances', prisoners had wilfully damaged government implements as a result of some 'imaginary grievance', but this is unconfirmed. However, a farmer-member of Essex EC, giving evidence to a POWEC enquiry in July 1918, said that the behaviour of the prisoners (whom he had employed on his own farm) was satisfactory, and that they did not annoy the civilians with whom they necessarily came into contact.[95]

On the quality of the prisoners' work, there was agreement that they worked well, but slowly.[96] The reasons adduced for slow work were three: natural slowness, idleness, and inadequate feeding. The first two are subjective, but there is some evidence to support the third. The interval between breakfast and the evening meal for prisoners was normally twelve hours (6 am–6 pm), and to sustain them for this period, the permitted ration was four ounces of broken biscuit and one ounce of cheese. The Ministry of National Service report which contains this information, described it as 'not really enough to enable a man to perform hard manual work', which seems an understatement.[97] There is testimony by farmers and camp commandants that the paucity of the midday meal was largely responsible for the slow work of the prisoners, and that, when farmers supplemented the ration (e.g., with potatoes or coffee) output rose more than sufficiently to cover the extra cost.[98] It may have been the POWEC hearings which persuaded the War Office in July to supply the prisoners with a midday meal.[99] It was against regulations for farmers to supply the prisoners with food, although one commandant was reported as having been to see the local farmers, and told them to use their common sense and give the prisoners some food during the day.[100] Other local initiatives may have been taken; Worcs. EC instructed the local commandant to issue extra rations to prisoners doing overtime work during the 1918 hay and corn harvests.[101]

There were other hindrances to the expansion of effort by the prisoners. Camp commandants were on the whole not interested in exercising control over the prisoners' work, and so the guard assigned to them had little incentive to make them work. Although farmers recognised that a guard with a commanding personality could get much more work from the prisoners, especially if he was interested in, and had knowledge of, farming, the general view of the farmers was that the guard was as much of a hindrance as a help – and required feeding at midday into the bargain.[102]

Even if the commandants had shown an interest in the work, the system of guarding was not designed to maximise output. There were four types of guard: a civilian foreman, whose function was to supervise the work done; a British NCO, who was to prevent idling; a German NCO, and a guard from the Royal Defence Corps, who was required only to escort and guard the prisoners. It depended on local conditions which type of guard was used. The British NCO got most work out of the prisoners, but there was only one of them available per 200 prisoners. None of the guards were paid in ratio to the work performed. A further confusion was that prisoners and guards might answer to different superiors. The prisoners were responsible to the camp commandant, the British guard to an officer of the Royal Defence Corps; where British soldiers assisted in the work of the prisoners (e.g., as gang leaders or horse keepers), they were under the control of the local Agricultural Company.[103]

In conclusion, the expansion of the prisoner labour force was accomplished swiftly, smoothly (especially in 1918), and on a very large scale. It rendered substantial assistance to the food production programme, perhaps most notably in providing ploughmen at a very critical time in early 1918. The programme also proved administratively flexible when required, especially in the matter of guards. Its weakness lay in the failure to promote efficient work by the prisoners, due to an inefficient guarding system and poor nourishment outside the camp.

WOMEN

After 1916 it is difficult to trace the employment of village women in agriculture. The Board of Agriculture report on the WWACs up to August 1916 had recorded 57,497 women registered for work on the land, and 28,767 actually working;[104] an earlier report showed 140,000 registrations in February 1916.[105] Subsequent statements are usually rather rougher approximations. The FPD stated that in September 1917 there were 200,000 women at work on the land in England and Wales. The War Cabinet estimated that by the end of 1917 there were 270,000 at work, and considered that this represented an increase of 140,000 above pre-war. At the same time, it was admitted that there was no complete return available of the numbers involved; the figure of 140,000 is also suspiciously identical with the number of women registered in February 1916.[106]

In 1918, estimates begin to conflict. The War Cabinet's 1918 resort began by downgrading its own estimate for the end of 1917 to 260,000. For the summer of 1918, estimates vary from 230,000 (Middleton) to 260,000 (FPD), and for the autumn from 'at least 300,000' (War Cabinet) to 320,000 (Lord Ernle).[107] There is clearly a lot of guesswork in these figures, and they are only overall estimates. The only detailed analysis by counties is for August 1918 prepared by the Women's Branch of the FPD (Table 9.6).

This estimate covered most of the civil parishes in England and Wales (9,383 out of 13,702), so that it represents a much firmer base for calculation than the previous estimates, about whose origins we are uncertain. If the unsurveyed parishes had employed women at the same rate as those surveyed, total employment would have risen to some 263,000, which is close to the estimate of the FPD above.

Table 9.6: Village women working in agriculture in England and Wales, August 1918

	England	Wales	Total
On farms	129,717	36,221	165,938
On market gardens	14,137	448	14,585
Totals	143,854	36,669	180,523

Source: Bedford RO, WWA 6/1, 'Quarterly return of women land workers, exclusive of the Women's Land Army'

The official estimates are probably nearer the truth than those in the Board of Trade Z8 surveys, which seem unduly low. Apart from the methodological defects noted, it may be that farmers regarded registered women as 'official' labour and, in accordance with their instructions, excluded them from the returns.

In assessing the supply of village female labour, we have averaged the various official estimates for 1917–18. The next problem is to make allowance for part-time working. It seems clear that most of the village women were part-time. The 1918 AWB enquiry considered that 80 per cent were part-time. Lord Ernle thought that 210,000 of his estimated 300,000 on the land in the summer of 1918 were part-time. For our purposes, it was decided to adopt the figure of 80 per cent part-timers.[108]

As to the length of the working year of the part-timers, there is little information. We have estimated the working year of part-timers before the war as equivalent to 3 months. For wartime part-timers, the figure was probably shorter, although the evidence on this point is meagre; the fact that the AWB report on farm labour early in 1918 showed only 20,000 women at full-time work (when the total number in the labour force may have been c. 200,000),[109] and the fact that in 1916 the government did not think it worth rewarding those in agricultural work for more than thirty days. The final estimate can only be a matter of guesswork, but it seems safe to conclude that the wartime part-timer worked for a shorter period than her peacetime counterpart, and for purposes of calculation we have adopted the period of one month. Having converted the resulting estimate into man-units by the procedure detailed above (ch. 4), the final problem is to make a deduction for the numbers employed before the war. Since the 1908 census of production is the most comprehensive survey of the pre-war labour force, and apparently forms the basis for the War Cabinet's estimate for the pre-war labour force (90,000), we have used this census estimate. When this is deducted from the estimates of wartime employment, the net influx of village women into agriculture, which had been equivalent to 6,000 man-units in 1916, rose to 25,000 in 1917 and 30,000 in 1918.[110] Seen thus, the supply of village women was less important than that of soldiers in the last year of the war, and about equivalent to that of prisoners of war.

It is perhaps surprising that the supply of village female labour was at its height during the last year of the war; unlike the other forms of replacement labour, it was not under direct official control. The explanation may lie to some extent in the relationship between the cost of living and the level of allowances made to the families of soldiers and sailors. There seems no doubt that the real value of allowances had deteriorated by 1917 (Table 9.7).

Table 9.7: Family allowances and the cost of living, 1914–18

Cost of living index		Allowances	
July 1914	100	Sep. 1914	100
1915	120	Nov. 1914	120
1916	135	–	
1917	160	Jan. 1917	151
1918	180	July 1918	165

Source: Bowley, *Prices and Wages*, 106; Dewey, thesis, 287

The relationship improved in favour of allowances in the first months of the war, and deteriorated later. This deterioration was partly due to policy. In January 1917 the War Cabinet decided against a general raising of allowances, fearing that the incentive for women to work would be diminished.[111]

The distribution of female labour followed closely that of the family farm and the dairying areas. The 1918 AWB enquiry had shown certain counties as outstanding in female employment: Cornwall, Devon, Cheshire, Gloucs., Lancs., Somerset, Yorks.

(W.R.), and Cardigan.[112] A similar pattern was shown in August 1918, except that Gloucester was not as prominent as before, and Essex, Norfolk, Lincoln, and the Isle of Ely were also shown as large employers, as were Carmarthen and Pembroke. West Kent was outstanding, with almost 7,000 women in farming, presumably because of the hop harvest. Unfortunately, neither of these sources tells us what the pre-war level of employment was, so that estimates of the wartime increase in particular counties are not possible. However, it can be said that in so far as there was an increase in 1918, it was largely in the arable counties.

The general rise in the female labour force had certain consequences for areas of traditional female employment. In Northumberland, where the 'double hind' system of husband and wife farm servants had persisted up to 1914, it was noted that the wife was often carrying on alone. The entry of the WLA into the labour market also affected women. In Staffordshire, they were thought to be working harder than usual, to dissuade farmers from employing the WLA. In Essex, jealousy of the WLA had the opposite effect, and some village women refused to work. In Rutland, the use of the WLA excited great interest, but village women were usually prevented from joining them at work by family commitments.[113]

In all, although the village women were a useful source of labour, it is surprising that comparatively little official energy went into their mobilisation. There is little new in policy after 1916 which might have contributed to that end. The one positive measure which might have had an effect – the establishment of creches by local authorities – was intended to be part of a Local Government Bill, which was still under discussion by the War Cabinet in July 1918.[114] On the whole, policy after 1916 tended to the organisation of the skilled or educated woman, and seemed to hope that the village woman would thereby be induced to emulate her (largely urban) counterpart. This was a policy of indirect action, which was relatively unproductive.

With the adoption of the food production policy, a new impetus was given to women's work organisations on the land. While the existing organisations such as the WNLSC continued in being, and the WWACs continued to encourage village women to take up farm work, the Board of Agriculture created a wholly new organisation, the Women's Land Army. The intention was to supply a force of trained, permanent (yet mobile) skilled labour, which would be

130

useful *per se*, and also encourage village women to come forward by its example. There were also features of the WLA which caused much public interest; that it was run by women, the distinctive uniform adopted, and the quasi-military flavour of the organisation. However, in terms of numbers, the WLA was a minor source of replacement labour. Its working strength varied over the period (Table 9.8).

Table 9.8: Women's Land Army: working strength 1917–18

July 1917	5,000
5 Oct. 1917	6,000
24 Nov. 1917	6,672
March 1918	7,665
Sep. 1918	16,000
31 Dec. 1918	11,529

Source: Andrews and Hobbs, 73–4; IWM, LAND V, F. 7; Cd. 25, county reports, Ernle, *Land*, 128; War Cabinet, *1918 Report*, 237

There were four periods in the recruiting history of the WLA. There was an initial rush in the spring of 1917, a period of slow growth in the autumn and winter following, a large and successful recruiting drive in April 1918 consequent on the renewed conscription of farm labour, and the peak of late summer and autumn of 1918.

The response to the initial appeal for recruits in March 1917 was enthusiastic. Over 45,000 candidates applied, of whom only 5,000 were accepted. Lord Ernle wrote that this high rejection rate was due to the high standards of physical fitness required. This was clearly important, but probably not the dominant consideration; up to October 1918, only 16 per cent of applicants had been rejected on medical grounds,[115] so other factors must have been at work. The Selection and Allocation Committees of the WWACs, on whom fell the task of choosing recruits, also paid much attention to character, since they were mindful of the high standards required of young women going to work, perhaps alone, in the countryside. An impression of these early candidates may be had from the minute book of the Hertfordshire committee:[116]

D.M.: seemed unsuitable in her general health and appearance. Looked irresponsible. Refs. taken up.
L.B.: had been at Girls' Club and was known to be nice type.

Had been in munitions and was discharged owing to ill health. Refs. taken up.

M.L.: Doubtful family. Willing girl. Lower class than B. Took up refs.

F.M.: No good. Rejected. Told to try and get temp. outdoor work for 6 months. Mrs. Odell knew family, reported bad health, shocking.

The committees tended to favour the more educated candidates. Although not explicitly aimed at educated women, the WLA thus acquired a strong educated and middle-class flavour.[117]

If the new recruit was already skilled, employment was at once found. If not, then training was arranged. Since, as Ernle records, some 23,000 WLA received training, the majority must have been unused to agriculture. Thus the establishment of the WLA involved a substantial expansion of training for women. The training was offered initially for four weeks. This, as Ernle admitted, did little more than toughen the muscles. When later extended to six weeks, the benefit was marked. The syllabus covered general work, and also tried to provide for local needs.[118]

The WWACs tried to establish new depots or hostels where training could be given, and renewed their appeals to local farmers and landowners to assist in training. Hertfordshire had 62 training places available as early as mid-April (nine in a hostel, the rest on farms). Lindsey accepted 159 WLA members initially; 20 were passed on to instruction depots, and 42 were given bursaries to train with farmers and landowners. Wiltshire, which had been to the fore in women's work for some time, having formed a Ladies' Sub-committee of the WAC in January 1916, had by October 1917 three training schools, although there were only 15 girls in training.[119]

The initial rush of recruits was succeeded by a bleak period in the summer of 1917, when it was apparent that farmers were not keen to have the services of the Land Army, for a variety of reasons; anti-female prejudice, a fear that to do so would mean the risk of losing male labourers to the forces, and the difficulties of providing accommodation on farms were the main ones.[120] In Lindsey, 24 WLA girls were unemployed in August, and it was feared that there would soon be more. Several had 'run away'. The committee was sufficiently depressed about the prospects to advise the FPD to abandon the scheme, and concentrate on local labour.[121]

However, the demand for female labour was growing, even in the slack season of winter 1917–18, as the food production programme made headway. The Oxford women's committee reported in January 1918 that, having begun with 31 girls in April 1917, it had now trained 71. Winter unemployment was still a problem; Herts. had 113 WLA enrolled, but only 82 of them were at work in January.[122] In the late spring, seasonal demand and the new recruiting drive transformed the picture. In Lindsey, numbers at work had fallen considerably over the winter, and did not regain their September level (83) until March 1918. Then they grew rapidly, reaching 115 in July and 308 at the Armistice.[123] Most counties showed a similar pattern.

The new recruiting drive attracted fewer applicants than that of 1917, but a higher proportion were accepted – about a quarter of the 28,393 who applied between March and July.[124] The fresh expansion meant more work for the selection committees. The candidates were a varied group:[125]

B.H.: The worst type of munition worker. Flashy, and very yellow as to hair. Quite inexperienced, except as to horses; her father was a dealer in them. Not suitable.

W.O.: A nice girl. Domestic servant class. Not over strong. Wishes to work with horses.

Mrs H.: Slightly mad. Has tended her own horses. Wishes to train as horsewoman. Very assertive and imperious. Age 39.

The special needs of the WLA had already spawned an elaborate welfare organisation. Every village registrar was asked to befriend the Land Army girls. County organisers inspected the billets, training centres, depots and hospitals, and the WWACs appointed voluntary workers in each county to look after the welfare of the girls. In addition, there was a WLA journal (*The Landswoman*), which was distributed to members.[126] The welfare organisation was elaborated in the summer of 1918. The spur to this was a fear of deteriorating quality. As the Director of the Women's Branch of the FPD (and thus the head of the WLA), Miss M. Talbot, wrote in June 1918:[127]

The supply of girls of sufficiently high character to make it safe to send them out to live alone on the farms or in cottages is running short. The Selection Boards all over the country are quite rightly rejecting a large proportion of the recruits who come before them.

The feared disaster did not occur, and relatively few cases of seriously bad behaviour were recorded. In Lindsey, cases were recorded of girls 'running away' from centres and farms. From Lindsey also comes the only case of dismissal for drunkenness so far traced. The same county had a minor disaster in October 1918, when the lack of a cook at a hostel precipitated the flight of 21 girls. In Gloucester it was noted that ten girls had been dismissed for bad behaviour in the first year of the WLA's existence. In Norfolk, it was found that 7 per cent of the WLA were 'failures'.[128] The problem was met by the expansion of the welfare service. By early November, 43 welfare officers and their deputies had been appointed, and it was planned to raise the total to 80, so that there would be one officer for every 200 WLA members, the total strength of the WLA being then at its maximum of 16,000.[129]

Not all members of the WLA worked on farms. Early in its existence, it was decided to persuade suitable candidates to work in the Forage Department of the War Office, the Timber Supply Department of the Board of Trade, or the Forestry Department of the Board of Agriculture. Those accepting such work remained WLA members. It was felt that such an arrangement avoided competition for labour between different departments, was economical, and led to greater continuity of employment for the women. Of the total of 23,965 women who had been at some time members of the WLA up to the end of April 1919, 21,127 had been engaged in agriculture, 2,267 in forage, and 571 in timber work.[130]

The nature of the work performed by the WLA is not known in detail. In August 1918 there were 12,657 WLA at work, the largest group being engaged in milking (5,734) and field work (3,971), although most types of farm work were represented, from tractor driving to thatching.[131] The WLA women were not evenly spread over the country. The earliest record of their distribution (early 1918) shows few in Wales or north-east England. Of the 7,665 recorded, 4,000 were alleged to be in Norfolk. This very high figure is suspect; not only did it represent over half the total in existence, but as late as October 1917, only 141 WLA were recorded by the

EC as having been placed in Norfolk. Norfolk apart, the highest figure was for Lancashire (800), followed by Gloucs. (269), Somerset (230), and Cheshire (212). In the other 39 countries making returns, employment was below 200 in all cases.[132]

The post-war distribution of the Land Army still reflected to some extent a bias towards the dairying counties. At the end of April 1919 Lancashire and Cheshire employed 784 out of the total in England and Wales of 10,103. Other prominent counties were East Kent (441), Hampshire (432), Warwick (387), Surrey (353), and Gloucester (315). There was also a large contingent (267) threshing in West Kent. Again, Wales had comparatively few WLA; only 988 in total.[133] On the whole, the distribution of women fits in with the analysis of types of work done – chiefly dairy and field work. This did not entirely match the original intention, which had been that the WLA were to be a force of skilled workers, tending animals, milking, tractor driving, and leaving the less skilled village women to do the general field work. In practice, although the WLA seem to have turned their hands to every type of work, they were probably less of a labour aristocracy than had been hoped.[134]

An important element in the usefulness of the WLA was its mobility. Recruits had to promise to go to work where directed.[135] Thus at short notice WWACs could arrange a supply of labour for special tasks. Ernle recorded the case of hoeing corn on Romney Marsh, where the proposed use of prisoners was forbidden at the last moment, since it was near the coast. A force of WLA women stepped into the breach, and did a creditable job.[136] WWACs were always in the process of 'exporting' or 'importing' members. In Gloucester, there were about 450 Land Army girls at work in September 1918, but 67 had been exported, and 40 imported by then. In Lindsey in March 1918, 83 WLA girls were on the land, but 24 of them had been imported.[137]

On the whole, the reaction of farmers to the WLA was favourable, although there still remained pockets of prejudice, even at the end of the war. Farmers in Bedfordshire and Sussex appeared to be most dubious, but great satisfaction was expressed in Norfolk, Cheshire, and Northants. There were some complaints of laziness, and giggling rather than working; it was noted that: 'This appears to be confined to those who are ex-domestic servants, etc.' A comment from Worcestershire was: 'Trained women in Worcester-shire do very well, but they are unsuitable for heavy work. If they come from a good family they are useful, but if from the poorer classes they are not so good, and take every advantage.' Generally, the WLA seem to have deserved the verdict of a Northants farmer – 'plucky, patriotic and keen'.[138]

The opinion was expressed that the WLA was satisfactory, but expensive.[139] In fact, the rates of pay fixed for the WLA were lower than those of the ordinary farm labourer, so the charge of expense loses much of its force. At the inception of the WLA, the minimum wage guaranteed by the Board of Agriculture was 18s (90p) a week. By the spring of 1918 it was 20s, which became 22s 6d after three months' service, and 25s after six months. By April 1919 the minimum rate had risen to 25s (more if the local AWB rate was higher).[140] Roughly, the WLA minimum rate during the war was about four-fifths of the rate for the ordinary unskilled male labourer. Interestingly, a Board of Agriculture report rated the physical efficiency of women as about four-fifths that of men.[141] On that basis, it could be said that the cost-efficiency of WLA labour was the same as the labour it replaced. But this is to ignore that all the WLA were supposed to have been trained, and that a high proportion were in skilled work, such as milking. If the WLA received only the official minimum wage, then farmers were getting more or less skilled labour for less than the cost of unskilled labour.

MISCELLANEOUS LABOUR

The system of exempting children from school for agricultural work continued into the latter half of the war. While there are no national returns of the number exempted after October 1916, a count of the numbers exempted in five counties at the end of 1917 showed 2,629 (2,168 boys and 461 girls), compared with only 1,339 when the last returns had been compiled on 16 October 1916. For other counties, information is fragmentary. In 1917 in Somerset, 408 children were exempted from school for agriculture at some time during the year, compared with 488 on 16 October previous.[142] In Kesteven (Lincs.) there had been 976 exemptions in 1914, half of which were thought to be for agriculture; in March 1918, the number of exemptions was 772, and there were 641 temporary wartime exemptions, of which 500 were thought to be for agriculture.[143] In Kent in 1918 there were a very large total number of exemptions (3,980), compared with only 331 at the October 1916 return.[144] However, the demand for labour in Kent was highly influenced by hop-picking, and so untypical. The most that can be said is that agricultural exemptions in 1917–18 were much greater than in 1914–16, but to what extent is not clear.

A further addition to the labour force was made by children working part-time out of school hours. The extent of this pre-war is not known. The only wartime enquiry into it was carried out in 1917 by the Board of Education. It concerned 91 rural schools in five adjacent dairying counties. Out of 2,379 boys on the registers of the schools, 700 were doing part-time milking or other farm work; out of 2,317 girls registered, only 102 were so engaged.[145]

In addition to schoolchild exemptions, there were special camps set up to deal with the harvesting of certain crops. Ernle refers to the use of 5,000 public schoolboys for the 1917 corn harvest and 15,000 for the 1918 harvest. This was part of a wider scheme set up by the National Service Department to use boys and masters from public and secondary schools. The full size of the scheme is unknown, although the Lindsey committee refers to an allocation of 500 boys for Lincolnshire for the 1917 harvest. Individual schools may have supplied quite large contingents; Uppingham School provided 50 in 1917 for the corn harvest in Cumberland, and proposed to send 150 in 1918 to two camps at Penrith and Cockermouth.[146]

As well as military prisoners of war, attempts were made to use interned aliens as farm labour. These were not successful. As early as June 1916, the Home Office had permitted them to be released on parole, and employed on farms in non-prohibited areas. A further precaution against espionage was taken by restricting the scheme to Austro-Hungarian or Turkish nationals. The aliens would be boarded with the farmer, and paid at the current rate for English agricultural labour. The scheme was extended in May 1917, when aliens were allowed into formerly prohibited areas. The only area still absolutely prohibited was the east coast.[147] In spite of the fact that they would be paid, and escape the tedium of camp life, few aliens volunteered for any sort of work, and few instances of their use in agriculture have been traced. Ernle wrote of 'under 2,000' being employed.[148] An unpublished FPD report is more circumspect, stating that 1,912 aliens 'have been employed', so that this may have been a cumulative figure.[149] There is little evidence that employment was ever as high as this at any one time. Montgomery writes that about 500 were employed in farming in May 1917, but even this is probably an overestimate; the War Cabinet report for 1918 lists the main types of replacement labour supplied to farmers by the FPD; aliens would be included in 'other' labour, which stood at only 200 on 1 January 1918, and only 430 a year later.[150] In January–February 1918, the AWB found 20 aliens working in Kesteven, and in Shropshire 40 were at work in April 1917.[151] Even when specialist working camps were set up, little use was made of aliens in farming. In the last months of the war, the Ministry of National Service carried out a survey of 39 PoW camps (the 'general' type). Of these, two were solely for aliens – Leighterton (Staffs.) with 247 men, and Bulford (Wilts.) with 212 men. In neither camp were any men working in agriculture.[152] Where aliens were employed, the quality of their work is largely unknown. Montgomery states that farmers considered them: '. . . invariably willing and useful, and gave no trouble'. On the only occasion that they were mentioned in the Board of Trade Z8 reports, a Herefordshire farmer was quoted as saying: 'Since I obtained the help of six aliens I have been able to manage very well, and they do farm work well now after a little training, although all were waiters'.[153]

The most complete failure in making use of a potential labour supply was in the case of conscientious objectors. Here, the problem was the strength of public hostility. As a result, few were employed. Ernle says their numbers in agriculture 'scarcely rose above 200'. The only trace of their employment is in June 1918, when 214 were recorded as working in agriculture; there were also 500 working on land reclamation on Dartmoor.[154]

Two attempts were made during the war to obtain British volunteers to work on the land. The first was in February 1917, when the Ministry of National Service tried to obtain volunteers from less essential industries to work in agriculture. A 'large number' volunteered, but only a few hundred were actually employed, since many volunteers were unsuitable.[155] A more successful scheme, the War Agricultural Volunteers, was tried in May 1918. This aimed to make use of men who, by reason of age or medical condition, were more likely to be of use on the land than in the forces, the age-limit for military service having just been raised to 51. Under the scheme, any man who had reached the age of 45 could, irrespective of his position as regards military service, enrol as a WAV.

Thus in effect men aged over 45 could avoid military service by volunteering to work in agriculture. Men under 45 could do so if they were in medical categories B3, C3 or Grade III, or were not liable for service. The scheme produced 3,904 men for agriculture by the end of the year, of whom a high proportion had been gardeners, or had had experience of agriculture when younger.[156] This, the largest group of miscellaneous labour supplied to agriculture, has left little trace in the records. A final temporary form of assistance came from the Metropolitan Police; to help in the supply of ploughmen, 150 policemen volunteered in 1917 to resume their previous calling, and were employed on the land.[157]

LABOUR SHORTAGE IN AGRICULTURE, 1914–18

In considering the likely variations in the civilian labour supply in the first two years of the war, certain assumptions have been made; chiefly, that farmers were not recruited into the forces; that the Board of Trade Z8 surveys are a reliable guide only to variations in the size of the hired labour force; and that the propensity of male members of farmers' families to join the forces was only half of that of hired labour. These assumptions have been applied to the labour force data for 1917–18 given in the Z8 reports, to yield an estimate of the 'conventional' labour supply during the whole war period (Table 9.9).

Table 9.9: 'Conventional' labour supply in agriculture, 1915–18 ('000 man-units)

	Pre-war	1915	1916	1917	1918
	1,541	1,429	1,377	1,337	1,347
As per cent	100	93	89	87	87

Source: Appendix F

The second half of the war saw a much slower rate of labour loss, as the government adopted a policy of protecting agricultural labour from military service. In addition, great efforts were made to supply replacement labour to farmers (Table 9.10).

Figures for the combined conventional and replacement labour supply are shown in Table 9.11.[158]

139

Table 9.10: Replacement labour in agriculture, 1915–18 ('000 man-units)

	1915	1916	1917	1918
Soldiers	11	14	28	66
PoWs	0	0	3	14
WLA	0	0	3	8
Village women	0	6	25	30
Miscellaneous	4	10	15	17
Totals	15	30	74	135

Source: Appendix G

Table 9.11: Total labour supply in agriculture, 1914–18 ('000 man-units)

	Pre-war	1914	1915	1916	1917	1918
Conventional	1,543	1,543	1,429	1,377	1,337	1,347
Replacement	0	0	15	30	74	135
Totals	1,543	1,543	1,444	1,407	1,411	1,482
As per cent	100	100	94	91	91	96

Source: Tables 9.9, 9.10

The effect of replacement labour was thus to reduce the fall in the labour supply to 9 per cent in 1916, and 4 per cent in 1918. It is clear that replacement labour more than offset fresh conscription in 1917–18. Thus the fall in the labour supply was much less than historians have hitherto assumed; it should be reiterated that these calculations should not mislead by a spurious precision, since there are many elements of uncertainty in the statistics. However, any revision of the orthodox view which takes into account the contribution to the labour supply made by farmers and their relatives (male and female) is bound to conclude that the fall in labour supply was much less than conventionally assumed, since it takes account of the fact that a large proportion of the total labour force was not vulnerable to recruiting to the forces.

The fall in the supply of labour is, however, not necessarily the same as *shortage* of labour. The fact that the structure of production changed after 1916, with a shift to the more labour-intensive activity of tillage rather than livestock, makes it advisable to consider whether labour *demand* rose, so as to worsen the shortage of labour in 1917–18. The demand for labour may be calculated by using estimated work-norms for 1911 (Table 9.12).[159]

Table 9.12: Man-hours required for the main farm tasks, 1911

	Hours per annum (per acre or per head of livestock)
Pasture or rotation grass	9.5
Arable land	90.0
Cattle	125.0
Sheep	11.0
Pigs	32.0
Horses	105.0

Source: A. W. Ashby and J. L. Davies, 'Farming efficiency and the agricultural depression', *JPAES* 1 (1929), 101–2; Dewey, thesis, 190–2

While these estimates are based on Welsh rather than English conditions, and thus may be less applicable to Britain as a whole, they may be used to give an idea of variations in the total agricultural work-load, if not its absolute level. Applying them to the acreage and livestock data in the annual agricultural statistics produces the series shown in Table 9.13.

Table 9.13: Labour demand in British agriculture, 1914–18 (million man-hours p.a.)

	1909–13	*1914*	*1915*	*1916*	*1917*	*1918*
	2,606	2,577	2,608	2,619	2,626	2,738
As per cent	100	99	100	100	101	105

Labour demand was more or less constant for most of the war, but in 1918 it rose by about 4 per cent, reflecting the change in production structure brought about by the food production policy. Comparing the demand for, and supply of, labour, enables a view to be taken on the relative changes in the degree of labour shortage throughout the war (Table 9.14).

Table 9.14: Labour shortage in British agriculture, 1914–18

	1909–13	*1914*	*1915*	*1916*	*1917*	*1918*
Demand	100	99	100	100	101	105
Supply	100	100	93	91	91	96
Shortage	100	99	107	110	111	109

['Shortage' = Demand/Supply × 100. If result is >100, then shortage is greater than pre-war, and vice versa]

Thus when replacement labour supplies have been taken into

account, the labour shortage was by 1917 of the order of 11 per cent greater than pre-war, and it fell to about 9 per cent greater than pre-war in 1918. In 1918, the higher labour requirements stemming from the food production policy were slightly offset by the rise in the supply of replacement labour; however, this did not make good the existing labour shortage which had developed by the end of 1916.

NOTES

1 CAB 23/1, 5(2), 31 Dec. 1916.
2 CAB 23/1, 42(6).
3 Montgomery, *Labour Supply*, 13–16; CAB 23/3, 170(1), 27 June 1917; Middleton, *Food Production*, 185.
4 No report has been found for July 1917; the July figure is from the October 1917 report, 10.
5 Middleton, *Food Production*, 285; Ernle, *Land*, 162.
6 Ernle, *Land*, 163.
7 Cheshire EC, Report, 12.
8 Lindsey EC minutes, 25 June 1918.
9 CAB 23/7, 438(11), 1 July 1918.
10 Lancashire EC Report, July 1918, 3.
11 Herts. EC minutes, 24 June 1918.
12 Middleton, *Food Production*, 267; Ernle, *Land*, 163.
13 Middleton, *Food Production*, 267.
14 Board of Trade, *Report on the State of Employment . . . (1917–18)*.
15 Ibid., July 1918, 8.
16 Ibid., 1917–18. The 1917–18 percentages are calculated from the estimates of the current male labour force in the Z8 reports.
17 Board of Agriculture, *Report on Wages and Conditions of Employment in Agriculture* (1919), Cmd. 24 and 25, PP 1919, IX.
18 Cmd. 24, paras. 229–56.
19 Cmd. 24, para. 272.
20 Cmd. 24, paras. 285–8, 290–314.
21 Bowley, *Prices and Wages*, 70, 74; Board of Agriculture, *Report of the Enquiry into the Financial Results of the Occupation of Agriculture and the Cost of Living of Rural Workers* (1919), Cmd. 76, PP 1919, VIII, 37.
22 S. Pollard, *The Development of the British Economy 1914–1980* (3rd edn, 1983), 42–3; Winter, *Great War*, 230–7.
23 *Royal Commission to enquire into the prospects of the agricultural industry* (1919), interim report, Cd. 473, PP VIII, 1919, para. 16; A. W. Ashby, 'The work of the Agricultural Wages Board in 1918', *JRASE* 79 (1918), 139, 141, Appx, Table V.
24 Cmd. 76, 70; Beveridge, *Food Control*, 313.
25 Bowley, *Prices and Wages*, 70.
26 Ibid., 74.

27 Ashby, *JRASE* 1918, 138–45.
28 CAB 23/1, 42(6), 23 Jan. 1917.
29 Ernle, *Land*, 125.
30 CAB 23/3, 170(1), 27 June 1917.
31 Ernle, *Land*, 126.
32 Somerset EC minutes, 5 March 1917.
33 'Soldier labour', *JBA*, December 1918, 1112; Ernle, *Land*, 126.
34 CAB 23/2, 116 (Appx 1), 10 April 1917.
35 Salop EC minutes, 24 April 1917.
36 Lindsey EC, Report to 31 March 1918, 8.
37 Oxford EC minutes, 28 Jan. 1918.
38 Ernle, *Land*, 126–7.
39 CAB 23/3, 170(1), 27 June 1917.
40 CAB 23/4, 258(1), 26 Oct. 1917; 266(1,2), 6 Nov. 1917.
41 War Cabinet, *Report for the year 1918*, 237.
42 Worcs. EC minutes, 22 Aug. 1917.
43 Hereford EC, K29/2, Executive Officer's report, 26 Sep. 1917.
44 Ernle, *Land*, 143; CAB 23/4, 297, 24 Dec. 1917.
45 Montgomery, *Labour Supply*, 33.
46 Ibid., 35–40.
47 *JBA*, December 1918, 1112; Montgomery, *Labour Supply*, 607; but it may have only been 1,000 for 2 months – CAB 23/4, 296(16), 12 Dec. 1917.
48 Lancs. EC Reports: May 1917, 3, Dec. 1917, 2; Gloucs. EC minutes, 2 Feb. 1918.
49 CAB 23/4, 371(8), 23 March 1918.
50 CAB 23/4, 455(19), 7 Aug. 1918 and War Cabinet *1918 Report*, 236; Montgomery, *Labour Supply*, 41, suggests 20,000.
51 *Seventh Report of the Board of Agriculture for Scotland*, PP 1919, IX, lv; War Cabinet *1918 Report*, 241.
52 CAB 23/4, 371(8), 23 March 1918.
53 Cmd. 25, p. 136, para. 15.
54 Ernle, *Land*, 125.
55 Norfolk EC minutes, vol. 2, Report of labour sub-committee, 12 Sep. 1917.
56 Somerset EC minutes, 26 March 1917.
57 Cmd. 24, 121–2.
58 Cmd. 24, 126.
59 Herts. EC minutes, 7 Jan. 1918.
60 Salop EC, Report to 31 Dec. 1918, 5; Lindsey EC, Report to 31 March 1918, 8.
61 Cmd. 25, p. 179, para. 18.
62 Salop EC, Report to 31 Dec. 1918, 5.
63 Cmd. 24, para. 123.
64 Lindsey EC, Report to 31 March 1918, 8.
65 Cmd. 24, para. 123.
66 Cmd. 24, para. 126.
67 Cmd. 24, para. 123.

68 Lancs. EC minutes, 14 Feb. 1916.
69 Ibid.; Oxfordshire WAC minutes, 28 Feb. 1916.
70 West Sussex WAC minutes, 17 March 1916.
71 Cheshire EC, Report to 31 March 1918, 11.
72 Lancs. EC, minutes, Board of Agriculture circular A209/L, 16 Jan. 1917.
73 Cheshire EC minutes, 17 Feb. 1917; Herts. EC, Report, 16 Feb. 1917; Oxford EC minutes, 29 Jan. 1917; West Sussex EC minutes, 15 Jan. 1917; Wilts. WAC minutes, 8 Dec. 1916.
74 Somerset EC minutes, 26 Feb. 1917; Norfolk EC minutes, 22 June 1917.
75 Montgomery, *Labour Supply*, 42–3.
76 Ernle, *Land*, 127.
77 Somerset EC minutes, 26 Feb. 1917; Norfolk EC minutes, 14 July 1917; West Sussex EC minutes, 8 March 1917.
78 Montgomery, *Labour Supply*, 43.
79 Hereford EC, Executive Officer's report, 27 June 1917; Bedford EC minutes, 14 July 1917; Worcs. EC minutes, 11 Aug. 1917.
80 Lindsey EC minutes, 17 Oct. 1917; Report to 31 March 1918, 9.
81 War Cabinet, *1918 Report*, 237; PRO, NATS 1/132, L. 1/627, *Prisoners of War Employment Committee, first interim report*, Appendix B(1).
82 CAB 23/6, 297(7), 13 Dec. 1917.
83 Montgomery, *Labour Supply*, 44–5.
84 Ibid., 45.
85 CAB 23/5, 227(9), 3 Sep. 1917; 245(3), 4 Oct. 1917.
86 Cheshire EC, Report to 30 March 1918, 11; Hereford EC minutes, 5 April 1918–20 June 1918; Herts. EC minutes, 18 Feb. 1918, 25 March 1918; Lindsey EC, Report to 31 March 1918, 9; Salop, Report to 31 Dec. 1918, 5.
87 Montgomery, *Labour Supply*, 46–8.
88 Ibid., 47.
89 NATS I/132, L. 1/626/28 (Appx IV), Ben H. Morgan's report.
90 Montgomery, *Labour Supply*, 47–8.
91 NATS I/32, L. 1/627, *POWEC first interim report*, Appendix A.
92 Lindsey EC, Report to 31 March 1918, 9.
93 Beds. EC minutes, Sep.-Nov. 1918.
94 Worcs. EC minutes, German PoW labour sub-committee, 28 Aug. 1918; Worcs. EC minutes, cultivation sub-committee, 26 May 1919; NATS I/132, L. 1/627, *Notes by the FPD as to the present system of employing prisoners of war in agriculture*, n.d., 5.
95 NATS I/132, L. 1/626, POWEC meeting of 7 June 1918, evidence of Mr J. Steel, of Lock's Hill, Rochford, Essex, 6–7.
96 Ibid., 3, and evidence of Mr. W. P. Theakston, 21.
97 NATS 1/123, L. 1/627, para. 9.
98 Ibid., para. 9(f); Evidence of Lieut. Parker, POWEC meeting, 21 June 1918, 12.
99 Montgomery, *Labour Supply*, 47.
100 POWEC meeting, 7 July 1918, 15.

101 EC minutes, German PoW labour sub-committee, 3 July 1918.
102 POWEC meeting, 7 June 1918, Steel p. 6; Theakston p. 16.
103 NATS 1/132, L. 1/627, POWEC, *Remuneration of prisoners*, para. 2; *Notes by the FPD. . . .*, para. 5. In spite of the remarks made above on prisoners' inefficiency, they have been classed here as equivalent to adult male labourers when calculating the size of replacement labour flows (above, p. 140). This is unsatisfactory, but there is no alternative basis for calculating prisoners' level of efficiency.
104 MAF 59/1, L. 29369, *Work of the Women's War Agricultural Committees for the year ending August 1916*, 2.
105 Andrews and Hobbs, *Economic Effects of the War on Women* (2nd edn, New York, 1920), 71.
106 MAF 42/8, 40171/D, *Statement on the Work of the Food Production Department since the Government change in December 1916*, 1; *Report of the War Cabinet for the Year 1917*, 161.
107 War Cabinet, *1918 Report*, 237; Middleton, *Food Production*, 222–3; MAF 42/8, 40171/0, *Report of the Food Production Department (England and Wales) to the 1st June 1918*; Ernle, *Land*, 177.
108 Cmd. 24., 134; Ernle, *Land*, 128–9; his estimate of 0.3 million differs from that in *Land*, 177.
109 Cmd. 25, 248–9.
110 See Appendix G.
111 CAB 23/1, 31, Appx II.
112 Cmd. 25, vol. II, *Reports of Investigators*, county entries.
113 Cmd. 25, 138–9.
114 CAB 23/1, 31(12), Appx II, 10 Jan. 1917; CAB 23/7, 449(15), 19 July 1918.
115 Ernle, *Land*, 128; Mrs A. Lyttleton, 'The Women's Land Army', *JBA*, Oct. 1918, 808.
116 Herts. EC minutes, AEC/8, WWAC Selection and Allocation Committee, 4 July 1917.
117 Ernle, *Land*, 128.
118 Ibid., 182–3.
119 Herts. EC minutes, 18 April 1917; Lindsey EC minutes, 20 July 1917; Wilts. EC minutes, 12 Oct. 1917.
120 Ernle, *Land*, 174–5.
121 Lindsey EC minutes, 3 and 31 Aug. 1917.
122 Oxford EC minutes, 28 Jan. 1918; Herts. EC minutes, *Review of EC work since January 1918*, 17 Feb. 1919.
123 Lindsey EC, Report to 31 March 1918, 13–14.
124 Anon., 'Women's work on the land', *JBA*, July 1918, 455.
125 Herts. EC minutes, 26 April 1918, 5 July 1918.
126 MAF 42/8, 40171/D, 11.
127 MAF 42/8, 33867, memorandum by Miss M. Talbot, 1–2.
128 Lindsey EC minutes, 31 Aug. 1917, 22 June 1917, 11 Oct. 1918; Gloucs. EC minutes, 26 March 1918; Norfolk EC minutes, 27 Oct. 1917, Appendix.
129 MAF 42/8, 33867, minute of 5 Nov. 1918.

130 MAF 42/8, 40171/D, 11; IWM, LAND V, List W.L.18 of 26 April 1919, and letter of 24 May 1919 by Miss Talbot.

131 Ernle, *Land*, 183.

132 Cmd. 25, county entries.

133 IWM, LAND V, List. W.L.18, 26 April 1919. The WLA do not appear to have worked in Scotland.

134 Cmd. 25, para. 142.

135 IWM, LAND V, *WLA Handbook*, 7.

136 Ernle, *Land*, 184.

137 Gloucs. WWAC General Committee meeting, 21 Sep. 1918; Lindsey EC minutes, 15 March 1918.

138 Cmd. 25, paras. 143–5.

139 Ibid., para. 143.

140 Ernle, *Land*, 184; IWM, LAND V, *WLA Handbook*, July 1919, 7.

141 Cmd. 25, para. 205.

142 Board of Education, *Annual Report of Chief Medical Officer of the Board of Education for 1917*, Cd. 9206, PP 1918, IX, 143; Board of Education, *School Attendance and Employment in Agriculture*.

143 Cmd. 24, para. 148.

144 Board of Education, *Annual Report for 1918 of the Chief Medical Officer of the Board of Education*, PP XXI (1919), Cmd. 420, 189.

145 Cd. 9206, 152–3.

146 Ernle, *Land*, 129; West Sussex WAC minutes, 25 June 1917; Lindsey EC minutes, 10 July 1917; Cmd. 24, 153.

147 Montgomery, *Labour Supply*, 49–50.

146 Ernle, *Land*, 128.

149 PRO, MAF 42/8, 40171/D.

150 Montgomery, *Labour Supply*, 50; War Cabinet, *Report for 1918*, 237.

151 Cmd. 25, county entries; Salop EC minutes, Report to 24 April 1917.

152 NATS I/132, L. 1/626, *Reports on Prisoner of War Camps*, by Ben H. Morgan, 8 Oct. 1918, Nos. 9 and 32.

153 Montgomery, *Labour Supply*, 50; Board of Trade, *Report on the State of Employment at the end of July 1917*, 6.

154 *Report of FPD to 1 June 1918*, MAF 42/8, 40171/D, 8.

155 Ibid., 8; Middleton, *Food Production*, 186.

156 *Report of FPD . . .*, 9; War Cabinet, *Report for 1918*, 237.

157 Ernle, *Land*, 144; Middleton, *Food Production*, 210.

158 Replacement labour estimates are for England and Wales only. The estimate for soldier labour in 1917–18 has been altered from that originally published [Dewey, *EcHR* 1975, 104):

	1917	1918
Original	40	45
New estimate	28	66

For Scotland, information is fragmentary; for spring cultivation, 1,850 soldiers were loaned in 1917, and 6,000 in 1918. Assistance with the harvests of 1917 and 1918 amounted to 3,000 and 10,000 (although another estimate for the 1917 harvest is 15,000 soldiers).

By the end of 1918, some 9,000 soldiers were recorded in Agricultural Companies. Other forms of replacement labour were smaller; the largest are 2,000 schoolboys (1917 harvest), 762 (?village) women in 1917, and 600 PoWs in 1918; *Report of the Board of Agriculture for Scotland* (1917 and 1918), PP 1918, v, p. xxv; 1919, ix. p. lv; War Cabinet, *Report for 1917*, 160; *Report for 1918*, 241.

159 I am indebted to the late Mr J. L. Davies for information on the 1929 article, supplied in July 1973.

Chapter Ten

TRACTORS AND MACHINERY

The transformation of policy in 1916–17 had important effects on the supply of agricultural machinery. Whereas farmers had been subject to increasing shortages up to the end of 1916, these were now overcome as part of the plough policy. They also saw an important new development: the introduction of the tractor for the first time on a large scale.

Even before the adoption of the plough policy, there had been organisational changes. On 24 November 1916, the War Committee had decided to make the Ministry of Munitions responsible for the supply of agricultural machinery. On 2 January 1917, S. F. Edge was appointed as the first Director of the Agricultural Machinery Branch of the ministry. The functions of the AMB were to place contracts, to control manufacture, and to meet the requirements of the FPD. At the same time, regulation of purchase by the public was altered. The existing system of priority permits was abolished; purchase was now unregulated, but manufacture was prohibited without a licence from the Ministry. When a licence had been given, priority for materials was granted, and manufacture could begin.[1]

Home manufacture for private customers continued, but on a reduced scale; imports also continued, but on a much reduced scale.[2] The bulk of supply, whether home or imported, was now in the hands of the Ministry, which in 1917 and 1918 placed orders for machinery worth £4.7 million. The orders were for cultivating machinery of most existing types, with the novel addition of tractors (Table 10.1).

Broadly, the programme consisted in ordering tractors from the USA and other cultivating machinery and implements from home

Table 10.1: Ministry of Munitions orders for agricultural machinery, 1917–18

6,000 Fordson tractors (from USA)
3,750 Oliver ploughs (from USA; for use with the Fordsons)
2,632 International Harvester Co. Titan tractors (from USA)
500 Caterpillar tractors (Clayton and Shuttleworth)
400 Saunderson tractors
65 sets of steam ploughing tackle (Fowler & Co.)
6,500 harrows
5,000 binders (USA)
6,000 two-furrow Fordson ploughs
393 threshing machines

Source: *History of the Ministry of Munitions*, XII, Pt. VI, 8–9

producers. However, given the pre-war dependence on the USA for field machinery, and the wartime pressure of munitions production, home producers could not keep the whole of the non-tractor list to themselves. Thus the binders were largely from the USA; Hornsby & Co., a large producer before the war, when it produced £37,400-worth, was only producing £24,900-worth in 1916. Although this rose briefly to £29,400 in 1917, it fell to £20,600 in 1918. Since meanwhile the average price of a binder had risen from £30 to £65, the real value of output was much reduced.[3] On the other hand, Ransomes, a plough specialist, experienced a rise in output, from an average of £95,000 p.a. in 1909–13, to £342,000 in 1918.[4]

The extent of dependence on imports for both tractors and other machines and implements can be indicated in a rough way by the British trade statistics; retained imports of agricultural machinery, which had been worth £572,000 p.a. in 1909–13, rose in 1917 to £3.56 million, and in 1918 to £5.69 million.[5] By 1918, retained imports were about the same value as the whole output of the home agricultural machinery industry before the war.

The growing dependence on imports was also a growing dependence on the USA. This is clearly so in the case of 'prime movers' (chiefly tractors and their spares). Although negligible before the war, the trade had been essentially from the USA, and this continued to be the case. Of the imports in 1916–18, which averaged £1,254,000 p.a., 97 per cent came from the USA. Some 60 per cent of 'other machinery' also came from the USA.[6] A more detailed view of the types of machinery obtained from the USA may be had from the USA trade statistics (although the values are not comparable with the British statistics). Of the $6.79 million of US exports of machinery to the UK in 1917 and 1918, $2.01 million was of ploughs and cultivators, and 'other' machinery (chiefly tractors and their spares) amounted to $3.29 million.[7]

Since these figures are in current prices, allowance must be made for wartime inflation, which also affected the USA, although less severely than Britain. When the USA export figures are deflated by the US wholesale price index, it becomes apparent that US exports, which had fallen off early in the war, had still not quite recovered even in 1917, although there was an enormous increase in 1918, which took US exports in real terms to about 2.6 times the 1909–13 level (Table 10.2).

Table 10.2: USA machinery exports to Britain, 1916–18

[1909–13 prices, $'000]				
1914	1915	1916	1917	1918
1,182	757	944	993	3,197

Source: see n. 7 below, and Bureau of the Census, *Historical Statistics of the USA*, 351

By 1917, the supply of both home-produced and imported machinery had been curtailed for two years. However, this is unlikely to have led to serious deterioration in the quantity or quality of farm machinery. In so far as the machinery supply gave concern in 1917–18, it was most notably in threshing, and the problem was often lack of labour or coal rather than machinery. The Lindsey EC reported in March 1918 that there were plenty of threshing sets in the county, but not enough labour to work them. In Salop, 'numerous complaints' of difficulty in obtaining threshing machines were made in 1917, and lack of labour again seems to be the reason. The Wiltshire EC in April 1918 thought that there were a sufficient number of threshing sets to go round, if farmers would loan them out, but that the main difficulty would be labour. As late as August 1918, Lindsey EC noted a serious shortage of coal for steam cultivating and threshing. The difficulty of obtaining steam coal had been earlier referred to in Norfolk, as had the insufficiency of steam ploughing tackle.[8] The latter had already been recognised as a national problem by the FPD; a census of steam sets in January 1917 showed that nearly half the total number of 500 sets were out of action, needing either drivers or repair. Action was taken on both counts, and Ernle records that all but 40 sets, which were obsolete, were at work by June 1917. This concern is also reflected in the FPD order for 65 new sets from Fowlers of Leeds.[9]

Apart from tractors and ploughs, the new policy required an expansion in the supply of cultivating and harvesting machinery. Most of this went to the ECs, permitting them to offer a wide range of services to farmers. By January 1918 Salop had received 34 of the 40 disc harrows requested, and all of the 17 disc drills. By March, Lindsey had 10 disc harrows, 3 land presses, 10 land rollers and 16 cultivators. For the 1918 harvest the ECs had a considerable number of binders to offer; 4,250 were supplied to them by the FPD. They were also supplied with threshing machines, of which 19 are recorded for Salop (25 had been requested).[10]

Farmers were adopting the tractor before the advent of the FPD. The first British tractor, the Ivel, had been produced in 1902 (S. F. Edge being a director of the company), and 900 of them were eventually produced before the company became insolvent in 1921. Other attempts were made before the war, and in 1910 the Royal Agricultural Society held its first tractor trials, fielding two Ivels, two 'Universal' tractors by Saunderson & Mills (Bedford), and three steam engines; the steam engines won. Antipathy to the petrol-engined tractors derived from their heavy weight, cost, and (allegedly) fear of the dangers attending the use of petrol.[11]

The war spurred the development and marketing of tractors. An editorial in the *Farmer and Stock Breeder* said in July 1915: 'Horses are now so dear that the motor manufacturer never had a better chance to push his goods in agricultural circles'.[12] As early as November 1915, the *Journal of the Board of Agriculture* reported on the result of tractor demonstrations organised chiefly by certain county councils. Not all the machines were motor tractors; there were four motor ploughs and two steam tractors, as well as eight motor tractors. While the motor ploughs were favourably received, some of the tractors were thought to be too heavy and expensive for ordinary farmers; the heaviest weighed over four tons, and the most expensive cost £500. Very favourably commented on was the Overtime (a USA model), which, at 2 tons 3 cwt and costing £231, was described as 'a light tractor at a moderate price'.[13]

Even during the first year of the war, farmers had a choice of tractor; the Ivel and four models of Universal were on the market, as were two types of motor plough (Garrett-Crawley and Wyles). The IHC Mogul (25 HP) appeared in April 1915. There was also a steam tractor by Mann & Co. In December 1915, the Highland and Agricultural Society of Scotland held a motor tillage trial, with five entrants: a Wyles, Mogul (16 HP), Mann, and two new USA tractors (Sandusky and Overtime). In April 1916 two more types appeared from the USA: the Emerson-Brantingham and the Avery (which came in six versions, from 5–10 HP to 40–80 HP).[14]

In the succeeding months before the plough policy, the use of tractors grew, as the import statistics suggest. Estimates of the numbers in use are uncertain; the manufacturers of the Overtime advertised it prominently in the farming press ('Sell 3 of your horses and buy an Overtime. Immediate deliveries.'), claiming in February 1917 that there were 1,400 in use, although by then the price had risen to £325.[15] The claim may have been an exaggeration; the earliest record of private tractor numbers in a county (Herts., spring 1917) is 53; even assuming each of the 87 counties in Britain had the same, it is unlikely that Overtimes constituted over a third of the total tractor stock.[16]

During 1915–17, further models made their appearance. At least eight types can be traced, excluding the Overtime and those appearing in the 1915 trials,[17] but including a ploughing attachment for the Ford Model T motor car ('the Eros attachment'), and, more significantly, the IHC Titan, accompanying their existing Mogul model.[18] By March 1918 there were at least a further five models on the market. Altogether, a conservative estimate of the different models on the market by the end of the war is 26 (although this includes two steam tractors). British and USA manufacturers were almost equally represented.[19]

The FPD commitment to tractors thus took place in a rapidly developing market. To begin with, ECs obtained tractors from existing owners – either hiring, buying, or borrowing them. In April 1917, 13 of the 15 government tractors at work in Hertfordshire were private machines temporarily taken over by the EC, with a promise to plough the owner's land before that of others. In Somerset, the EC bought its first tractor (an Overtime) from a farmer in February 1917. In March it received FPD permission to buy a second, more expensive, tractor (a Mogul). The farmer wished to hire it out, but the committee preferred to buy; the farmer was to be allowed to first plough his own arable with it. In West

Sussex, two machines (the first to be operated by the EC) were lent by their owners in March 1917.[20]

By late spring, the committees were beginning to obtain tractors from the FPD. Salop initially asked for eight; six had arrived by late April, to join the nine already 'commandeered'. These were due to be returned by 1 May, but six replacements were expected from the FPD.[21] While the types are unknown, they are likely to have been Moguls or Titans. Moguls had already received Prothero's endorsement,[22] and Titans figure prominently amongst the early models operated by ECs. The earliest list of EC tractors, (Worcs., September 1917) comprises fifteen, ten of which were Titans, the rest being Moguls (two), an Avery, Bates 'Steel Mule', and an Overtime. The early prominence of the Titan is also suggested by an (unconfirmed) estimate that 2,000 of them were imported into Britain in 1914–18.[23]

The government tractor supply was by the summer of 1917 still in its infancy. By the end of May, the FPD employed 666, of which 477 were owned by the government, 135 were privately owned but controlled by the ECs, and 54 were caterpillar tractors, originally built for the Russian government, but temporarily loaned to the FPD. Spread over the 54 counties of England and Wales (excluding London), this supply would not go very far, being twelve to thirteen per county, and the distribution was uneven; Hertfordshire and Salop had fifteen each, but Somerset still had only three.[24] It is not known how many of the 'government' machines had been supplied new, or had been purchased from farmers. In all, it was a hastily improvised programme.[25]

During the summer and early autumn of 1917, the FPD stepped up the tractor supply. While no national estimates are available, the tractor stock of nine counties at the end of October stood at 225, making an average of 25 per county. Again there were large variations, the best-supplied counties being Somerset and Norfolk, with 43 and 69 respectively. On this basis, the FPD tractor stock in England and Wales may have been about 1,375. This is roughly confirmed by a War Cabinet memorandum at the end of October giving the number of government tractors at work as 1,550, and a statement that there were 1,600 in EC hands at the beginning of 1918. But there were still more private machines than government machines in England and Wales – an estimated 3,500 in October 1917.[26]

Titans and Moguls were still the dominant models; the Cheshire EC stock for the ploughing season of 1917–18 was 25 (eight 25-HP Moguls, four 16-HP Moguls, twelve 20-HP Titans, and one Overtime). In Lindsey, the eight Titans at work early in July 1917 were complemented by a delivery of eleven 16-HP Moguls later in the same month, although the EC considered them only suitable for light land, and expressed a preference for a more powerful machine.[27]

Committees were experiencing a shortage of tractors in the autumn and early winter of 1917–18; Somerset sent an anguished telegram to the FPD in September asking for more. The Department promised 24 machines. While 10 of these had arrived by the end of the month, the full complement was not at work until the end of November. Meanwhile, the EC had declined an FPD offer of three caterpillars, on the grounds of weight (15 tons each), and shortly afterwards reported that its ten Averys were constantly breaking down, and asked to exchange them for 20-HP Titans.[28]

At the root of the problem lay the delay in Fordson deliveries. In June 1917 it had been agreed with Ford that 5,000 (later raised to 6,000) should be manufactured in Britain, with Ford supplying specifications and assistance. However, in the same month, it was decided to change the recently established factories over to aircraft production, Ford then agreeing to manufacture the tractors in the USA. This caused much delay. According to Ford's chief assistant, Sorensen, delivery thereafter was rapid, with the first tractors being sent out in October 1917. However, there seems to have been a lengthy interval (seven weeks) before they reached the ECs. The War Cabinet recorded that they did not arrive in quantity before the beginning of 1918, and Ernle wrote that they did not arrive in large numbers until February. As late as 29 January, Somerset had to accept three Overtime and ten Parrett or Interstate tractors in place of the promised Fordsons.[29] No cases have been found of Fordsons delivered to ECs before 1918. Cheshire received 'a few towards the end of the ploughing season'. In Huntingdonshire, Fordsons (three only) were not obtained until 4 May. Lindsey first received some (four) in March, but only had ten in June. Norfolk had to wait until July for its Fordsons, but its patience was rewarded, since it then obtained 46. Somerset and Worcestershire both received ten Fordsons in April, and Somerset received a further delivery of 59 in May; West Sussex only obtained ten in May.[30]

Slow Fordson deliveries implied slow growth in the total tractor stock until the spring of 1918. There were 519 machines in the hands of 11 English ECs by the end of April, or 47 per county on average. For the 54 English and Welsh counties, this implies a total of 2,538 machines. This is rather less than a national estimate of 3,240 by the end of the spring. It was substantially behind schedule; the War Cabinet had hoped to have 6,000 at work by the end of March. The uneven distribution noted earlier persisted; outstanding were Lindsey (74), Norfolk (121), and Somerset (109).[31]

Ironically, most Fordsons were superfluous when they did arrive. They came too late for the main part of the 1917–18 ploughing programme and, although useful for the harvest of 1918, were not essential for it. Thereafter, the next task was winter threshing, for which the existing steam engines and tractors were more than adequate. Above all, the plough policy was in its final stages, the 1919 programme having been effectively abandoned even before Lord Lee's resignation in June. Thus the tractor programme began to be wound down; as early as 1 June, the FPD released 1,000 tractors from the ECs for sale to the public.[32]

The arrival of Fordsons in large numbers gave the FPD the opportunity to curtail the large number of different models employed by the ECs. At one time there had been more than 20 types, and this had given rise to acute problems of spares supply. In the second half of 1918, they were reduced to six: Titan, Overtime, Clayton and Shuttleworth (caterpillar), Saunderson, 25-HP Mogul, and the Fordson. The Somerset machinery sub-committee recorded that the scheme implied the disposal of: twelve 16-HP Moguls; five 25-HP Overtimes; four 25-HP Averys; four 16-HP Averys; ten 25-HP Parretts and nineteen 25-HP Samsons. In this case the FPD did not get its wishes. The sub-committee requested the Department to consider their retention of the Moguls, and the replacement of the other tractors on the list by Titans, as 'it is necessary to have in Somerset, stronger engines than Fordsons'. Shortly afterwards, most of the Averys and Samsons on the list were put up for sale, the Moguls presumably being retained.[33]

Substantial numbers of tractors were disposed of in this way. In addition to the 1,000 for sale in June must be added those sold later. The War Cabinet reported that about 3,000 had been sold by the end of the year. The FPD's Mechanical Cultivations Commissioner wrote that 3,000–4,000 had been sold in 1918. While the 1,000 for sale in June were of the 'less suitable' types, large numbers sold later were likely to have been Fordsons, sold direct to farmers without having been used by the ECs. Somerset had 110 tractors in mid-May, but in spite of a large delivery of 59 Fordsons, which brought the number to 169, the maximum number of tractors at work never exceeded 85, and three months later there were still 41 in storage; there is a strong presumption that they were Fordsons.[34]

These large disposals, and the late Fordson deliveries, make it likely that the total number of tractors in the hands of the ECs fell short of the orders placed with the manufacturers. These had amounted to 9,532 (of which 6,000 were Fordsons). By the end of May 1918, only 4,500 of all types had been delivered to the FPD. In October, ten English ECs had an average of 76 each, which, if a national average, would produce 4,104 in England and Wales. At the Armistice, there were 3,925 in England and Wales. The War Cabinet reported that the EC tractor stock at the end of the year was 4,200.[35] Assuming that the number of disposals by then was the 3,000–4,000 suggested by Hutchinson, then the highest number of EC tractors is unlikely to have been more than 7,000–8,000, and a large proportion of these probably never saw service.

Since at first the ECs had to take what tractors they could find through commercial channels, the result was a variegated stock. Of the more than 20 types originally operated by the ECs, 14 have been traced. In so far as their technical data, origins, and prices are known, they are given in Table 10.3 on the following page (prices are those of 1919).

Apart from the Universal (a pre-war model) there was no dominant British tractor, although there were several British motor ploughs on the market. Since the tractor was in its technical infancy (the first experimental Fordson appeared in 1916),[36] most suffered from certain disadvantages. The principal one was a low power/weight ratio. This was partly because manufacturers preferred heavy machines, to improve gripping power on the soil,[37] and partly because of the method of construction, which favoured a large rigid frame as the basis of the machine. This in turn called for a large engine, so that the final weight of the tractor was also large, even in the case of some early tractors with a not unfavourable power/weight ratio. The best example of the latter was the Overtime, and even that weighed two tons. Its chief advantage was low cost; it

Table 10.3: Tractor types operated by Executive Committees, 1917–19

Type	HP	Weight (cwt)	Origin	Price (£)
Avery	28	65	USA	500
Clayton & Shuttleworth[a]	35	–	Br.	650
Bates Steel Mule	30	50	Br.	485
Fordson[a]	22	34	USA	280
IHC Mogul[a]	30	85	USA	580
IHC Mogul	16	45	USA	–
IHC Titan[a]	25	55	USA	410
Interstate	–	–	USA	–
Overtime[a]	28	40	USA	368
Parrett	25	–	Br.	–
Samson	–	–	–	–
Saunderson & Mills Universal[a]	25	55	Br.	510

Notes: [a] selected for final FPD list
– = not available

Source: Wright, *Old Farm Tractors*, 12–13; *JBA*, November 1915, 762; *FSB*, 18 March 1918

was the cheapest model on the market until the advent of the much smaller-framed Fordson, which was supplied to the FPD at an initial price of £150 (= cost + $50),[38] making it much the cheapest model available. With the Fordson, the FPD reaped the advantages of cheapness, high power/weight ratio, and general technical superiority.[39] Another disadvantage of the early tractors was that they usually required two-man operation; one man drove the tractor, and one sat on the plough, which was trailed behind the tractor. Most Fordsons worked likewise, but a start was made by Ford in pioneering the self-lift plough.[40] More generally, tractors suffered from exposure of working parts to grit and dust, chain drives that failed or clogged, and a need for frequent lubrication of inaccessible parts. Here again the Fordson was an improvement, having more enclosed workings, and semi-automatic lubrication.[41]

The final selection of tractor types by the FPD was the result of the accumulation of experience during the war. By this time, the strengths and weaknesses of the various models had emerged. The FPD Mechanical Cultivations Commissioner judged them as follows: the Titan was very good on all types of land, and useful as a stationary engine for threshing, cutting chaff, and sawing; the Overtime was a satisfactory general utility model; the Clayton caterpillar was powerful but expensive, and best used on heavy land;

the Universal was especially superior in road haulage; the (larger) Mogul was best confined to threshing, since it was too heavy for use on wet land; the Fordson was probably the cheapest on the market, and overall the best if its limitations were borne in mind; it was not powerful enough for stationary work, but an 'acknowledged success' for cultivation, even on heavy land.[42] However, the Somerset machinery sub-committee would have demurred at some of these statements, preferring to retain Moguls rather than accept Fordsons for the cultivation of heavy land.[43]

Even the Fordson, however, had disadvantages. In particular, its longitudinal stability was poor. It reared up rapidly when the plough hit an obstacle, and several drivers were allegedly killed in 1918 as a result. This feature became so notorious that one company marketed a device which depressed the clutch as soon as an obstruction was hit; in 1919 Ford introduced a release mechanism for the draw-bar for this reason.[44]

The disadvantages which attended early tractor design could not be avoided in the early days of tractor work. There was, however, one major technical flaw in the programme which should have been foreseen: the failure to provide suitable ploughs. The model originally selected (with the Fordson in mind) was the American Oliver pattern, of which 3,750 were ordered.[45] The Oliver suffered from the error which afflicted all early designs of tractor plough: the tendency to copy the shape of the plough breast from a horse plough. Since tractors were faster than horses, this design tended to break and scatter the plough slice, instead of neatly inverting it unbroken. In addition, the Oliver originally produced too wide a furrow (14 inches) for English conditions, and a plough giving a 10-inch furrow eventually had to be adopted.[46]

The ECs soon discovered the drawbacks of the Oliver. As early as July 1917 the Somerset machinery sub-committee instructed its secretary to write to the FPD and complain that Oliver ploughs (and a type known as the Moline) were useless in that county; Cockshutt ploughs (another USA model) were preferred. In April 1918, it was noted that the Olivers were designed for stubble breaking rather than grass ploughing, and that a new type was being manufactured. In West Sussex, the committee noted that Olivers were not suitable for ploughing for grain, the furrow being too wide, but that the FPD was now (June 1918) supplying a conversion kit to reduce the Oliver furrow to 10 inches. In Huntingdonshire, ploughing had been much hindered by having to work with unsuitable ploughs, and as early as September 1917 a local firm was experimenting to devise a plough combining the best features of British and USA models.[47]

Apart from the waste of time, irritation, and poor ploughing caused by the Oliver fiasco, it increased the number of plough types, further complicating the spares problem. At the end of March 1918, Lindsey operated five different types of tractor, but seven types of plough; it had just received its first Fordsons, but even before that, it operated four tractor and five plough types.[48] The government did not publicise this embarrassment during the war.[49] Eventually, the FPD was obliged to order 6,000 special ploughs for the Fordson; it seems unlikely that the order would have been as large but for the disappointment over the Oliver.[50]

Tractors and ploughs were the items ordered in the greatest quantities by the FPD. The next largest order was for 5,000 self-binders; although the final delivery total is not known, the War Cabinet reported that the FPD operated or hired to farmers 4,250 during the 1918 harvest, and released for sale a further 524. High in value, if not in numbers, were 66 steam ploughing sets and 438 threshing machines manufactured to FPD order. There was also a wide range of cultivating implements, of which 1,600 cultivators, 730 disc harrows, and 200 land presses are known to have been delivered to the Department by 31 May 1918, although they fell short of the total numbers ordered. Finally, the plough policy also involved placing orders for horse-drawn equipment; 500 ploughs and 1,000 carts were ordered for horse use, as well as a certain number of disc harrows.[51]

Analysis of the steps taken to increase the supply of agricultural machinery and implements in 1917–18 leads to several conclusions. The first is that the stock of machinery by the end of 1916 was adequate for the existing demands made upon it. It is noticeable that the FPD did not think it necessary to provide for a revival of production of the full range of machinery and implements then found on farms. It confined its attentions to the extra machinery for field cultivation consequent on the adoption of the plough policy. The only large order for non-arable equipment was for milk churns and some cheese preparation utensils.[52]

Secondly, the machinery programme was above all centred upon

the supply of tractors and their implements. At 1918 prices, tractors
and tractor ploughs ordered had approximately these values:[53]

	£ million
6,000 Fordsons @ £150	0.9
2,632 Titans @ £400	1.05
400 Universals @ £450	0.18
9,750 ploughs @ £9.84	0.095
Total	2.22

Since the total value of FPD orders in 1917–18 came to £4.7
million, tractors and ploughs accounted for almost half of the total.
The order for 66 steam ploughing sets from Fowler and Co. would
have been worth about £200,000, and the binders would have been
worth about £330,000 (both at 1918 prices).[54] Apart from tractors
and their equipment, steam sets and binders, the FPD ordered what
in retrospect appears to be a modest amount of machinery and
implements – only about £1.9 million in value.

Thirdly, the selection of tractor types was commendable. Of the
pre-Fordson types, the Titan was probably the best (although the
Overtime had much to commend it). It was also cheaper and lighter
than the 30-HP Mogul, and had the prospect of being supplied in
quantity. The Fordson was in a superior class altogether, being in
effect the pioneer of a novel approach to tractor construction, and
one which provided the basis for future design. It also undercut the
price of existing tractors by a large margin.

However, the programme was substantially marred by delay (and
to some extent error). Some difficulties were unavoidable; the FPD
could do little about the multiplicity of tractor types on the market,
and the subsequent spares confusion. Some could have been
avoided; the delay in getting tractors from the USA to the counties
comes to mind. The largest of the avoidable mistakes was the Oliver
fiasco, in which no attempt seems to have been made to hold
proving trials before settling on the plough type, and the possible
unsuitability of a USA model for British conditions does not seem
to have been considered. The larger delays in the programme were
due to confusion over political or military priorities; the six-month
delay in 1917 before approving the 1918 ploughing programme was
a serious handicap in all aspects of the food production policy, and
the machinery programme was further seriously delayed by the
decision to switch Fordson production to the USA.

NOTES

1 Ministry of Munitions, *History of the Ministry of Munitions*, XII, Pt. VI, 3.
2 On 23 February 1917 imports without a licence were forbidden; ibid., 11.
3 Lincoln RO, Ruston archive; Cmd. 76, 61.
4 Ransomes archive, Institute of Agricultural History, Reading University.
5 *Annual Statement of Trade*, 1909–18.
6 Ibid.
7 USA, Dept. of Commerce and Labor, *The foreign commerce and navigation of the United States for the year ending June 30 . . .* (1909–18), (Washington, 1910–19).
8 Lindsey EC minutes, 5 May 1918, 13 Aug. 1918; Salop, Report of the EC to 12 Jan. 1918, 6; Wilts. EC, 3 April 1918; Norfolk EC, 18 and 25 June 1917.
9 Ernle, *Land*, 130; *History of the Ministry of Munitions*, XII, Pt. VI, 8–9.
10 Salop EC, Report to 12 Jan. 1918, 5, 6; Report to 31 Dec. 1918, 3; Lindsey EC, Report to 31 March 1918, 6. War Cabinet, *Report for the year 1918*, 239. Clayton & Shuttleworth, a leading manufacturer, placed a notice in the *Mark Lane Express* on 2 September 1918 (p. 194) to say that all its output was now taken by the FPD.
11 P. A. Wright, *Old Farm Tractors* (1962), 1–5.
12 *FSB*, 26 July 1915, 1369.
13 'Demonstrations of motor ploughs and tractors', *JBA*, November 1915, 760–6.
14 *IMR*, 1 July 1914–1 April 1916.
15 *MLE*, 3 Jan. 1916, 31; FSB, 12 Feb. 1917, 275.
16 EC, Report, April 1917, 7.
17 Wright, *Old Farm Tractors*, 53.
18 *FSB*, 10 Dec. 1917, p. 1877, 4 March 1918, p. 553. Wright, *Old Farm Tractors*, 19, notes 3,500 Titans imported between 1914 and 1920.
19 *FSB*, 4 March 1918, 553; this estimate is derived from Wright, *Old Farm Tractors*, 12–23, and *JBA*, 'Demonstrations', Nov. 1915, 762.
20 Herts. EC, Report, April 1917; Somerset EC, 19 Feb. 1917–5 April 1917; West Sussex EC, 12 March 1917.
21 Salop EC, Report, 24 April 1917.
22 *JBA*, Jan. 1917, 937, report of speech at Bedford.
23 Worcs. EC, cultivation sub-committee, 19 Sep. 1917; Brigden, *Ploughs and Ploughing*, 26.
24 Herts. EC, Report, April 1917; Salop Report of EC, 24 April 1917; Somerset EC minutes, 5 March–21 May 1917.
25 MAF 42/8, 40171/D; *Report of the Food Production Department (England and Wales) for the period up to the 1st June 1918*, 12; Ernle, *Land*, 131.
26 War Cabinet, *1918 Report*, 238; CAB 23/4, 297, quoting memo GT 2767; many of the private tractors were said to be idle due to lack of fuel.

27 Chester EC, Report to 30 June 1918, 9; Lindsey EC minutes, 10–24 July 1917.
28 Somerset EC minutes, 6 Sep.–18 Dec. 1917.
29 Ibid., 29 Jan. 1918; Ernle, *Land*, 142–3; C. E. Sorenson, *Forty Years with Ford* (1957), 236–8; War Cabinet, *1918 Report*, 238; CAB 23/4, 297, GT. 2767, 2.
30 EC minutes for these counties.
31 J. Sheail, 'Land improvement and reclamation: the experiences of the First World War in England and Wales', *AgHR* 24, II (1976), 116; CAB 23/4, 297; 3; EC minutes for Lindsey, Norfolk, and Somerset.
32 MAF 42/8, 40171/D, 14.
33 G. T. Hutchinson, 'Government tractor cultivation in England and Wales', *JBA*, December 1918, 1046–52; Somerset EC minutes, 11 June, 27 Aug. 1918.
34 Hutchinson, 'Tractor cultivation', 1046; Somerset EC, machinery sub-committee, SH/A/1 & 2.
35 FPD report to 1 June 1918, 13; Herts. WAC, 18 Nov. 1918; Sheail (1976), 116; War Cabinet, *1918 Report*, 238. The Scottish tractor contingent reached a maximum of 198 in 1918; *Seventh Report of the Board of Agriculture for Scotland* (1918), PP 1919, IX, p. xlv.
36 Sorensen, *Forty Years*, 236.
37 T. Close et al., 'The Lincoln tractor trials', *JBA*, October 1919, 687.
38 Ministry of Munitions, *History*, XII, Pt. VI, 6; Sorensen, *Forty Years*, 238.
39 Wright, *Old Farm Tractors*, 31.
40 Hutchinson, 'Tractor cultivation', 1052; the Overtime had earlier been advertised with a self-lift plough; *MLE*, 24 Jan. 1916.
41 Wright, *Old Farm Tractors*, 31.
42 Hutchinson, 'Tractor cultivation', 1052.
43 EC minutes, 11 June 1918.
44 C. Fraser, *Harry Ferguson, Inventor and Pioneer* (1972), 47–8; Hutchinson, 'Tractor cultivation', 1053.
45 The Ministry of Munitions order list stated that the Olivers were intended for use with the Fordsons, but they were used with other machines before the Fordsons arrived; *History of the Ministry of Munitions*, XII, Pt. VI, 8–9; Hutchinson, 'Tractor cultivation', 1049.
46 T. Close, 'Modern labour-saving implements', *JBA*, Aug. 1919, 487; 'The Lincoln tractor trials', *JBA*, Oct. 1919, 687; Hutchinson, 'Tractor cultivation', 1052.
47 Somerset EC, 9 July, 18 Dec. 1917, 11 April 1918; West Sussex EC, 14 and 21 June 1918; Hunts. EC, 31 Aug., 1 Sep. 1917. See also Close, 'Implements', 486.
48 Lindsey EC, Report to 31 March 1918; EC minutes, 5 March 1918.
49 Not surprisingly, it is not mentioned in the 1918 War Cabinet report. Surprisingly, it is absent from the unpublished reports of the FPD (destined for the War Cabinet) in the PRO.
50 Ministry of Munitions, *History*, XII, Pt. VI, 8–9.

51 War Cabinet, *1918 Report*, 238–9; MAF 42/8, 40171/D, 13; Ministry of Munitions, *History*, XII, Pt. VI, 8–9.
52 Ministry of Munitions, *History*, XII, Pt. VI, 8–9.
53 Ibid.; prices from advertisements in *FSB*, *MLE*, *IMR*, various issues.
54 Ministry of Munitions, *History*, XII, Pt. VI, 8–9; prices from *FSB*, 4 Feb. 1918; Wright, *Old Farm Tractors*, 4; Cmd. 76, 61. The steam ploughing sets were not operated by the ECs, but were sold to contractors; H. Bonnett, *Saga of the Steam Plow*, 143, writes that the contractors buying the sets paid £3,000 a set.

Chapter Eleven

FERTILISERS AND FEEDS

FERTILISERS

During the second half of the war, the problems of curtailed imports and shipping difficulties persisted, and could only be partially mitigated. The competition from munitions factories for materials such as sulphuric acid also continued, and munitions still had priority over agriculture. The novel feature of 1917–18 was the food production policy. Since this was a policy for converting grassland into tillage, it required a large increase in the supply of fertiliser. In May 1917, the agricultural departments of the UK estimated the fertiliser requirements of the plough programme.[1] The War Cabinet was particularly impressed with the need for phosphates, and accepted Lord Milner's proposal at the end of May that an extra 50,000 tons a month of phosphatic rock should be imported for the next five months. This programme was implemented, but not entirely successfully. In December, Sir Arthur Lee reported that only 149,000 tons had been imported.[2] However, the programme, although lagging, was continued. The average pre-war import had been 492,000 tons a year (1909–13). By 1916 it had fallen to 333,000 tons, and fell further to 277,000 tons in 1917. However, it revived substantially in 1918, to 465,000 tons – only slightly below the pre-war level. At the same time, the other bottleneck in superphosphate production, the supply of sulphuric acid, was tackled. Acid produced by the superphosphate manufacturers, formerly diverted to munitions, was redirected to its original purpose.[3] In addition, some alleviation was provided by the near-cessation of superphosphate exports, compared to pre-war.

Thus the supply of the most widely used fertiliser in British farming was revived. Our estimate is that the extra imports of rock in 1917–18 permitted home production to rise almost to the pre-war level. When the near-cessation of exports is taken into account, the available supply for farmers was somewhat above the pre-war level, although not providing extra supply for the food production programme on the scale envisaged by the government.[4]

Little was done about the shortage of sodium nitrate. Imports, which before the war had been some 94,000 tons annually (1909–13) had already fallen considerably by 1916, to only 21,000 tons. In 1917 only about 1,000 tons came in, and in 1918 only 300.[5] The government preferred to develop the existing policy of encouraging farmers to use ammonium sulphate instead of sodium nitrate, as a source of nitrogen. Early in February 1917, the War Cabinet decided to make available 200,000 tons of ammonium sulphate, at a fixed price of £15.50 (ex-works), or £16.00 anywhere in the UK. No time limit was set for this offer. It was anticipated that farmers would have taken up about 80,000 tons of this by the end of May. Unfortunately, the distribution arrangements were faulty, and there were many complaints. Responsibility for distribution was then transferred to the FPD, and matters improved, such that by the end of May 90,000 tons of sulphate had been supplied at the fixed price.[6]

The virtual disappearance of sodium nitrate from the market had already had the effect of stimulating ammonium sulphate consumption; Middleton estimated that it had already reached 80,000 tons in 1916.[7] By the spring of 1917 consumption was rising rapidly. The Acland Committee reported at the end of March that agricultural consumption between July 1916 and April 1917 was estimated at 110,000 tons. However, the potential was even greater. Production was still at (or slightly above) the pre-war level, at 430,000 tons, and export had been greatly reduced, being only permitted to certain British allies and possessions as a political gesture. Even given the fact that a large demand for sulphate had developed from the munitions industry, to the extent of 200,000 tons a year, there was still, the War Cabinet and the Acland Committee thought, the possibility of raising agricultural usage to 230,000 tons a year; the final consumption level for the fertiliser year 1916–17 had been 150,000 tons.[8]

In order to stimulate consumption, a further inducement was offered. This centred around a technical problem. Ammonium sulphate being slightly deliquescent, in time it absorbed atmospheric moisture and turned hard. Thus both the private manufacturers and the Ministry of Munitions (which also manufactured it) wished to clear their stocks as quickly as possible. In the case of the commercial manufacturers, there was the additional factor of the costs of storage to be considered. On the other hand, farmers did not wish to purchase until January, in order to apply it in January–April, and to avoid the problems of storage themselves. The Board's solution was a sliding price scale, beginning at £14,875 in June–September, rising to £15.75 in January–May 1918. Additionally, export would only be permitted 'in the national interest', and in any case only between June and December.[9]

This scheme was adopted to considerable effect, although hopes that consumption would rise to 230,000 tons were dashed by the end of the year. In December, Sir Arthur Lee reported that the demand for sulphate for munitions had been greater than anticipated, and that the prospective agricultural supply would fall short by 40,000 tons. Later in December, a memorandum from Prothero to the War Cabinet confirmed this, but quoted a slightly lower original target of 220,000 tons. Deducting 40,000 tons from this would leave only 180,000 tons.[10] Even if government hopes were not entirely fulfilled, there seems no doubt that farmers had substantially increased their usage.

The scheme inaugurated for the supply of sulphate was continued in 1918. As a further inducement, it was decided that the maximum price for 1918–19 should be the same as in the preceding year. The system whereby ECs drew up lists of approved agents was also continued. This was designed to counter the storage problems facing farmers, and (presumably) to enable them to place orders with confidence; the fertiliser industry had long been notoriously prone to complaints of poor quality and adulteration. The final consumption figure for the calendar year 1918 is estimated to be 230,000 tons, so that the War Cabinet target had been reached at last.[11]

In the case of basic slag, difficulties were minor. There was no shortage of the raw material, although there was some shortage of slag suitable for grinding, and there were delays in transport. The greatest problem was a shortage of labour in the slag factories. There were only about 20 of these works, and the difficulty was soon overcome by drafting Army Reserve Munition Workers into them; by March 1917 all except one had their full complement of labour. It is possible that, after the Ministry of Munitions assumed responsibility for manufacture, output rose slightly. It seems more likely that output was maintained at roughly the pre-war level. By 1916, the export trade had fallen considerably, and in 1917 and 1918 it was almost negligible (2,000 and 1,000 tons respectively, having been 194,000 p.a. in 1909–13). Given the adequacy of the raw material supply, and that slag was essentially a grassland fertiliser, demand is unlikely to have exceeded supply by much, especially in view of the reduction in permanent grass in 1917–18. On the basis of the method of calculation in ch. 6 above, we estimate agricultural consumption of slag as being 258,000 tons in 1917 and 238,000 in 1918 (1909–13 = 263,000).[12]

The only other fertiliser of importance whose supply was affected by the war was potash, usually supplied as 'kainit'. Potash supplies before the war were almost all imported from Germany, and were almost entirely cut off in 1914. This led to much apprehension, especially among potato growers. By 1917, the Acland Committee thought that the effect of potash shortage was being felt seriously, especially on potatoes; the only other source in prospect was Abyssinia, and this seemed unpromising. However, in spite of the fact that the supply did not revive in 1917–18, the shortage does not appear to have had a perceptible effect on crop yields.[13]

FEEDSTUFFS

Before 1917, feedstuffs had been affected to some extent by the reduction in imports of oilseeds and oilseed cake. However, the supply of cereal feeds had been largely maintained, with the exception of the slight reduction in supply caused by the poor harvests of 1916, and the beginning of liquor control. In 1917–18, the position deteriorated sharply, especially during the last year of the war, when a rationing scheme for feedstuffs was prepared; however, it was never fully implemented, and was abandoned at the Armistice.[14] There were two main reasons for the deterioration: imports were much more severely curtailed, and a large amount of cereals and cereal products were diverted to human consumption.

The restrictions on importing were most acutely felt in the case of prepared feeds such as cake, since the raw materials were imported. In 1917 imports of prepared cake continued to decline, but the most dramatic fall came in 1918, when imports of all three major forms of cake almost vanished. Imports of raw seed continued, albeit at a reduced level, so that cake could still be produced in the UK. Even so, the decline was potentially serious. Our estimate is that, compared with a pre-war level of 899,000 tons a year, consumption in 1917 was down to 492,000 tons, and to 393,000 tons in 1918.[15] For 1918, this is roughly confirmed by the War Cabinet calculation that supply of all oilcakes in the first eight months of 1918 was 300,000 tons.[16]

Import reductions also affected cereal feeds. This was most obvious for maize, which had been entirely imported. In 1909–13, the net import of maize had been on average almost 41 million cwt a year. By 1916, this had already been reduced to 34 million, and fell increasingly rapidly thereafter, to 25 million in 1917 and 14 million in 1918. Reductions were also severe in the more important cases of wheat and barley; by 1918, wheat imports were not much more than half their pre-war level, and those of barley were only about one-third.[17] These reductions were partly involuntary (e.g., maize) and partly a result of shipping policy. But much larger losses of feed were caused by another policy, that of breadstuffs. This entailed a sharp reduction in the supply of milling offals. Since wheat offals formed much the largest cereal feed pre-war, accounting for about half of expenditure on cereal feeds, this had serious consequences for the feed supply as a whole.

The cornerstone of the breadstuffs policy was to economise on flour by raising the milling extraction rate, i.e., the proportion of the wheat grain which was to be made into flour. In peacetime, this had been about 70 per cent: of the weight of grain entering the flour mills, about 70 per cent emerged as wheat flour. The residual 30 per cent, being almost entirely the shell or husk, was utilised for animal feed, under the name of 'millers' offals'. The raising of the extraction rate began in November 1916; the highest level reached was in April 1918, when it was 91.9 per cent. Thereafter it was allowed to fall to about 87 per cent, where it remained for the rest of the war.[18]

The breadstuffs policy chiefly affected wheat and barley. The supply of barley feed was also reduced by the increasingly severe restrictions on brewing and distilling which began in 1916, leading to a reduction in the supply of brewing, malting, and distilling offals. By 1918, the production of beer had more than halved, and what was produced was using less barley per barrel; the production of spirits had also more than halved.[19]

While precise figures of the supply of millers' and brewers' offals are not available, a rough estimate of cereal feed supply may be made. In the case of wheat, figures for home grain supply are shown below (Appendix C), import figures are available from the trade statistics, and the milling rates are given by Beveridge. Barley output is also estimated in the Appendix. It is assumed that the proportion of barley output sold off farms for feed was the same during the war as before it until 1917, when it sank to negligible amounts. Maize consumption, being entirely derived from imports, can be estimated from the trade statistics. The resulting estimate is that (roughly), cereal feed consumption in 1917 fell to about 2 million tons, and to about 1 million tons in 1918.[20] The 1918 estimate may be somewhat pessimistic; the War Cabinet estimated that cereal feed supply in the first eight months of the year was 1.07 million tons, but the reduction was certainly very large, compared with pre-war consumption of 2.65 million tons.[21]

NOTES

1 CAB 23/2, 135 (Appx), 9 May 1917.

2 Ibid., 153 (1), 31 May 1917; CAB 23/4, 297(10), 13 Dec. 1917, 5.

3 Cmd. 29, 6; this had probably been about one-fifth of the acid produced by those superphosphate manufacturers making their own acid; MAF 36/58, Fertiliser Committee, 30 Nov. 1915, 6.

4 See Appendix I.

5 *Annual Statement of Trade*, 1909–18.

6 Middleton, *Food Production*, 187; CAB 23/2, 150 (23), 30 May 1917.

7 Middleton, *Food Production*, 149.

8 CAB 23/2, 150(23), IV; MAF 36/62, Fertiliser Committee, 27 March 1917; Middleton, *Food Production*, 187.

9 Watson and More, *Agriculture*, 67; War Cabinet and Fertiliser Committee minutes in as n. 8.

10 CAB 23/4, 297(10), 5, 13 Dec. 1917; CAB 23/4, memorandum of 24 Dec. 1917, GT 2767, 5.

11 CAB 23/4, 399(12), 5; Oxford EC, 25 Sept. 1916; Chester EC, Report to 30 June 1918, 14; Salop EC, Report to 31 Dec. 1917, 6; Report to 31 Dec. 1918, 6; Middleton, *Food Production*, 228.

12 MAF 36/60, 15 Jan. 1917 and 36/62, 21 March 1917; Middleton, *Food Production*, 187; *Annual Statement of Trade*, Cmd. 29, 14.

13 Middleton, *Food Production*, 35–6, 111; MAF 36/60, memo of 8 Jan. 1917, 4.

14 It was due to come into effect on 17 November 1918; Beveridge, *Food Control*, 258.

15 See Appendix J.

16 CAB 23/40, 333(12), GT 3434, section A.
17 *Annual Statement of Trade*, 1909–18.
18 Beveridge, *Food Control*, 375.
19 Ibid., 100–2; Mitchell and Deane, *Abstract*, 253, 259.
20 See Appendix J; Beveridge, *Food Control*, 375; *Annual Statement of Trade*, 1917–18. See also CAB 23/40, GT 3434, which suggests very little barley going for animal feed in 1918. However, this does not include on-farm feed, which is excluded from the present calculations,
21 CAB 23/40, 333(12), section A and Appendix; this figure excludes oats.

Chapter Twelve

THE WORK OF THE COUNTY EXECUTIVE COMMITTEES

The adoption of the food production policy led immediately to the evolution of local organisations to implement it. From the first, the aim was to carry out the policy by decentralisation; as Lord Ernle pointed out: 'several hundreds of thousands of separate businesses could not be treated, like factories, as controlled establishments'.[1] The framework already existed, in the form of the County War Agricultural Committees. However, these were large, and did not have executive powers. They were now asked to form small Executive Committees, of not more than seven members. To each EC was added a county representative from the Board of Agriculture. They were given executive powers by the Cultivation of Lands Order, and informed of the new policy by the Board. In order to carry the policy down to local level, the ECs appointed District Committees (usually on the basis of existing Rural District Council areas), and in some cases, Parish Representatives. Apart from the need for decentralisation, the government felt that farmers were more likely to take advice from, or comply with the requests of, local farmers rather than persons unacquainted with the locality.[2]

The ECs were composed of farmers and landowners, with others interested in agriculture. The composition of the Lancashire EC was: 'One representative landowner, Two land agents, Four representative farmers.' On the whole, they escaped the dominance of county councillors which had marked the WACs (in Lindsey, however, the dominance of councillors continued on the EC). Once on the EC, members tended to remain for the rest of the war, although there was some movement due to illness, or finding other jobs. In Lancashire, a member of the EC resigned in 1918 to become Deputy Executive Officer for a District Committee (he later became a District Executive Officer). In 1918 some interest was shown in having representatives of labour on the committees, and one was appointed in Wiltshire in July. Norfolk, however, had one from the beginning, in the person of the agricultural trade union leader, George Edwards. The absence of the titled persons who had often acted as chairmen of the WACs is notable, although Lord St. Audries acted as chairman of the Somerset EC.[3]

The powers of the ECs were far-reaching. Effectively, they could either compel farmers to cultivate as directed, or take over farm land and cultivate it themselves. Nor was there any appeal possible above county level until the passing of the Corn Production (Amendment) Act in August 1918. Until then, farmers could only appeal against orders of the District Committees to the county EC itself. Thus the committees were effectively judges in their own cases.

Carrying out the new policy required full-time staff. Committees appointed Executive Officers, who became the persons responsible for implementing the policy. Generally, EOs were knowledgeable about county conditions. The Cheshire EO had been acting land agent to the county council; the Kent and West Sussex EOs had been the county agricultural education organisers. The FPD defrayed the cost of office accommodation and secretarial assistance. The post of EO became very onerous (the Salop EO suffered a breakdown in health, allegedly through overwork), and the FPD later recognised this by recommending the appointment of deputy EOs.[4]

The first task of the new policy, in most cases slightly antedating the establishment of the ECs, was to carry out a rapid survey of the land which could be made to yield more crops in 1917, either through improving existing arable land or breaking up grassland. The FPD suggested the form that the surveys might take. The model chosen was a survey recently carried out by the Essex WAC, which had graded farms into three types: well farmed, indifferently farmed but capable of improvement, and derelict. The ECs were notified of the Essex procedure, and were supplied with large-scale maps by the Ordnance Survey.[5]

The WACs or ECs delegated the survey work to the District Committees, when these had already been formed. The procedure may be illustrated by the case of Westbourne DC (West Sussex). The WAC asked it on 21 December 1916 to obtain a report on land not properly cultivated, from three of the 'most prominent' local farmers. The three men visited well-known local farmers on 28 December, and obtained their assistance in delivering forms of enquiry. 'Very many' of the forms had been returned by 30 December, and the three farmers spent the next few days poring over them, visiting farms about which they were doubtful, and classifying farms as 'satisfactory', 'unsatisfactory', or 'derelict'. Their final report was given to the DC on 17 January. West Sussex was quick off the mark, and the final result was fairly comprehensive; forms were returned covering 259,097 acres, which accounted for most of the 280,000 acres under cultivation in the county. A negligible quantity of land was considered to be derelict, but about one-quarter of both arable and grassland was considered to be unsatisfactory.[6]

This preliminary survey was directed to the 1917 harvest. Committees were also requested to make a second, more detailed survey for the 1918 harvest. They were told that in the summer they would be allocated a quota of ploughing for the two harvest years combined.[7] The second survey was not as hasty as the first. However, ECs were very concerned with cost, and the time of committee members, so that the coverage of the survey differed between counties. In Cheshire, only holdings of eight acres or above were considered. In Hereford, survey forms were only distributed to farms of 20 acres or above. In Lancashire, 'the utmost possible latitude' was allowed to District Committees in carrying out the survey. In Salop, it is possible that the survey did not cover holdings of less than 50 acres. In Somerset, the survey definitely did not deal with holdings of less than 50 acres; it was proposed to deal with them by direct approach from the DCs.[8]

These early surveys revealed many cases of poor farming. In Cheshire in February 1917, the case of a farm of 110 acres was noted.[9]

good workable farm, sub-soil light, friable . . . let at 40/– per acre. Exceedingly badly cultivated, the produce is in a deplorable condition, the stacks not being yet thatched, and portion of root crops still in the ground . . . of the 26.5 acres arable, none yet ploughed . . . 65 acres pasture carries only 20–25 head of cattle . . . the farm is in its present condition on account of Mr A.'s generally dilatory methods, and not from lack of labour or implements etc.

A month earlier, the West Sussex EC had found an estate of 573 acres in a deplorable condition:

> The Mansion House is in need of repair, and is apparently quite useless to the owner . . . The Park is neglected . . . The hay stacks are not thatched and are partly rotten. In some of the fields the hay has not even been carried in and tons of good hay, which could have been used for the Army or cattle, have been absolutely wasted . . .

The sub-committee added that it was impossible to overstate the amount of neglect and waste occurring on the land and the buildings, representing the accumulated neglect of 25–30 years.[10]

The second survey, and the ploughing orders to which it gave rise, was well under way by the time that the ECs were informed of their ploughing quotas on 14 June 1917. In Lindsey, the survey resulted in the scheduling for ploughing of 30,000 acres of grass; this was reduced to 25,788 acres after farmers had appealed to the EC. This did not satisfy the FPD, which fixed a quota for the county of 90,000 acres, although this was later reduced to 65,000 acres. The shortfall in grass to be broken necessitated a third survey being carried out towards the end of the year, which produced only a further 8,126 acres of scheduled grassland. In Salop, the initial quota was 80,000 acres. This was later reduced to 50,000 acres, the initial quota having only produced 27,116 acres for ploughing. Again, the FPD urged compliance with the revised quota. The EC did not mount a further survey, but raised the quotas for the District Committees to a new level of 53,995 acres.[11]

Orders to plough or to improve cultivation followed speedily on the surveys. On the whole, committees were very conscious of the need to persuade farmers to agree to the proposed course of action, rather than simply to inspect the farm and issue an order. The Norfolk EC procedure must have been very common:

> Mr. George Sands attended the Committee when the valuer's report was read and after a discussion Mr. Sands agreed to stock the 38½ acres at once and to plough up the land before the end of July and he undertook that if he could not carry

out the ploughing he would inform the Committee so that other arrangements could be made.[12]

Even in cases where farmers offered to plough land voluntarily, the FPD advised committees to issue a formal ploughing order, in case a claim might later be made under the DORA regulations. This was partly because the Department had accepted the principle that losses which might be made under the plough policy could be offset by compensation, and partly to protect tenants who had to break covenants forbidding the ploughing up of grassland.[13]

Even with the legal powers at the disposal of the ECs, and with the limited rights of appeal available, the ploughing orders issued in 1917–18 sometimes provoked considerable opposition. The ECs had to set up 'appeal courts' in the districts to hear objections. A large number was raised; in Lindsey, 1,600 had been dealt with up to the end of March 1918. The EC and its sub-committees did not invariably confirm the orders; the area scheduled for ploughing in Lindsey was reduced on appeal from 30,000 to less than 26,000 acres. The Lancashire committee was less sympathetic; in spite of the 'considerable number of appeals', it found itself: '. . . with few exceptions, in full agreement with the action of the District Committees'. In Cheshire only 15 appeals came up to the EC. a small proportion of the 9,000 ploughing orders issued. Herefordshire did not hold many appeal meetings; only three are recorded, and: 'Except in special cases very few appeals were allowed.'[14]

The appeals gave rise to more work for the members of the ECs over a considerable period. In Worcestershire, there were at least 45 meetings, extending from September 1917 to May 1918. A specimen of the kind of objections raised concerned the tenant of a 60-acre farm, ordered to plough 10 acres:

> The tenant stated that he only went into the farm in 1916 and it is in a very poor state indeed, and he does not think it possible for him to work more land. He usually keeps two horses, but lost one last week as it met with an accident. If the Committee send horses to plough the land the tenant will do his best, but the fields are so large they will require a lot of fencing. The only field which would not require fencing has a large pit in the centre and is too wet.

The EC decided that: 'it is useless pressing this man.'[15]

Given the way in which the surveys had been carried out, it is likely that the larger farms came to the attention of the ECs before the smaller. In Salop, where by the autumn the FPD was pressing the county to meet its ploughing quota, the EC reported that the farmers of under 50 acres had previously not been pressed to plough, but it was felt that now was the time for them to take a share, 'when holding land that can conveniently be ploughed'. Somerset had a similar policy.[16]

However, the ECs did not overlook the importance of small farms or plots of land, either in the matter of ploughing orders or in the improvement of cultivation. Instances of concern with small plots, whether called 'farms' or not, abound, and some were very small indeed. The smallest were allotment and garden lands; Wiltshire served cultivation orders on allotments as small as 5 perches, and on gardens as small as 20 perches (160 perches = 1 acre). Norfolk was asking farmers to plough areas as small as 1.5 acres as early as the end of January 1917, and took notice of a patch of derelict land of 2.5 acres, reported by George Edwards. Somerset issued a cultivation order for a market garden of 30 perches, and took over a 1.5-acre patch of arable which was in a foul condition. By the end of March 1918, Cheshire had taken possession of 41 holdings, ranging from a large farm of 146 acres down to a plot of 1.5 acres; the smallest plot described as a farm was 5.4 acres.[17]

Not only did the ECs grind small, but they were no respecters of persons. Between them the ECs of Cheshire, Norfolk, Wiltshire, and Worcestershire served ploughing or cultivating orders on Lords Orford, Drayton, Sandys, and the Rt. Hon. W. H. Long MP (Colonial Secretary); entered on lands belonging to Sir Frederick Banbury, Lady Arundell, and a Colonel Turnor; and recommended the determination of a tenancy on land belonging to a member of the WAC.[18]

A glimpse of the plough policy in action may be had by looking at a not untypical page from the list of cultivation orders served by the Somerset EC in January–March 1918. The orders are not only for farms, but also for market gardens, and even kitchen gardens and house gardens. The areas are small, the smallest being gardens of 1 rood (=1/4 acre), the largest being a pasture field of slightly over eight acres. The small size of the areas presumably reflects the fact that larger farms and holdings had been dealt with earlier. The orders are usually highly specific, and give a date by which the

176

SOMERSET WAR AGRICULTURAL EXECUTIVE COMMITTEE

Special Cultivation Orders under Defence of the Realm Regulation 2 M (I) (e)

Name and Address of Occupier to be served with Order	Name of Farm or other description for identification of land	Parish	No. of field on 25 in. Ord. Map	Area of each field A.	R.	P.	Whether pasture, arable, or ley	Requirements of Order	Date before which work to be completed	Name and Address of Owner of land	Remarks
1	2	3	4	5			6	7	8	9	10
									1918		
AXBRIDGE Frank Tucker	Hall Farm	Wedmore		6	–	20	pasture	plough	15 Jan	Crutwell Daniels & Collings Solicitors, Frome Agent for Mrs Woollen.	
				8	3	29	pasture	crop to corn plough crop to corn	28 Feb. 15 Jan 28 Feb.		
Mrs John Say, Churchill.	Market Garden	Cheddar	part 109	1	–		market garden	cultivate, clean & crop with potatoes.	15 Apr.	Mrs John Say, Churchill.	
Dr. Wm. Wall, Pembroke.	'The Lilacs'	Wedmore	1900	–	1		2 villa gardens	cultivate, clean & crop with potatoes	15 Apr.	Occupier.	
J. Bennett Latchen, Wedmore.	arable field situate near occupant's house	Wedmore	part 3002	1 (approx)	–		arable	To lift potatoes in 7 days cultivate & clean	28 Feb.		
Henry House, Wood Farm, Theale. Wedmore.	Kitchen garden and pasture field on Wood Farm	Theale	part 2661	3	–		kitchen garden – pasture –	cultivate & clean cut & burn the brambles	28 Feb. 31 Mar.		
BATH G. Broad, Eagle House Farm, Batheaston.	Eagle Hse Farm	Batheaston	155	4	3		pasture	plough by 15th Jan. and crop for 1918 harvest		G. Broad, Eagle House Farm, Batheaston.	

Figure 12.1: Cultivation orders issued by Somerset County Agricultural Executive Committee, January–March 1918

work has to be done. Individual fields are identified by use of Ordnance Survey maps, and entries are typed on to specially printed forms. Overall, the impression is one of efficiency and lack of fuss.[19]

There were still complaints remaining after the appeals; farmers in Worcestershire complained in July 1917 that, having agreed to plough up land, they were not being supplied with the necessary equipment – a common complaint in the early days of the food production policy. A Lindsey farmer complained that his 30-acre field scheduled for ploughing was unsuitable, had not in fact been seen by the inspection committee, and that the Machinery Officer refused to work it with a tractor. The EC referred the problem back to the district committee. Sometimes farmers were not dealt with so easily. The Hereford EC felt obliged to threaten a lady with the call-up of her son unless she improved the cultivation of her land; a tactic that was probably *ultra vires*. The threats were not all one way; a Hereford farmer ordered to improve his methods told the EC that he would not take a soldier to work for him while his son was still serving in the forces.[20]

In making the orders, and in seeing that they were carried out, the committees relied above all on persuasion. Farmers were usually given a chance to improve their cultivations, and further inspections were made before action was taken. In December 1917 a Hereford farmer was 'very severely cautioned', told to improve his cultivation, and informed that another inspection would be made in February.[21] Even when orders had been made, but not obeyed, caution was necessary. In February 1918, the Worcestershire EC noted that no progress had been made on a farm run by an aged widow. A further inspection was decided upon; the position would be explained to her before recommending further action. In more difficult cases, a farmer might be urged to give up his holding in favour of his son, or to leave the farm for a year and let his friends manage it.[22]

Only if persuasion failed was prosecution contemplated. In mid-March 1918, there were no less than 176 cases of non-compliance outstanding in Worcestershire. The occupiers were told to start the work within five days, and complete it within a fortnight, or prosecution would follow. This threat seems to have worked; two weeks later, only eight prosecutions were being contemplated, and only one by early April, since work was now in progress on the other farms. The committees only prosecuted after a long period had elapsed; Bedford decided in January 1918 to press a prosecution on a ploughing order made as long ago as June 1917, since it was felt that a prosecution was required 'to move matters on in that district'. The national figures of prosecutions reflect this unwilling-ness; only 254 prosecutions were mounted, convictions being secured in 236 cases.[23]

Apart from prosecutions, the ECs had two other weapons: to authorise landowners to determine a tenancy and place it under other management, or to take over the land and farm it themselves, either directly or with the aid of another farmer. Neither of these devices was particularly favoured, although the totals sound impressive; 317 tenancies were determined (in respect of 20,197 acres), and the ECs took possession of 27,287 acres of badly farmed land.[24] But these were comparatively small amounts. Taken together, they covered only about 0.15 per cent of the total area of crops and grass (excluding rough grazings) in Britain, and averaged only 374 acres and 505 acres per county in England and Wales. The reluctance of ECs is reflected in the report of the Cheshire EC:

> In most other cases the warnings of the Committee to induce better cultivation proved effectual without the necessity for drastic action, and it had been found that as a general rule inferior farmers have been willing to take the tactfully offered advice of one or more good local farmers.[25]

Cheshire had determined only 11 tenancies by June 1918. In two more cases, tenants had been allowed to remain on probation. In Lancashire, by July 1918, only 31 tenancies had been determined, and the agents had arranged new tenants in most of these cases; in four cases, the EC had taken over the running of the farms. In addition, there were a number of farms where tenants had been allowed to remain on probation.[26]

Where there seemed no alternative to entering on land, the preferred course was to arrange for another person to cultivate it. By June 1918, Cheshire had taken over 1,000 acres, but only culti-vated 224 acres of it directly. By the end of 1918, Salop only worked directly 118 acres of Ludlow racecourse, and a farm of 115 acres, which the committee used as a depot for horses. In Bedford, only 161 acres had been entered on by June 1917. Some counties were keener than others to take over land. Somerset took over its first farm in April 1917 (93 acres); it is not known whether the committee proposed to work it directly or find a farmer to run it. The next entry, in the same month, was in respect of only 1.5 acres, which it was proposed to let to a market gardener. The committee eventually took over a much larger acreage than the national average; in May 1919, it still held 1,274 acres. Most of this (849 acres) was accounted for by three large farms. In addition, some 115 acres had been taken over in order to create allotments.[27]

Taking over a farm, especially a large one, was a potentially hazardous undertaking for the ECs. Much depended on the condition of the land and buildings, and whether it required further investment before being made productive. A further consideration was whether the condition of the farm would deter a future lessee, or would make it necessary for the EC to farm it directly for some time. Thus decisions were *ad hoc*. In West Sussex, Brightams Farm (108 acres), having land in a 'deplorable' condition, but 'useful' grassland and 'excellent' buildings was thought worth entry, and the Executive Officer recommended that it should be taken over by the EC, paying the owner £150 a year rent for it. But similar action was not recommended by the district committee in the case of the large and very neglected Coolhurst Estate; at 573 acres, mainly grass, without farm buildings, it would require much expenditure on manures. However, the EC decided to proceed with entry. The kind of renovation required may be detailed in the case of Foxley Farm (719 acres), entered by the Wilts. EC in April 1918. The two members of the EC detailed to watch over its running recommended that 650 acres of it should be let to a named tenant at £550 a year. This rent, already low by current standards, was to be subject to a rebate of £100, spread over four years, in respect of the expenses of repairing 'live' fences (i.e., hedges), cleansing water courses, and erecting new post and wire fences. The farm was still in the hands of the EC in June 1919, when the two members reported that it was in much better condition.[28]

The reluctance of the ECs to enter on land, and the problems which could arise if they did so, is illustrated by the case of Powers Farm (Worcs.). Comprising 110 acres, its owner, Lord Sandys, was served a cultivation order in August 1917. Following failure to comply, the EC decided to prosecute and request FPD permission to enter on the land. This was granted, and the EC took over 106 acres of the farm (ECs could not enter the dwelling house of a farm) on 14 March 1918. This required supplies, such as a ton of ammonium sulphate. Further expense was in prospect when Lord Sandys claimed the large sum of £1,003 9s. 4d. for tenant right and loss of profit. This was settled in June 1918 at £313 16s. od. for the live and dead stock of the farm. The last reference to it was in September 1918, when the EC were trying to get £500 from the FPD to stock it.[29] Not only did this saga drag on for a long time, presumably cause considerable expense, and take the time of the EC members concerned, but the secretarial load was very heavy; over 2,000 letters and papers were generated by this case alone. Where ECs took over above-average amounts of land, it seems likely that this was due to the presence of a few large, badly managed farms. Even in the small-farm county of Cheshire, almost half of the acreage entered on and subsequently run on behalf of the EC was accounted for by five farms.[30] Taking over farms could prove a financial and administrative burden, which the ECs were keen to avoid. Lord Ernle was right to insist that farming could not be carried out from Whitehall; the ECs tried hard to avoid farming from County Hall.

Overseeing the progress of the ploughing programme was the main work of the ECs. Their next concern was to assist farmers to fulfil the ploughing quotas, by supplying labour and the services of tractors, horses, machinery, fertilisers, and other supplies. Much of the work was carried out under the supervision of sub-committees of the main committees. Their establishment had been suggested by the FPD in May 1917, although some ECs had done so beforehand.[31] By 1918 most ECs had sub-committees for the most important branches of their work: Labour, Machinery, Supplies, and Finance. Most also seem to have had a Cultivation, and some a Survey sub-committee, although sometimes these were combined; the Salop Survey Sub-committee seems to have been transformed into a Cultivation Sub-committee during 1918.[32] However, some ECs preferred to keep these functions in the hands of the main committee.[33] In 1918, two other sub-committees were usually also added: Horticulture and Drainage.

In addition to the sub-committees, the ECs had the network of District Committees first developed under the WACs. These seem to have contained the same personnel as before. The only reorganisation was in January 1918, when the FPD suggested the appointment of District Executive Officers, to whom many of the EC powers were delegated. At the same time, the DCs were urged to divide

181

their districts into small groups of townships, to more effectively pursue the policy at the local level. In retrospect, it seems clear that this was a response by the FPD to the disappointing progress of the plough policy. The suggestions were not always carried out completely. In Lancashire, only 13 of the 16 DCs thought it necessary to appoint an Executive Officer. The ECs themselves were not further reorganised, although they grew in size. The Salop EC numbered 15 by the end of 1918. The Lancashire EC, which had decided (with FPD approval) that each of the districts must be represented on the main EC, numbered 19 by the end of 1917.[34]

In the first few months of the ECs' existence, their direct cultivating activities were limited by the slow growth of FPD supplies of tractors, machinery, and horse ploughs. Only in the case of soldier labour could it be said that they had a substantial supply of a necessary factor of production. Other than organising soldiers (and, where available, the first of the prisoners of war and WLA), the ECs were occupied with issuing ploughing and cultivating orders, continuing the survey work inaugurated in the preliminary survey, distributing what supplies they could acquire, and requisitioning their first tractors.

Work on cultivation for the 1917 crop was well ahead by early summer. The Lancs. EC reported in May that, of the 19,769 acres marked for improvement or ploughing for 1917, 12,063 had been dealt with. By this time, the committee was in the throes of the re-survey ordered for the 1918 programme, and hoped to complete it by 16 June. Substantial assistance had already been afforded by soldiers; 1,301 ploughmen had been supplied from military depots in Lancashire, and three Agricultural Companies had been established in the county. Tractor work had begun, chiefly with the hire of privately owned machines, but the lateness of the season when work began meant that only 900 acres had so far been ploughed, and since farmers had already completed most of their ploughing, the tractors had to work small areas in scattered places. A start had already been made in using tractors for cultivating, with about 140 acres dealt with; the FPD had at first objected to this, but, when told that the machines would otherwise be idle, had aquiesced. The EC had also dealt with the cases of agriculturalists exempted from military service, persuaded a landowner to withdraw a proposed rent increase, and considered what to do in two cases where notices to quit had been served. These actions may be contrasted with that of Cheshire EC, which decided that it had no power to deal with complaints about rent increases. Other matters dealt with were the destruction of rooks, the increase in trespass cases due to the absence of gamekeepers on military service, the provision of credit to farmers (18 applications were made, six of which were granted), problems of flooded land, the best use of golf courses for food production, assistance to local councils in acquiring land for allotments, and clarification of Army regulations on selling and disposing of hay. In all, the pace of the programme was increasing, and the EC was having to make decisions in many spheres which were probably not originally contemplated.[35]

The ploughing programme had proceeded by the early autumn, but the limiting factor was still the supply of tractors. Lindsey had noted in August that there was an urgent need for more tractors, since the committee still had fewer FPD tractors (nine) than tractors borrowed from private owners (twelve). Ploughing was still a slow business, the tractors seldom managing more than 13 acres each per week. The supply of tractors improved by early November, when there were 41 in the county, but only 31 were at work, and the weekly acreage per machine had fallen to a little over 10, due to bad weather.[36] The same story of inadequate numbers and slow progress came from Norfolk. Although better provided for than Lindsey, having 66 tractors by the end of September, the EC thought that 100 more were required immediately; in the week ending 29 September, only 635.25 acres were ploughed, and 87 cultivated; an average of only 10.9 acres per machine. There were occasional bursts of achievement, since in the week afterwards, the (now 69) machines at work ploughed and cultivated an average of 17 acres each, but this was exceptional.[37] Nor did the work always give satisfaction; Lindsey reduced the bill for one farmer who complained of the quality of the work, since: 'the early tractor ploughing was more or less an experiment'. A further problem came from drivers refusing to work overtime; since they were not paid for it, this hardly seems surprising.[38] On the other hand, if the work proceeded slowly, it proceeded fairly continuously; by the end of October, the Somerset tractors, now 43 in number (although only 16 as recently as August) had ploughed 3,473 acres and cultivated a further 820.[39]

By the end of 1917 there were signs of strain; the Lancs. EC found the reviewing of over 6,000 cases for exemption from military service onerous, as also the survey of land for the 1918 crop, which necessitated the scheduling for ploughing of about 50,000 acres of grass, and the service of notices on owners and occupiers – 'an immense amount of work', according to the Chairman.[40] Hertfordshire thought it worth while to point out the heavy burdens involved: by the end of 1917 it had sent out 25,000 letters, issued 750 cultivation notices (in quadruplicate), dealt with applications for 400 shotgun ammunition licences and 284 petrol licences, and authorised the sale of 752 agricultural horses.[41]

The strain was not mitigated by the realisation that the tractor programme was proceeding more slowly than the FPD wished. This was partly still due to slow tractor deliveries. Salop had asked for 90 in May 1917, but had only received 34 by the end of the year. In Lancashire there were only 25, and 16 in Hertfordshire.[42] It was also due to the season, mechanical breakdown, and a lack of spare parts; in Lindsey at the end of January 1918, for these reasons only 29 of the 43 EC tractors were working. In Norfolk, the average tractor acreage ploughed or cultivated was down to eight in the third week in December.[43] Problems of another sort had occurred in Somerset, where the Machinery Officer had forged a testimonial to obtain his appointment, and had been dismissed. The FPD were informed of the matter, but decided not to prosecute. When last heard of, the ex-Machinery Officer was trying to get the EC to pay for repairs to his typewriter; the Committee declined to do so.[44] A considerable irritation had been the inadequate petrol allowance permitted for the Machinery Officers, who used large amounts in travelling to arrange ploughing contracts. In Norfolk in August, his work was reported to be 'almost stopped' for this reason, and it was still causing concern in Somerset in December.[45]

In other spheres, though, the ECs now had more resources, especially in the form of labour and horse ploughing teams. In Herts. there were by the end of the year over 150 prisoners and 78 WLA at work, and the EC had 100 horses working in plough teams. There was also frustration here: the Lancs. EC had had problems in obtaining implements and horses, partly because of the delay of the FPD in approving the proposed scheme, and there had been sickness amongst the horses, but the scheme was now successfully launched.[46]

A new burden was the preparation of threshing facilities for the 1918 crop. In November, ECs had been asked by the FPD to take stock of the threshing machines in the county, and to arrange with the owners a coordinated scheme for the 1918 harvest. In addition, ECs ordered further machines from the FPD, and assessed the need for threshing labour.[47]

By 1918, the work of the ECs had swelled to the point where some reorganisation was necessary; the appointment of District Executive Officers was the result. The plough programme was about to move into higher gear, as most ECs had received more tractors during the winter; Somerset, which had only 29 in mid-September, had 68 by the new year. The prospect of improved weather was also going to make a great difference (Table 12.1).

Table 12.1: Worcestershire EC tractor performance, January–February and March–April 1918

| | Week ending: | |
	11 Jan.–1 Feb. 1918	15 March–5 April 1918
No. in county	24	24
Av. no. at work	20	20
Av. acreage ploughed	5.7	8.8
Hours each working tractor available per week	72	78
Per cent of available time:		
Working	33	51
Idle, due to:		
Weather	43	19
Repairs	18	19
Travelling	3	5
Other cause	2	5
Total[a]	99	99

Note: [a] Rounding adjustment

Source: Worcs. EC, Machinery sub-committee

To have tractors working for about half the time they were available was a fairly good performance by the standards of the ECs. Even in mid-September 1918, the Worcs. machines were only working for 54 per cent of the time possible.[48]. From the above table it seems that the weather was the greatest variable influence, given that other causes of idle tractors were fairly constant. In particular, the problem of a high level of repairs was never solved. Even at the Armistice, repairs occupied 16 per cent of the time of all the 2,993 government tractors working in England and Wales. Idleness due to poor weather accounted for 37 per cent, and the tractors only worked for 37 per cent of the time possible.[49] Given the fallibility of early tractors and the shortage of spare parts, this was probably insoluble.

The difficulties of ploughing were increased by the type of tractors used. Cheshire, which used mainly Moguls, Titans, and Overtimes, noted that these heavy machines (especially, presumably, the Moguls and Titans) were liable to be 'frequently held up on broken ground due to unfavourable weather conditions' (i.e., bogged down), and that 'Thirty minutes' heavy rain may mean 24 hours delay.' That the problems had not been greater was due to the fact that most of the ploughing so far had been of grassland, but the EC anticipated difficulties with these machines in the coming season, when most of the work would be on ploughland. These difficulties were not apparent with the few Fordsons operated by the Committee, which were much lighter than the other tractors. However, few ECs had any Fordsons until late in the spring. Somerset had none until 11 April. Worcestershire received its first a day later. Lindsey had none before the end of April.[50]

There were other irritations in the plough programme. On 1 January 1918, ECs were made responsible for the collection of all accounts for tractor work, the FPD having previously performed this task. This threw a further administrative burden on the committees. They also had to cope with certain excesses of bureaucracy; in March 1918 the FPD decreed that separate contracts should be issued for each field ploughed; protests were made, and the idea was soon dropped.[51]

The government tractor scheme was at last into its stride. Between 1 October 1917 and the end of May 1918, the FPD estimated that 360,000 acres had been ploughed under the scheme. Adding an estimated 130,000 acres to cover the period between the start of the scheme and 1 October, government tractors had ploughed almost half a million acres, and also cultivated most of them.[52] To this should be added an unknown amount of ploughing by EC horses. This came in three ways: by the EC hiring horses (and perhaps tackle) to farmers; by the use of soldier ploughmen and their horse teams; and by prisoner ploughing teams. All these seem to be included in the reported total number of horses employed by the ECs, as cited in the War Cabinet's 1918 report; the number rose from 4,600 at the beginning of 1918 to 10,000 at the end. A very rough calculation, taking the average of these figures, and multiplying by the 50 acres which could be dealt with by a pair of horses before the war gives an estimated acreage ploughed (and cultivated) in 1918 of 182,500 acres. This is a very rough estimate, but it seems clear that EC horse ploughing was much less important than the tractor programme; in Lancashire, the 1918 tractor ploughing was 5,925 acres; horse ploughing was 3,270 acres. On the other hand, it must have proved very useful to the smaller farmer, for whom it was intended, and who often had neither the knowledge nor the equipment necessary to break up grassland. If, as seems likely, Machinery Officers favoured the use of tractors on larger fields rather than smaller, in spite of the disapproval of the FPD, then the horse teams must have been particularly useful to the small farmer; the chairman of the Cheshire machinery sub-committee had instructed ploughing officers not to tractor-plough irregular fields or those of less than eight acres.[53]

As well as coping with the organisation of ploughing schemes, the ECs had by the spring of 1918 large and increasing amounts of labour. The number of soldiers on the land was now nearing its maximum; most of the extra men promised in June 1917 had by now arrived, so that by the end of May 1918 there were 57,952 on farms, and a further 3,721 engaged in training, indisposed, or awaiting employment. Much of the administration of this scheme, and that of prisoner labour, was carried out by the staff at the military camps which sent the soldiers out to farms. But the ECs were directly responsible for the employment of the WLA; our estimate is that in March there were 7,665 at work, or less than half the final contingent. In addition, there were the village women, over whose labour the WWACs held a watching brief, and concerned themselves with training. All these responsibilities meant further work for the committees. Thus by late September 1918 the Gloucs. WWAC was organising the labour of 450 WLA women, the Machinery Officer was responsible for 64 tractors, and the Horse Officer for 482 horses (332 FPD, 66 on loan from the Army, and the rest at five of the prisoner of war camps). In Herts., about 90 WLA, 21 tractors, and 55 horses in February 1918 had increased to 308, 31, and 117 by the end of July.[54]

The summer and early autumn of 1918 was the peak of the ploughing programme. Many earlier difficulties had now been solved. There seems no doubt that the workforce had become much more skilled, both in general work and in ploughing, about which few complaints were now made. The supply of substitute labour reached its maximum, as did that of tractors and other machinery, and of fertiliser and other supplies. Work for the 1919 programme was now under way. Aided by good weather, and the large number of tractors at their disposal, the ECs ploughed on. In Worcestershire, which had managed with only 24 tractors until April, there were by October 59 (although only 42 were at work), and the record weekly ploughing acreage of 435 was reached in the second week in September, never having previously exceeded 210.[55] In Somerset, the tractors did as much ploughing in the second half of the year as in the first (Table 12.2)

Table 12.2: Somerset EC tractor work, 1918

| | | Cumulative acreage ploughed and cultivated from March 1917 | | |
		Ploughed	Cultivated	Tractors at work
To:	2 Jan. 1918	6,971	856	35
	4 June 1918	16,020	11,818	64
	17 Dec. 1918	26,709	15,344	40

Source: Somerset machinery sub-committee

In the summer, the attention of the ECs turned to harvesting. Tractors and horses and their equipment were made available for reaping and binding; in Somerset, 2,057 acres had been worked by binder by the end of August, and in Salop 1,530 acres. In threshing operations, the plans made earlier in the year bore fruit: in Salop, the scheme called for the FPD to supply 19 threshing boxes and 15 Mogul 25-HP tractors. All the boxes, but only seven of the tractors, had been delivered by the end of the year.[56] In Bedford, the labour problem was partly solved by getting a few prisoners to do threshing. In Kent, 276 WLA were engaged in the work. When the threshing season arrived, shortages of coal were probably of more concern than those of labour. To organise the work more efficiently, the ECs allotted areas of work to the contractors in the county, and drew up a scale of charges.[57]

In spite of the fact that the ECs were still ploughing large areas in the autumn of 1918 and the spring of 1919, these were largely on already broken land, and the tillage area in Britain in 1919 was less than in 1918 by some 346,000 acres. Ploughing orders were still issued, but the virtual collapse of the powers of the ECs to enforce them, given the passage of the CP(A) Act in August, led to a large number of appeals over ploughing orders, and a much higher proportion of these were allowed than in 1917–18. In Gloucs., 18 meetings were held, to hear 1,537 appeals in respect of orders covering 20,181 acres. Since orders had originally been made in respect of 34,000 acres, the appeals covered well over half of the acreage scheduled by the EC. Table 12.3 shows the final result of the 1919 ploughing order process in the county.

Table 12.3: Gloucestershire: results of ploughing orders issued for 1919 harvest

	Acres
Total cancelled	8,533
To be inspected	3,932
Postponed by one year	1,213
Total	13,678
Confirmed on appeal	5,342
Already ploughed	4,137
Agreed to plough	2,611
No appeal and confirmed	8,232
Total	20,322

Source: Gloucs. EC, CWAM 4/1, cultivation committee
Summary of results of ploughing orders for 1919 harvest

Clearly, it was worth appealing against a ploughing order, since there was a considerably greater chance of it being cancelled or postponed than upheld. The EC was pessimistic about the chances of inspections turning in its favour, noting that it did not expect more than a third of the orders referred to the Farm Inspector to stand.

Apart from directly influencing cultivation, the ECs had responsibility for a wide range of matters which bore, directly or indirectly, on the extension of tillage. These were the improvement of drainage, control of pests, the sale of farm horses, promotion of small-scale food production, the provision of credit to farmers, and the distribution of miscellaneous supplies.

The chief of these, and the most important long-term legacy of the ECs, was the improvement of drainage. The extent to which poor drainage impeded farm work was a matter of guesswork, but the government thought that it was a considerable problem, affecting about a million acres in England and Wales.[58] Since time was too short for major engineering works, attention was paid to the more limited tasks of clearing watercourses which had become impeded, and repairing river and watercourse banks which had been neglected. Under the Cultivation of Lands Order, the ECs could direct owners and occupiers of watercourses to prevent the flooding of land. Where cooperation was not forthcoming, the EC could carry out the work if the owner failed to act within seven days of receiving a drainage order; the cost would be later recouped from the owner.[59]

Drainage seems to have been a problem confined largely to coastal counties; of the EC records surviving, those showing evidence of concern about drainage are Cheshire, Lancashire, Lindsey, Norfolk, Somerset, and West Sussex. These either had large areas of low-lying land, or large catchment areas drained by major rivers (e.g., the Norfolk Ouse). An exception is the West Riding of Yorkshire, where 82,700 acres were recorded as drained by the ECs during the war.[60] The county most troubled by the question of flooding was Lancashire; about 30 areas liable to flooding were brought to the attention of the EC, and they comprised 'many thousands of acres'. The EC thought it worthwhile to make drainage a special department of its work, and eventually got Treasury permission to appoint the County Bridgemaster as advising engineer. The general policy was to press riparian owners to improve drainage, but sometimes more drastic action was necessary; the Croston Drainage Commissioners were persuaded to hand over their functions to the EC. In the case of the areas known as Hest Bank and Black Dyke, efforts at voluntary action proved fruitless, and the EC persuaded the Board of Agriculture to set up an enquiry, with a view to creating a Drainage Board. At Aldingham, it was found that no authority was responsible for draining some 250–300 acres, and the Cultivation of Lands Order was invoked, so that the EC could undertake the work itself.[61]

A notable feature of EC drainage work was the extent to which it made use of prisoner of war labour, which became available in large amounts in 1918. There was also the consideration that drainage work was unlikely to bring prisoners into contact with members of the public, and it avoided having to press prisoners on reluctant farmers. The Lindsey EC considered in October 1917 that farmers' hostility would vitiate the use of prisoners on farms, and thus they would be better employed on drainage schemes.[62] In Norfolk, five of the seven drainage schemes initiated by the EC between the summer of 1917 and November 1918 were manned by prisoners, a total of 360 being employed.[63] Similar reliance on prisoners is seen in Cheshire, where a total of 635 helped in the work, although a contribution was also made by soldier labour. The biggest scheme was the cleaning of 19 miles of the rivers Birkett, Fender, and Arrow, which took the labour of 250 prisoners, and affected some 5,000 acres.[64]

Increased awareness of the problem of drainage on a national scale was reflected in the Land Drainage Act 1918, which came into effect on 30 July. ECs had been to the fore in pressing for this amendment to the inadequate 1861 Act. The result was to make it easier to establish a Drainage Board for an area liable to flooding, thus cutting through the problems posed by the previous conflicts of interest. This change came too late for the ECs, but even without its aid, considerable progress had been made. As early as September 1917, schemes were in hand for improving the drainage of 80,000 acres.[65] By the end of May 1918, the figure had risen to 120,000, and by the end of the year it was 150,000.[66] These may be conservative estimates; a later report referred to a total of 405,500 acres in England and Wales which had benefited from EC drainage work during the war, with most of the work (280,400 acres) being performed in the counties of Norfolk, Cumberland, East Suffolk, Essex, Yorks. (West Riding), and Lindsey.[67]

Concern about the destruction of crops by vermin was present throughout the war, and rose with the emphasis on food production. In 1917, the Board of Agriculture introduced both a Rabbits Order and a Rookeries Order, authorising ECs to take action to control these animals where necessary. Bedford was employing its own rabbit-catcher in July 1917.[68] The Lancs. EC communicated with a large number of rookery owners, and in 17 cases where insufficient control had been exerted, entered upon land in order to destroy the birds. It also took the initiative in trying to persuade landowners, shooting tenants and land agents to organise woodpigeon shoots. DCs were asked to encourage similar action in their localities.[69] In 1918, the Ministry of Food introduced a Rats Order, which allowed local authorities to intervene where landowners failed to cooperate. In 1918 also, the Board of Agriculture urged the ECs to take action against sparrows. Many ECs responded by encouraging the formation of Rat and Sparrow Clubs; Lancashire offered bounties at the rate of 1s per dozen rat tails, 3d per dozen heads of fully fledged house sparrows, and 1d per dozen sparrow eggs. The Herts. EC recorded the destruction in 1917–18 of 103,512 rats, 40,586 fully fledged sparrows, 8,670 unfledged sparrows, and 19,216 sparrows' eggs.[70] An indirect form of control was provided by the issuing of licences to purchase shotgun cartridges for vermin control. However, supplies were limited, and permission for the ECs to purchase them in the first place had to come from the Ministry of Food. Thus authorised, Salop distributed 5,000 cartridges in 1918.[71]

In organising the food production programme, the FPD became worried that insufficient numbers of farm horses would be available. In particular, concern was caused by the purchase of horses for the Army. The Director of Remounts was buying some 3,000 a month, mostly from industry and urban transport. These were replenishing their supplies by purchasing farm horses. The Sale of Horses Order (June 1917) was intended to stop this trade; the sale of farm horses was forbidden without a licence from the EC. The licence could be granted only if the animal was surplus to the farm's requirements, and was being sold to another farmer or authorised person.[72]

This regulation caused the ECs much work. Norfolk issued licences for the sale of 8,500 horses between June 1917 and the end of December 1918. Salop issued 6,810 licences until the withdrawal of the Order on 23 November 1918. Lancashire had issued 3,455 licences by July 1918. Cheshire had issued 3,140 by the same date, and the EC noted that the work required almost the whole time of a clerk. The Order spawned a comparatively large number of prosecutions, compared with those attending the issuing of cultivation orders – 17 in Cheshire, and 7 in Norfolk.[73] The early stages of the Order's implementation were marked by confusion, and Lancashire thought that it operated 'somewhat harshly, especially in the cases of farmers with young horses newly broken and ready for farm work'. However, the EC thought that it had gone a long way towards meeting its object, and Lindsey concurred. The most detailed appreciation of the working of the Order came in a report to the Norfolk EC. This concluded that the Order had achieved its objective, but if a shortage could be said to have existed, it was on farms of less than 200 acres. However, since the larger farms made use of tractors, their surplus horses trickled down to the smaller farms, so that 'The tractor has considerably releaved [sic] the horse question in Norfolk'.[74]

The FPD had made arrangements with the banks to advance credit to individual farmers for the purchase of supplies essential to food production. However, the applications had to be agreed by the ECs, which obtained a reputation for being strict in vetting applications. Cheshire received 15 applications for sums totalling £3,798, but only agreed to recommend advances totalling £343. Lindsey received 16 applications, and recommended 10 of them, for a total of £1,027. Over all England and Wales, 478 applications had been made by June 1918, of which 303 were recommended by the ECs, but the total sum involved was only £21,077.[75]

The war saw a considerable expansion of the allotment movement. In 1918, an additional 184,000 allotments were created; the Board of Agriculture estimated that in the war the number had increased from 570,000 to over 1,400,000.[76] The ECs were encouraged to promote the extension of allotments, and the yield of food from them. In 1918, the FPD urged them to form horticultural sub-committees: 'to organise and increase the supply of food grown on Small Holdings and Allotments and Private and Market Gardens'. Cheshire organised a marketing scheme for allotment holders, and promoted the keeping of rabbits, bees, and poultry. Lancashire assisted local councils which were experiencing difficulty in obtaining land for allotments. Most ECs were already involved in the question to some extent, since they took on the distribution of seed potatoes, which were intended primarily for the smallholder. Salop distributed 200 tons 'in lots of less than 5 cwts to cottagers and small cultivators' in 1917. The ECs acted similarly in organising the distribution of preserving sugar and glass bottles for fruit bottling.[77]

A particular problem attendant on the food production campaign was petrol supply. By late 1917, the government was rationing supplies, and the ECs had the function of granting applications for petrol allowances. Cheshire had dealt with 734 applications by 30 June 1918, and Salop dealt with 824 applications in 1918. Lancashire went further in trying to curtail consumption; it advised tractor owners to have carburettors modified so as to run on paraffin, and stipulated that petrol would be available only for starting the engines. It also arranged that users of paraffin for agricultural purposes should have priority over ordinary consumers, and advised the distributing agents of the oil companies accordingly.[78]

The work of the ECs continued into the post-war period. Some of their responsibilities disappeared fairly quickly, such as those regarding the supply of soldiers. Wiltshire had ceased to employ them by the end of February 1919, although prisoners lingered on until the end of May. But there was still plenty of unfinished business. There was the problem of collecting payments due on the horse and tractor ploughing accounts, which were still troubling Wiltshire as late as May 1919. The ECs were still concerned with vermin control; as a result of the Rats Order (1919), Wiltshire distributed a ton of poison, gratis. There was also the problem of offences allegedly committed by the ex-supplies clerk (a soldier), and the continuing management of farms taken over by the committee; the tenancy of Foxley Farm (q.v.) was extended until October 1919. The Ladies' Sub-committee continued in being until the demise of the WLA on 30 November 1919.[79]

The official dismantling of the FPD came on 31 March 1919. This did not spell the end of the ECs. They were dissolved and reconstituted, designed to assist the Board of Agriculture in implementing Part IV of the Corn Production (Amendment) Act of 1918. The new structure of the ECs was eight members nominated by the county councils, and four by the Board of Agriculture. The new ECs also had officers; the post of Chief Executive Officer for Wiltshire, with a salary of £500 a year, attracted 93 applicants. The ECs were concerned with much the same objectives as the old ones, and still issued cleaning or cultivating orders. However, the effectiveness of the committees had been considerably weakened by the 1918 Act. The effective end came with the fall in agricultural prices in 1921, and the repeal of the 1920 Agriculture Act, which would have extended the system of guaranteed prices indefinitely, subject to four years' notice of withdrawal. The subsequent rapid price fall led to a decline in the tillage area, unchecked by the ECs. By 1922 they had become mainly concerned with agricultural education, advisory work, and the policing of certain agricultural regulations.[80]

NOTES

1 Ernle, *Land*, 108.
2 Some WACs had appointed ECs earlier – Lindsey and West Sussex in June 1916 – but they were to deal with urgent matters that the full WAC could not consider, and had no executive powers. Some WACs had already appointed District Committees before the ECs were established; Cheshire appointed 10 DCs at the first WAC meeting in October 1915, as did Lindsey; Report of Cheshire EC to 30 June 1918, 1; Lindsey EC, Report to 31 March 1918, 1.
3 Lancs. EC minutes, 5 Feb. 1917, Report of EC to July 1918, 1; Lindsey EC, Report to 31 March 1918, 2; Wilts. EC minutes, 10 July 1918; Norfolk EC minutes, 3 Feb. 1917; Somerset EC minutes, 8 Feb. 1917.
4 Cheshire EC, Report to 30 June 1918, 3; J. Sheail, 'The role of the War Agricultural and Executive Committees in the food production campaign of 1915–1918 in England and Wales', *Agricultural Administration*, 1974, 147; Salop EC, Report to 12 Jan. 1918. 7.
5 Middleton, *Food Production*, 171–2. In Scotland, surveys were also made of deer forest suitable for sheep grazing; War Cabinet, *1917 Report*, 159.
6 West Sussex EC, Westbourne Rural District minutes and EC Report of Land Survey, 3; *Agricultural Statistics*.
7 Ernle, *Land*, 111.
8 Cheshire EC, Report to 30 March 1918, 5; Hereford, Executive Officer's report 1 Dec. 1917; Lancs. EC, Report to May 1917, 2; Salop EC minutes, 8 May 1917, EC Report to 12 Jan. 1918, 3; Somerset EC, survey sub-committee, 15 Oct. 1917.
9 Cheshire EC minutes, 17 Feb. 1917, report of Executive Officer.
10 West Sussex EC, Report on Land Survey, 6–7.
11 Lindsey EC, Report to 31 March 1918, 4–5; Salop EC, Report to 12 Jan. 1918, 2–3.
12 Norfolk EC minutes, 12 May 1917.
13 Middleton, *Food Production*, 218
14 Lindsey EC, Report to 31 March 1918, 4; Lancs. EC, Report to July 1918, 2; Cheshire EC, Report to 30 June 1918, 6; Hereford EC, Executive Officer's report, 1 Dec. 1917.
15 Worcs. EC minutes, Rock meeting, 4 Sep. 1917.
16 Salop EC, Report to 1 Dec. 1918, 3; Somerset EC minutes, 15 Oct. 1917.
17 Wilts. EC minutes, 27 March, 15 May 1918; Norfolk EC, 29 Jan., 16 March 1917; Somerset EC, 5 April, 11 Dec. 1917; Cheshire EC, Report to 30 March 1918, 7.
18 Cheshire EC, 8 Feb. 1918; Norfolk EC, 26 Jan. 1918; Wilts. EC, 13 March, 3 April, 15 May 1918; Worcs. EC, 25 July 1917, 15 Aug. 1918.
19 Somerset EC, 11 Dec. 1917–20 Feb. 1919.
20 Worcs. EC, 7 July 1917; Lindsey EC, 11 Jan. 1918; Hereford EC, 1 Dec. 1917.

21 Hereford EC, 1 Dec. 1917.
22 Worcs, EC, 28 Feb., 27 May 1918; Norfolk EC, 28 Sep. 1917.
23 Worcs, EC, 13 March–3 April 1918; Bedfordshire EC, 21 Jan. 1918; Ernle, *Land*, 146.
24 Ernle, *Land*, 147.
25 Cheshire EC, Report to 30 June 1918, 8.
26 Ibid.; Lancs. EC, Report to July 1918, 5–6.
27 Cheshire EC, Report to 30 June 1918, 7–8; Salop EC, Report to 12 Jan, 1918, 2; Bedfordshire EC, 28 June 1917; Somerset EC, *Report on work of the old AEC 17.12.18 – 27.5.19*, para. 8.
28 West Sussex EC, 5 and 26 March 1917, 19 Sep. 1918, Report of Land Survey, 6; Wilts. EC, 3 and 10 April 1918, 25 June 1919.
29 Worcs. EC, 25 July 1917–11 Sep. 1918.
30 Cheshire EC, Report to 30 June 1918, 7.
31 Sheail, 'Role of the WACs' (1974) , 147.
32 Salop EC, Report to 12 Jan. 1918, 1.
33 Cheshire EC, Report to 30 June 1918, 5.
34 Lancs. EC, Report to July 1918, 1; Salop EC, Report to 12 Jan. 1918, Appendix A. Lancs. EC, Report to Dec. 1917, 1.
35 Lancs. EC, Report to May 1917, 1–5; Chester EC, 15 June 1917.
36 Lindsey EC, 7 Aug.–6 Oct. 1917.
37 Norfolk EC, 20 Sept.–6 Oct. 1917. 17 acres would have been a very good performance; government tractors in Kent in September 1917 averaged about 12 acres ploughing a week; G. H. Garrad, 'The work of the motor tractor', *JRASE*, 1918, 14.
38 Lindsey EC, 4 and 11 Sep. 1917.
39 Somerset machinery sub-committee, Aug.–Oct. 1917,
40 Lancs. EC, Report to Dec. 1917, 1, 3, 6.
41 Herts. EC, Report to 7 Jan. 1918.
42 Salop EC, Report to 12 Jan. 1918, 5; Lancs. EC, Report to Dec. 1917, 2; Herts, EC, Report to 7 Jan. 1918.
43 Lindsey, EC, 29 Jan. 1918; Norfolk EC, 22 Dec. 1917.
44 Somerset EC, 4 Sep.–27 Nov. 1917.
45 Norfolk EC, 14 Aug. 1917; Somerset EC, 11 Dec. 1917.
46 Herts. EC, Report to 7 Jan. 1918; Lancs. EC, Report to Dec. 1917, 2, 5.
47 Salop EC, Report to 12 Jan. 1918, 6; Cheshire EC, 4 Jan. 1918 and Report to 30 June 1918, 10.
48 Worcs. machinery sub-commiteee, w/e 13 Sep. 1918.
49 Herts. EC, 18 Nov. 1918.
50 Cheshire EC, Report to 30 March 1918, 9; Somerset EC, 11 April 1918; Worcs. machinery sub-committee, 12 April 1918; Lindsey EC, 30 April 1918.
51 Salop EC, Report to 31 Dec. 1918, 2; Somerset EC, 5 and 26 March 1918.
52 PRO, MAF 42/8, 40171/D, *Report of FPD to 1 June 1918*, 13.
53 War Cabinet, *1918 Report*, 238; Lancs. EC, Report to July 1918, 2;

PRO, MAF 42/8, 40171/D, 14; Hereford EC, FPD circular, 7 Oct.
1918; Cheshire EC, 23 Nov. 1917.

54 Ibid., 9; Dewey, thesis, 267; Gloucs. EC, WWAC meeting 21 Sep.
1918, cultivation committee, 11 Sep. and 23 Oct. 1918; Herts. EC,
11–29 July 1918.
55 Worcs. machinery sub-committee, 11 Jan.–7 Oct. 1918.
56 Somerset EC, cultivation sub-committee, 27 Aug. 1918; Salop EC,
Report to 31 Dec. 1918, 2.
57 Bedford, WAV/10, PoWs time sheets; P. Horn, *Rural Life in England
in the First World War* (1984), 135; Lindsey EC, 13 Aug. 1918; Lancs.
EC, Report to July 1918, 3–4.
58 War Cabinet, *Report for the year 1918*, 235.
59 Ibid.; J. Sheail, 'Land improvement', 120.
60 'Land drainage', *JBA*, February 1920, 1089–90.
61 Lancs. EC, Report to May 1917, 4; Report to Dec. 1917, 4; Report
to July 1918, 4–5.
62 Lindsey EC., 17 Oct. 1917.
63 'Drainage operations in Norfolk,' *JBA*, July 1919, 381.
64 Cheshire EC, Report to 30 June 1918, 3
65 MAF 42/8, 40171/D, *FPD report since December 1917*, 2.
66 MAF 42/8, 40171//D, *FPD report to 1 June 1918*, 7; War Cabinet, *Report
for 1918*, 235.
67 'Land drainage', *JBA*, Feb. 1920, 1089–90.
68 Beds. EC, 28 July 1917.
69 Sheail, 'Land improvement', 121; Lancs. EC, Report to May 1917, 3.
70 Lancs. EC, Report to July 1918, 8; Herts. EC, Review of its work
since January 1818, WAC minutes, 17 Feb. 1919.
71 Salop EC, Report to 12 Jan. 1918, 7.
72 Sheail, 'Land improvement', 112.
73 Norfolk EC, 4 Jan. 1919, report by H. Overman; Salop EC, Report
to 12 Jan. 1918, 6, Report to 25 Jan. 1919, 7. Lancs. EC, Report to
Dec. 1917, 5, Report to July 1918, 6; Cheshire EC, Report to 30 June
1918, 14.
74 Lancs. EC, Report to Dec. 1917, 5: Lindsey EC, Report to 31 March
1918, 6; Norfolk EC, 4 Jan. 1919, Overman's report, 1–2.
75 Cheshire EC, Report to 30 June 1918, 14; Lindsey EC, Report to 31
March 1918, 7; MAF 42/8, 40171/D, *FPD report to 1 June 1918*, 7.
76 MAF 42/8, 40171/D, *FPD report to 1 June 1918*, 22.
77 Cheshire EC, Report to 30 June 1918, 15–16; Lancs. EC, Report to
July 1918, 4–7; Salop EC, Report to 12 Jan. 1918, 6.
78 Cheshire EC, Report to 30 June 1918, 6; Salop EC, Report to 25 Jan.
1919, 8; Lancs. EC, Report to July 1918, 7.
79 Wilts. WAC minutes, 12 March–10 Sep. 1919.
80 Ibid.; E. H. Whetham, 'The Agriculture Act, 1920 and its repeal –
the 'Great Betrayal', *AgHR* 22 (1974), 48; Murray, *Agriculture*, 18.

THE ACHIEVEMENT

Chapter Thirteen

THE SUCCESS OF THE PLOUGH POLICY

Since the aim of the plough policy was to increase the supply of food via an increase in tillage, the success of the FPD would be dependent upon the extent to which grassland (chiefly permanent) could be broken up for cropping. The extent to which this occurred, and the potential for further tillage extension are shown in Table 13.1.

Table 13.1: Agricultural land use in Britain, 1914–18 (million acres)

	1909–13 av.	*1914*	*1915*	*1916*	*1917*	*1918*
Tillage	10.46	10.38	10.38	10.23	10.57	12.36
Temp. grass	4.15	3.92	3.88	4.12	4.04	3.49
Perm. grass	17.45	17.61	17.58	17.49	17.25	15.90
Totals	32.06	31.91	31.84	31.84	31.86	31.75

Source: *Agricultural Statistics,* 1909–18

There was little change in land use in 1914–16. In 1917 the work of the FPD began to take effect, and about 340,000 extra acres of tillage were created. However, it was only in 1918 that there was time to appreciably extend tillage, so that it rose in 1916–18 by some 2.13 million acres, or 20.8 per cent of the 1916 level.[1]

In its own terms, the plough policy did not completely succeed. The targets for 1918 had been increases in tillage, above that of 1916, of 2.6 million acres in England and Wales, and 0.35 million acres in Scotland. These represented increases of 31 and 19 per cent respectively (29 per cent for Britain). In practice, the 1918 tillage area had increased in England and Wales by 1.856 million acres, and in Scotland by 0.276 million acres; increases of 22 and 15 per cent respectively (21 per cent for Britain). In rough terms, it might be said that the programme for England and Wales was two-thirds fulfilled, and that for Scotland three-quarters fulfilled. That the targets were not entirely fulfilled should not detract from the considerable achievement of converting over two million acres of grass to tillage in less than two agricultural years. To put it into perspective, the highest reliably recorded tillage area in Britain, which occurred in 1875 (nine years after official agricultural statistics were first collected), was 13.75 million acres. The changes of 1916–18 raised it from 10.23 million to 12.36 million acres. Thus the plough policy had reinstated some 60 per cent of the loss of tillage incurred since 1875.

On the other hand, it may be suggested that the plough policy could have been carried much further if necessary. The policy operated through a reduction in permanent (and to some extent temporary) grass in favour of tillage. The possibilities for carrying this process further were by no means exhausted by the achievements of the plough policy, or even by its stated aims. In 1875 there had been 31.42 million acres of agricultural land in Britain, divided as: tillage 13.75, temporary grass 4.35, and permanent grass 13.31 million acres. There thus existed in 1909–13 slightly over 4 million more acres of land in permanent grass than in 1875. It was this, rather than the lost 3 million acres of tillage since the 1870s, which represented the potential for an extension of tillage. Given that the plough policy only succeeded in extending the tilled area by 1.9 million acres, as compared with 1909–13, it could be said with some justification that a further two million acres could have been ploughed. Even allowing for the reconversion of the 660,000 acres of temporary grass ploughed in wartime, there still remained a further ploughable area of 1.34 million acres. Looking ahead to the Second World War, the maximum tillage area then achieved was 13.71 million acres (1944); the potential for further tillage expansion in 1918 was clearly available. However, the achievement of the FPD measured by the extension of tillage was considerable, in view of the fact that it was the result of little more than a year of activity, that it occurred under very difficult circumstances, and that it was a wholly novel experiment.[2]

Within Britain, considerable differences were seen in the degree to which tillage was increased. Generally, the rise in tillage in 1916–18 was about 21 per cent, but this varied from 15 per cent in

Scotland to 20 per cent in England, and 52 per cent in Wales (Table 13.2).

Table 13.2: Tillage increases in Britain, 1916–18 (acres)

Region[a]	Acres	Increased tillage %
England		
East	146,257	8.9
North-East	166,904	9.3
South-East	162,821	17.0
East Midlands	183,990	23.1
West Midlands	208,735	28.8
South-West	264,165	37.2
North	222,137	29.3
North-West	242,421	39.9
England total:	1,597,430	20.0
Wales	245,192	52.2
Scotland	275,793	15.1
GB total:	2,118,415	20.6

Note: [a] Board of Agriculture regions

Source: Agricultural Statistics

Within the English regions, there were considerable county variations (see Figure 13.1), from the lowest increase in Ely (4.3 per cent) to Monmouth (103.5 per cent). Monmouth was officially part of England, but agriculturally better considered with Wales. Leaving Monmouth aside, the highest increase for an English county was 65.4 per cent (Westmorland).[3] In England, the general pattern was for tillage to increase proportionately more in the west and north. The most appropriate dividing line is from the western boundary of Dorset to the mouth of the Humber. To the east of this line, only one county increased its tillage by more than 30 per cent (East Sussex), while six counties rose by less than 10 per cent. To the west, only three counties (Nottingham, Lindsey (Lincs.), and Durham) were below 20 per cent and three English counties were above 50 per cent (Westmorland, Derbyshire, and Leicestershire). In Wales, it was notable that eight of the twelve counties recorded increases of 50 per cent or more, the outstanding ones being Glamorgan (80.6 per cent) and Flint (74 per cent). The lowest increase was Cardigan, which, at 25 per cent, was still higher than the English average. In Scotland, there was a generally slighter increase than in England, and less variation between counties; the lowest was Shetland (4 per cent), and the highest Ayr (28.7 per cent). Apart from a ridge of counties, running north from the border to Perthshire, most Scottish counties recorded increases of between 10 and 20 per cent.

Variations in the degree of increase in tillage largely reflected the existing ratio of permanent grass to tillage; put simply, there was proportionately more grass waiting to be broken up in the regions of the north and west than in the south and east. Thus in 1916 the ratio of permanent grass to tillage had been 1.75 in England. This concealed substantial variations, from 0.59 in the Eastern division to 3.77 in the North-Western division. Thus the latter region approached the situation of Wales, where the ratio was 4.27. In Scotland, however, there was relatively little permanent grass, and the ratio was only 0.81, so that there was little scope for adding to the tillage area by breaking permanent grass.

There were other factors at work; the decline in tillage since the 1870s had been much more pronounced in some counties than in others, so that there were known to be large areas which had in the past been devoted to tillage rather than grass. Thus in England between 1870 and 1914, six counties (excluding Monmouthshire) had fallen in corn acreage by more than 45 per cent. Two of these (Middlesex and Surrey) had since been affected by urban development to a large degree, so that their potential for tillage increase was not great, but it is noticeable that two others (Derbyshire and Leicestershire) expanded their wartime tillage between 1916 and 1918 by over 50 per cent.[4] In Wales, the four southern counties of Monmouth, Glamorgan, Carmarthen, and Brecknock had also reduced their corn area by over 45 per cent between 1870 and 1914, and during the war all except Carmarthen managed to revive tillage by over 50 per cent. In Scotland, however, the decline in corn since the 1870s had been less than in England or Wales, and there was correspondingly less scope for reversing the process.

The plough policy had not in most cases attempted to dictate to farmers what they should grow on the newly broken land. Although instances of ECs specifying the planting of potatoes have been found, most farmers were given freedom of cropping.[5] In particular, as long as they obeyed the directive to sow 'corn', they were free to choose between wheat, barley, and oats. Barley not being favoured, due to the restrictions on alcohol production, the decline in the numbers of pigs, and possibly the fact that it did not enjoy

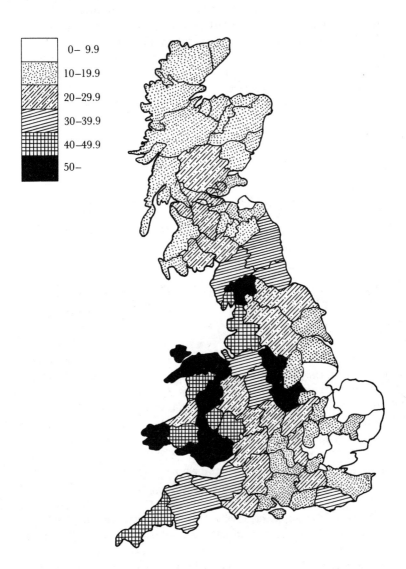

Figure 13.1: British county tillage increases, 1916–18 (%)

a minimum price, it was wheat and oats that were mostly chosen. In the event, oats were most popular, and the main effect of the plough policy was to produce a great expansion in the area sown to them. Even in England, where in large areas of the lowlands wheat had a climatic advantage over oats, the increase in the oats acreage was almost as large as that of wheat. In Wales and Scotland, oats were favoured more than wheat, so that for Britain as a whole the balance tipped strongly in favour of oats. However, in proportionate terms the rise in the wheat area was slightly greater than that of oats. The greatest proportionate increase was in potatoes (Table 13.3).

Table 13.3: Increases in individual crops in Britain, 1916–18 (acres)

	England	Wales	Scotland	GB	%
Wheat	598,484	45,969	15,979	660,432	33.4
Barley	150,222	18,511	(-)16,904	151,829	10.1
Oats	552,059	143,330	253,234	948,623	30.8
Potatoes	197,021	8,863	39,378	245,262	43.9
			Total	2,006,146	

Source: *Agricultural Statistics*

Given the type of policy adopted – the guaranteeing of wheat and oats prices, the reliance on breaking up permanent pasture, and the freedom of cropping given to farmers – the emphasis on oats was probably inevitable. But it calls into question the claim of the policy to be called one of food production. Oats were largely used as animal feed, which must have gone some way to offset the problems caused for farmers by the shortage of manufactured feeds. Even so, most of it was probably destined for horses, which on the whole did not suffer from the drop in manufactured feed supply. Nor were oats utilised as bread flour, so that the extra production did not help to eke out supplies of wheat, whether home or imported. On the whole, the emphasis on oats may be seen as a recognition of the technical obstacles to increasing the supply of wheat, and as providing an attractive market for farmers within the framework of the plough policy.

Another consequence of the freedom of cropping allowed to farmers was that the FPD had little information on the use to which the newly broken land was put. The only large survey on the subject was made in August 1918, when the ECs were asked to report on the use made of the new tillage, and of the crop yields obtained. Fifty-eight of the 61 ECs in England and Wales responded.[6] Results were compiled on the basis of a complete parish record for every 5,000 acres of land converted to tillage. The result was a survey of 78,000 acres of new tillage, which represented only 6.2 per cent of the 1,246,000 acres broken in those counties. On the basis of this sample, it was suggested that 850,000 of these acres had been devoted to oats, about 200,000 to wheat, 75,000 to barley, and 32,000 to potatoes, the rest being largely accounted for by pulses and minor corn crops.[7] Thus, although the estimates seem rather approximate, about 68 per cent of the new tillage was devoted to oats, about 16 per cent to wheat, and about 6 per cent to barley. Thus the plough policy would seem to be even more oats-oriented than the cropping figures above suggest. The disparity is explained by the fact that some existing root and green crops were abandoned in favour of cereals and potatoes.

Much interest was aroused by the question as to whether the yields of crops per acre on the new tillage would match those on the existing tillage. For Britain as a whole, yield estimates made by the Crop Reporters indicated that 1918 yields would be generally above the pre-war average (Table 13.4).

Table 13.4: Britain: crop yields per acre, 1909–13 and 1918

		1909–13	*1918*
Wheat	(bushels)	31.5	33.2
Barley	(bushels)	33.0	32.7
Oats	(bushels)	38.8	41.3
Potatoes	(tons)	6.2	6.7

Source: *Agricultural Statistics*

Estimated yields on new tillage were below the expected national average in 1918 for cereals (especially barley), although not for potatoes. It should be said that all these estimates were made before harvest, and the yields in practice, both on old and new tillage, may have been below these estimated levels. However, this does not alter the impression that new tillage was not quite as productive as the old, although the difference is not great.

These may be compared with the expected yields on new tillage in England and Wales, derived from the ECs' survey of August 1918 (Table 13.5).

Table 13.5: Expected crop yields on new tillage in England and Wales in 1918

Wheat	31.3 bushels/acre
Barley	28.8 bushels/acre
Oats	40.7 bushels/acre
Potatoes	7.1 tons/acre

Source: 1919 *Agricultural Statistics*, Pt. I, 4

The reasons for the slightly poorer yields on new tillage are somewhat conjectural. It was alleged that most of the new tillage was on the lighter land on higher ground, partly because farmers were reluctant to plough up the longer-established pastures in valley bottoms, and partly because the ECs were often reluctant to tackle the heavier soils.[8] Inadequate cultivation in the spring of 1918 was also blamed for the depredations of such pests as wireworms.[9] Given the comparative inexperience of FPD personnel and soldier ploughmen, especially in the early stages of the campaign, it is perhaps remarkable that the yields on new tillage were as good as they were. There seem to have been few substantial failures. A well-documented case of failure was south Hertfordshire. There, 1,122 acres were sown with oats, and produced a yield of only 30 bushels per acre; 226 acres failed completely, and had to be resown with barley, eventually yielding a crop of only 26.2 bushels per acre. The EC attributed this failure to the heavy soil, lack of drainage, late ploughing, and the ravages of London sparrows. Even this setback did not prevent the average oats yield in the county from reaching 43.5 bushels per acre, above that for England in 1918.[10]

Regional variations were apparent in yields on new tillage, as well as in tillage increases. For cereals, yields were generally higher above a line drawn between the Humber and the Bristol Channel than below it; the yields per acre from grassland counties were thus superior to those in the south and south-eastern counties.[11] This was probably due to the greater availability of good land for conversion to tillage in the grassland counties. By contrast, in the arable counties, farmers had greater difficulty in finding high-quality land for conversion to tillage. An additional factor may be present in Wales, where yields were often higher than those of the best English counties; a large amount of grass had been converted to tillage in 1915–16, so that farmers may be presumed to have acquired experience in the management of tillage which served them well in 1917–18.[12]

In the case of wheat, the best yields on new tillage were in Cornwall (38.5 bushels), Dorset (43.2), Monmouth (37.9), and the North Riding of Yorkshire (39.5). The lowest were in Sussex (18.3 bushels), Bucks. (19.3), Surrey (22.5), and Hunts. (23.8). In Wales, most counties exceeded a yield of 32 bushels per acre. Thus there were considerable variations in yield. This tendency was especially marked in the case of oats, where there were few average crops; the yields were either very good or very bad. On the new tillage, the highest yields were in Pembroke (57.9 bushels), Cumberland (50.1), Dorset (49.7), and Staffordshire (48.5). The lowest were in Surrey (27.4 bushels), Leicester (29.3), Huntingdon (29.6), and Herts. (30.0). For the oats crop as a whole, complete failure was reported for 12,000 acres, and it was estimated that a partial failure (24 bushels an acre or less) occurred on 85,000 acres. That in spite of these failures a relatively high yield for Britain as a whole was obtained is to be explained by the fact that the largest increases in acreage were found in western and northern counties, where yields were higher than the average. Barley was a more uniform crop, but apart from a small area in Wales and the north of England, gave a disappointing yield. Generally, no yield over 45 bushels was found, and no important case of failure was reported.[13]

It may be concluded that the effort of the FPD was largely successful, in that a large area of new tillage was created, and the yields of cereals on this land were not substantially inferior to those on existing tillage (with the exception of barley); the potato yield was perceptibly greater. On the other hand, the new tillage did not provide yields above those of old tillage, and the largest crop grown on it was oats, which contributed little to the supply of human food, either directly or indirectly. But in view of the scale and novelty of the experiment, it represented a considerable achievement, in circumstances of great difficulty.

NOTES

1 The decline in agricultural land in 1918 was due to a reclassification by the Board of Agriculture; Ministry of Agriculture, *A Century of Agricultural Statistics* (1968), 7.

2 *Agricultural Statistics*, 1875–1918.

3 Ibid., 1916–18. See map, p. 205.

4 The others were Worcestershire and Northumberland.

5 Somerset EC, SH/WA/2, Cultivation Orders.

6 J. A. Venn, *The Foundations of Agricultural Economics* (2nd edn. Cambridge 1933), 488; Middleton, *Food Production*, 248, finds 57. The missing counties appear to be Carmarthen, Anglesey, and Westmorland; Venn, *Foundations*, maps on pp. 491–5.

7 Venn, *Foundations*, 488–9.

8 Ibid., 488.

9 Ernle, *Land*, 148.

10 Middleton, *Food Production*, 250; Herts. EC, AEC/1, Review of EC work since January 1918, 17 Feb. 1919.

11 This had not been a noticeable feature of crop yields before the war; *Agricultural Statistics*, 1909–13.

12 Venn, *Foundations*, 490–2.

13 Ibid., 489–96.

Chapter Fourteen

THE OUTPUT OF
AGRICULTURE, 1914–18

It is now time to assess how British agriculture performed under wartime conditions. In this chapter an attempt will be made to estimate the output of agriculture during the whole war period. The starting-point for this estimate is the total production of agriculture, in the sense of all crops, livestock, and other items that are produced during an agricultural year. Total production may be derived fairly easily from the published agricultural statistics and other sources (Appendix A). But this measurement is too wide for our purpose, since a large proportion of total production never leaves the 'national farm', being used as raw material by other farmers, in the form of livestock feed and seed, or being consumed by the farming population itself (Appendix B). These items have been deducted from our estimate of total production, in order to leave an estimate of what is termed 'gross output'. Having estimated the physical quantities involved in the gross output of agriculture (Appendix C), these may be given financial values. If the prices per unit of output are held constant, we have an index of output in 'real' terms (Appendix D). This will enable us to trace the course of wartime output, to gauge the effect of shortages of factors of production, and to assess the impact of the food production policy.

The basis for our index is the average output of 1909–13. At £166.2 million, it is slightly higher than that shown in the 1908 *Census of Production* (£150.8 million).[1] However, the difference is largely accounted for by the rise in the prices of farm products between 1908 and 1914.[2] Our estimate of the variations in 'real' wartime output is shown in Table 14.1.

The striking feature of the 'real' output of agriculture is its comparative stability. Even in the last year of the war, output was

Table 14.1: Gross farm output in Britain, 1914–18, at 1909–13 prices (£ million)

	1909–13	1914	1915	1916	1917	1918
	166.2	171.5	168.3	162.3	162.1	154.9
As per cent:	100.0	103.2	101.3	97.6	97.5	93.2

Source: Appendix D

still only 7 per cent below its pre-war level, although the war had begun with output at about 3 per cent above it. To put the matter another way, at no time in the war did real output fall by more than 10 per cent, which is in itself a considerable achievement in comparison with the substantial falls which were seen in other wartime agricultural systems.

The comparative stability of output is more striking when it is realised that the type of measurement adopted tends to overstate the decline in output in 1918. The reason for this is that the measurement is based on the production structure of 1909–13. Since this structure changed quite considerably in 1918, this had implications for the way in which output is measured. The effect of FPD policy was to shift output away from relatively high value-added products to ones with lower values added per unit of labour (and other factors of production) employed. Since we are using market prices (of 1909–13) to measure output, this shift tends to exaggerate the decline in output in 1918. In other words, agriculture in 1918 was forced to become less efficient in market terms in order to become more efficient at producing basic foodstuffs.

Not only was the level of output surprisingly stable, but its structure was also stable until after 1916. This may be seen in the main output categories (Table 14.2).

Table 14.2: British farm output structure, 1914–18

	Per cent of total output					
	1909–13	1914	1915	1916	1917	1918
Cereals and potatoes	16.6	16.6	17.3	14.9	18.8	26.1
Dairy produce	16.8	17.7	17.1	16.6	15.2	13.9
Livestock	40.5	38.4	38.2	38.8	36.0	29.8
Other	26.1	27.3	27.4	29.7	30.0	30.2

Source: Appendix D

Structural changes before 1917 were conspicuous by their absence. The fall in the share of cereals and potatoes in 1916 reflects poor harvests (especially of potatoes) due to bad weather. There is some evidence of decline in the dairy sector, as milk yields per cow were beginning to fall, due to the shortage of artificial feeds. This fall was to continue and become more marked in 1917 and 1918, but for the moment it was relatively slight; down to 525 gallons per cow yearly from the pre-war average of 560.[3] Even with this adjustment, the dairy sector still held its pre-war position. The slight decline in the livestock sector in 1914–16 is due to depressed income from sheep and pigs, and particularly low horse sales in 1916, as farmers tried to rebuild their stocks following the heavy Army requisitioning of 1914–15.

The last area in which structural change may have been occurring in 1914–16 is in the category of 'other' products, where a slow but steady rise in importance is evident. Here, a certain caution is desirable, since the estimates are tentative. This is not of great significance for minor products such as hops, wool, poultry, eggs, and fruit. However, about half of the 'other' category in our estimate for 1909–13 consists of income from hay and straw. These were omitted in the 1908 census of production. However, we suggest that they were important income-generating products, which should not be ignored; there were before the war about 1.5 million non-agricultural horses in Britain, largely fed from British farms. During the war, the market for both hay and straw expanded with the rise in the numbers of military horses. Those in the UK were certainly fed on home produce (imports were negligible) and it is probable that a large number of the horses on the Western Front were similarly supplied. The War Cabinet was informed in March 1917 that the Army horses in France were consuming 70,000 tons of hay per month, which was bought in the UK and shipped across the Channel.[4]

The second half of the war saw great structural change. In 1918, the cereal/potato sector, which had accounted for about one-sixth of pre-war output, rose to about one-quarter, while livestock, accounting for over 40 per cent of pre-war output, fell to about 30 per cent. Dairy output fell by about a fifth. By the end of the war, cereals/potatoes, which had been slightly behind the dairy sector pre-war, contributed almost twice as much as dairying to the output of agriculture, and were almost as important as livestock.

The loss of grassland consequent on the food production policy did not play an important role in the decline of livestock output. It was notable that the number of cattle at the end of the war was slightly higher than at the beginning. The sheep flock fell, but only by about 10 per cent. The greatest fall was in pigs, whose numbers fell by 27 per cent. However, the loss of income from livestock was largely due to the decline in slaughter weights, a process which affected all three animals. This seems to have been due to animals being sent for slaughter at an earlier age. It was estimated that the average slaughter weight of cattle had fallen in 1918 to 579 lb; a fall of some 14 per cent on that recorded in the 1908 census of production. The average slaughter weight of sheep and lambs combined was thought to have declined from 61 lb before the war to 48.5 lb in 1918, and that of pigs from 160 lb to 132 lb.[5] Thus the decline in livestock output was due mainly to declining slaughter weights in the case of cattle and sheep, and to declining numbers slaughtered in the case of pigs.

A variety of influences accounted for the decline in livestock production. The background was the increasing shortage of artificial feeds in 1917–18, compounded by policy errors. Thus the mistakes made in fixing a sliding scale of cattle prices encouraged farmers to bring animals to market earlier than usual, so that there was a glutted market in the autumn of 1917, followed by a dearth of animals for slaughter in the spring of 1918. This process was also encouraged by the high price and scarcity of feed, which made farmers reluctant to feed animals over the winter. The shortage of purchased feeds also played an important part in the sharp fall (almost 50 per cent) in fertility of the pig population, and in discouraging farmers from raising calves for beef. In the case of sheep, relatively unfavourable prices seem to have been fixed, and the setting of a fixed price for all sheep sent for slaughter encouraged the selling off of ewes, which had usually fetched a lower price than other sheep. It was also felt that the decline of grass could be met with less disruption by a reduction in sheep rather than cattle. Finally, farmers may well have felt apprehension over the future of feed supplies, which was known to be uncertain.[6]

The shortage of purchased feeds also seems to have been at the root of the other major change in output structure during the war: the decline of the dairy sector. In constant price terms, output in 1918 was almost a fifth lower than before the war, mainly due to the decline in milk output. Since the milking herd in 1917 and 1918 was almost the same size as pre-war, this decline was due to the decline in milk output per cow which had begun in 1916, and proceeded at a faster rate in 1917 and 1918. In the latter year, a survey by the Ministry of Food showed that output per cow was only 436 gallons a year, compared with the pre-war (1909-13) average of 560 gallons – a fall of some 22 per cent. This large decline was attributed to the scarcity and high price of feeding stuffs, a decline in the quality of cakes and meals, and the lower efficiency of milking labour. The feed shortage, it was noted in an earlier report, was not of home grown materials such as hay and straw (since the War Office allowed producers to retain a reasonable amount for their own use), but of imported feeds.[7]

It may be a matter of surprise that British agriculture was comparatively successful in maintaining output during the war, in the face of considerable difficulties. In particular, there were substantial shortages of important factors of production. These may be illustrated in relation to the course of output (Table 14.3).

Table 14.3; Output and factor shortage in British agriculture, 1914-18 (per cent change on 1909-13)

	1914	1915	1916	1917	1918
Output	+3	+1	−2	−2	−7
Factor supplies:					
Fertiliser	+16	−10	−23	−17	+37
Purchased feeds	+4	0	−10	−32	−61
Horsepower	−13	−20	−15	−3	+14
Labour shortage	−1	+7	+10	+11	+9

Source: Appendices E, F, G, I, J

A degree of shortage of factors of production was becoming marked in some cases as early as 1915. This is especially true of the supply of tractive power in the form of horses, and of fertiliser (chiefly Chile nitrate). By 1916-17 the horse population was recovering, but the fertiliser shortage was now much greater; farmers had not yet replaced the missing nitrate with ammonium sulphate, and the shortage of phosphates and potash was acute. In addition, the supply of artificial feeds had taken a turn for the worse. There was also a clear labour shortage, of the order of 10 per cent. Thereafter, some supplies recovered, but only those of particular use for the new food production policy – tractive power in the form of tractors, and fertiliser in the form of ammonium sulphate and phosphates. The labour shortage was still apparent in 1918, and the supply of purchased feeds had fallen even more.

The question therefore arises: how did agriculture manage? To this question only tentative answers can be given. In the case of fertilisers, it was apparent that shortages did not have any discernible effect on yields per acre. Several explanations may be suggested. In the first place, there is the fact that artificial fertilisers were much less important in supplying fertilising agents to the soil than the traditional farmyard manure.[8] While criticisms had often been made in the past that farmers did not take adequate care of their manure supplies, it may be that in wartime they learnt to conserve them more efficiently. Secondly, the fertiliser shortage was comparatively brief, and enough stored-up fertility seems to have remained in the soil for yields to have stayed relatively stable. Finally, it may have been that artificial fertilisers were used less wastefully during the war.

The shortage of feed could not be thus obviated; it is noticeable that feed losses translated quite quickly into declines in milk yield per cow, and later into declines in slaughter weight (either directly, or by forcing the sale of immature animals). Faced with this situation, farmers coped by retaining animals whose loss would be most serious, both in terms of income forgone, and of the difficulty of rebuilding post-war populations. Thus sheep and (especially) pigs declined, and cattle were maintained. The surviving animals were less adequately fattened for market and fed for milk production, but sufficient home-produced fodder existed for their rearing and maintenance.

Labour shortage presents the greatest problems of explanation. That some degree of shortage existed is certain. The traditional view is that it was about one-third of the pre-war labour force. Our estimate is that it was probably not more than about one-tenth. Even this would be a potentially serious matter, especially in view of the fact that it took place within two years. Explanations of the apparent lack of connection between output and labour shortage are highly tentative, but some suggestions may be made.

In spite of the fact that British farms were on average larger than European farms, this is not the same as saying that the small farm was a thing of the past. Indeed, British agriculture had retained its small-scale (in British terms), family nature to an extent that was largely ignored by contemporaries, and has largely eluded historians. This is apparent from a consideration of the farming structure revealed in the census of production of 1908; while holdings of 50 acres or less only accounted for 14.7 per cent of the British agricultural area, they made up 67 per cent of all holdings. Even excluding the very small holdings of 5 acres or less still left 46 per cent of holdings in the 6–50 acre range, and, while some of these would have been fragmented holdings rather than discrete farms, many must have been independent family farms.[9] In this situation, the farm had reserves of labour, in the form of the farmer and his family, who could either work harder or be put to work in a more efficient way. This was less true of the large farm, where the labour of the farmer and his family formed a minor part of the whole labour supply. In addition, the larger farms, it has been argued, were more prone to the military recruitment of their manpower than were the small farms. The larger farmer, however, had some compensations. He was more likely to have labour to redeploy, in the form of junior horsemen, cattlemen, or grooms and gardeners. In addition, the larger farm areas benefited more than the smaller in the supply of extra labour organised by the FPD.[10]

More generally, the physical connection between labour supply and output was much looser than usually assumed. Many farm tasks could be subject to a greater degree of labour shortage without necessarily leading to a fall in output. In the case of crops, the main tasks were seedbed preparation, sowing, cultivating, and harvesting. The first three of these tasks were performed at times when the demand for labour was below its annual average, so that the effects of labour shortage were mitigated. Only in the case of harvesting did the demand for labour exceed the annual average.[11] On the livestock side, the main tasks were general supervision, feeding, cleaning, and milking. The first three of these could be spread so as to stagger the workload. Only milking could not so be treated, and required a high level of skill. Thus the two main tasks in which labour shortage might be expected to have the most serious consequences for output were harvesting and milking. In practice, however, considerable efforts were made by the authorities to supply harvest labour (from 1915), and milking labour (from 1917 especially).

The lack of connection between labour shortage and wartime

output is emphasised when it is realised that the main influences on output were the decline in the supply of animal feed, and the expansion of tillage in 1917–18. Labour supply had little connection with the former, and with the latter only in so far as an expansion of the labour supply was a prerequisite for the success of the plough policy. However, even with the revival of labour supply under the FPD, the existing labour shortage was not tackled, the extra labour being insufficient even for the extra tasks imposed by the food production policy.

The performance of agriculture may be summed up as follows: in the first half of the war, the output record is extremely creditable; output in 1916 had fallen only 2 per cent below pre-war (although 5 per cent below that of 1914), in the face of considerable shortages of fertiliser, feed, and labour. After 1916, the industry adopted a new tack, and to considerable effect; output of cereals and potatoes was 57 per cent above that of pre-war in 1918, although the FPD ploughing target was not achieved. However, this involved a further fall in overall output, some of which was due to policy. In particular, livestock pricing policy was inadequate in the autumn of 1917 and early in 1918. It was also the case that the serious and increasing feed shortage, to which most of the fall in livestock and milk production may be attributed, was itself partly the result of policy – in this case, the breadstuffs and liquor policies, and the policy of reducing imports so as to save shipping space. The latter was ill-conceived, and undid some of the effects of the food production policy; a higher level of feed imports need not have run counter to the primary aim of ploughing grassland. As it was, the rise in output (at constant prices) of cereals and potatoes was £16.6 million between 1916 and 1918, but this was more than offset by a fall of £22.9 million in the output of the dairy and livestock sectors.

NOTES

1 Board of Agriculture, *The Agricultural Output of Great Britain, 1908*, Cd. 6277, 25.
2 *Agricultural Statistics*, 1924, Pt. III, 140–1.
3 Astor Committee, Cmd. 483, para. 12.
4 PRO, CAB 23/2, 83 (Appendix II, 'Consumption of grain by horses.')
5 Guild, 'Variations in the numbers of livestock', 554–8.
6 Ibid., 540–50: Beveridge, *Food Control*, 258.
7 Astor Committee, Cd. 8886, para. 10; Cmd. 483, paras. 11–16.

8 E. J. Russell, 'On making and storing farmyard manure', *JRASE* 77 (1916), 3; *Farm Soil and its Improvement* (1923), 71.

9 *1908 Census of Production*, Cd. 6277, 17–19.

10 Dewey, thesis, 205–6.

11 W. H. Kirkpatrick, *The Seasonal Distribution of Farm Labour Requirements* (University of Cambridge, Department of Agriculture, Farm Economics Branch, Report no. 14, July 1930), Appendix A.

Chapter Fifteen

FARMING AND FOOD SUPPLY

In spite of the concern expressed over food supply during the war, the British people remained adequately fed. Sir William Beveridge's estimate of wartime food consumption in the UK showed that, in terms of calories, only a slight deterioration was evident (Table 15.1).[1]

Table 15.1: UK daily food consumption, 1914–18

	Calories per 'average man'	Per cent
1909–13 av.	3,442	100
1914	3,454	100
1915	3,551	103
1916	3,418	99
1917	3,320	96
1918	3,358	97

Source: Beveridge, *Food Control*, 313, Table X

The comparatively slight fall in consumption in the latter part of the war still left the average diet at an adequate level, even when losses of nutrition in transport, storage, and food preparation were taken into account. Seen in this light, the food problem of 1917–18 was one of distribution rather than actual shortage. This was recognised in the system of food rationing, which attempted to redistribute supplies to the benefit of the working-class consumer, rather than to reduce the level of average nutrition; the latter prospect was not absent from the minds of the administrators of the Ministry of Food, but it was obviated by the Armistice.[2]

The maintenance of the national food supply implied a larger wartime task for home agriculture, since imports fell. This was partly due to shipping difficulties (especially those due to the submarine campaign of 1917–18), and partly due to policy, as the Ministry of Shipping tried to save shipping space in order to transport the USA forces and their equipment to the Western Front in 1917–18. In terms of calories, the UK import supply varied as shown in Table 15.2.

Table 15.2: UK net food imports, 1914–18 (million calories)

	1909–13	1914	1915	1916	1917	1918
Cereals	14.0	16.3	15.0	16.5	16.6	15.2
Meat	3.5	4.0	4.0	3.8	3.4	4.6
Dairy produce	3.5	3.5	3.5	2.5	1.9	1.2
Sugar	6.6	8.5	7.4	6.5	5.9	5.4
Poultry and eggs	0.2	0.2	0.2	0.1	0.1	0.1
Fish	0.1	0.2	0.2	0.2	0.1	0.2
Fruit	0.9	0.9	0.9	0.9	0.4	0.3
Potatoes and vegetables	0.8	0.6	0.6	0.6	0.8	0.9
Totals	29.6	34.2	31.8	31.1	29.2	27.9
As per cent	100	116	107	105	99	94

Source: Dewey (1980), 81

Imports declined continuously during the war, falling well below the high level of 1914, and even, by 1918, below the level of 1909–13. Notable among the early losses were sugar and dairy products, both of which were affected by shipping difficulties. Both of these continued to decline in 1917–18, and were joined by cereals, whose reduction was largely due to the intentional reduction in imports. The supply of meat fell in 1914–17, but recovered in 1918, largely due to the importation of bacon from the USA.[3]

Seen in the light of the need to make up the gap left by falling imports, the task facing UK agriculture was not particularly great, although compounded by the shortage of labour and other factors of production. It will be recalled that the output of UK agriculture in 1909–13 was equivalent to about 21 billion calories. In order to restore food supplies in 1918 to their 1909–13 level, home agriculture would have had to make up a shortfall in imports to the equivalent of about 1.7 billion calories. This would amount to raising the level of home production by about 8 per cent. This modest target would seem to have been exceeded, if judged by contemporary and historical opinion. To be sure, some contemporaries had their doubts. Sir Henry Rew, a leading agricultural statistician, thought that when losses of nutrition due to the reduction of meat and milk supplies in 1918 had been taken into account, there probably had been a setback to food production by the end of the war.[4] But the proponents of the food production policy did not agree. Lord Ernle was particularly enthusiastic about the addition to bread supply brought about by the work of the FPD; taking into account the higher milling ratios, and the additives used in bread in 1918, he concluded that the UK, which before the war had only supplied its own bread for ten weeks of the year, had been enabled to do so for 40 weeks in 1918.[5]

The most comprehensive attempt at measuring the impact of the food production policy came from Middleton, who had been the first Director of the FPD. His account, which appeared in 1923, is the nearest approach to an official history of the campaign ever written. In it, he attempted to balance the gains in cereals and potatoes in 1918 with the losses of meat and milk. The conclusion he drew was that the net gain, above the home production of 1909–13, was 4.05 billion calories. Estimating home production before the war at 16.872 billion calories, he wrote that the work of the FPD had had the effect of raising home output by 24 per cent.[6] This figure has been accepted by subsequent authors as the measure of success of the food production policy.[7]

If valid, this estimate would mean that UK agriculture exceeded the target set by the reduction in food imports by a very large margin. However, even if this estimate proved to be acceptable, it would not tell us anything about the course of food output in 1914–17. We have therefore compiled our own estimates of the food value of UK food production for the war period (see Table 15.3 on the following page).

In 1916, and to a lesser extent in 1917, home food production was less than pre-war, so that the partial failure of agriculture was tending to worsen the situation. It was only in 1918 that the efforts of the FPD served to raise output back to the pre-war level. The decline in food production in 1916 would seem to be largely due to the poor cereal and potato harvests of that year. The influence of the weather is also discernible in the high output of 1915, assisted by the expansion in cereal acreage which took place in that year. By 1916, however, a reduction is evident in the output of milk and

Table 15.3: UK food production, 1914–18 (billion calories)

	1909–13	1914	1915	1916	1917	1918
Cereals	4.4	4.6	5.4	4.4	4.8	6.8
Potatoes	3.1	3.5	3.5	2.4	4.3	4.4
Meat	6.1	5.8	5.8	5.7	4.9	3.8
Milk	3.0	3.1	2.8	2.6	2.3	2.1
Other dairy produce	1.1	1.2	1.2	1.2	1.1	1.0
Poultry and eggs	0.1	0.1	0.1	0.1	0.1	0.1
Cottage produce	2.6	2.6	2.6	2.6	2.6	2.6
Vegetables	0.3	0.3	0.3	0.3	0.3	0.3
Fruit	0.2	0.2	0.2	0.2	0.2	0.1
Totals[a]	21.1	21.4	21.9	19.4	20.6	21.2
As per cent	100	102	105	93	99	101

Note: [a] Totals do not always agree with sub-totals, due to rounding

Source: Dewey (1980), 84

meat, and this grew more marked in 1917 and 1918. The efforts of the FPD were beginning to take effect in 1917, especially in potato output, and this was augmented by a substantial rise in cereals in 1918.

How is this apparently moderate performance – a rise of 1 per cent in food production in 1918 above the pre-war level – to be reconciled with Middleton's view that food production in 1918 was 24 per cent above that of 1909–13 – a view that, as we have seen, has become the accepted view amongst historians? The conflict is due partly to different methods and partly to differences of estimation. Middleton arrived at his figure of 24 per cent by taking the 1918 production of wheat, barley, oats, and potatoes, and converting the weights harvested into calories. This produced a figure of 4.78 billion calories. He then made a deduction for calories lost due to the fall in meat and milk production. This came to 0.73 billion calories. Deducting the meat and milk losses from the crop gains produced a net gain of 4.05 billion calories. Since he estimated the pre-war home production of food at 16.872 billion calories, the result was a net gain of 24 per cent in food production.[8]

This procedure can be criticised on several grounds. Firstly, the estimate of pre-war home food production is appreciably lower than that calculated by the Royal Society in 1916 (21.29 billion calories) or that presented above (21.1 billion calories). The effect of using this lower starting point is to exaggerate any gains made in 1918 when expressed as percentage increases above the pre-war level. The reason for the discrepancy lies in Middleton's restrictive defi-

223

nition of what constituted home food production. For his purpose, he attempted to define home production as that due solely to the produce of the soils of the UK. To that end, he excluded that part of home production which he felt able to attribute to imported animal feeds. In thus assuming that home output corresponded only to output from the soils (or products of the soils) of the UK, he is choosing a more limited definition than that of ourselves or the Royal Society; those estimates referred to the output of UK agriculture, whether due to home or imported materials. In adopting this approach, he seemed to have in mind that the best way to assess the performance of home agriculture was to exclude the effect of what amounted to outside assistance. Logically, this approach has much to commend it; a similar method was used by Murray in his official history of agriculture during the Second World War.[9] However, in practice, the performance of wartime agriculture and the work of the FPD were both affected materially by the availability of imported feed, which was already an important factor of production before the war, and it seems unrealistic to assess wartime agriculture as if it lived in a vacuum, immune from the outside world. It may also be noted that Middleton's approach lacks rigour, since he made no deduction for the contribution to soil fertility made by imported fertiliser.

Secondly, as a consequence of his desire to exclude the effect of imported feeds, Middleton underestimated the decline in meat and milk output in 1917–18; it seems clear that he included only those losses which he could attribute to the shortage of domestically produced feedstuffs. Since feed imports fell very considerably, this led him to underestimate substantially the losses of meat and milk; whereas he put these at no more than 0.73 billion calories, our estimate is that they amounted to 3.28 billion calories, which was almost enough to entirely offset the increase in calories due to the larger grain and potato crops of 1918.

There is also a disagreement on the size of the extra supply of calories made available by the cereal and potato harvests of 1918. Middleton's estimate is 4.78 billion calories; ours is only 3.63 billion calories. The main reason for this is that Middleton assumed that all of the extra wheat crop would have been made into bread, without deduction for seed, feed or waste on farms, whereas we have deducted 38 per cent of the crop for those purposes. In addition, he assumed that the (small) increase in the 1918 barley crop would have been consumed as beer; an unlikely outcome by then in view of the reduction in brewing.

The main differences between the traditional view and our own are summarised in Table 15.4.

Table 15.4: Net increase in UK food production from main crops and livestock, 1918/1909–13 (billion calories)

	Middleton	Revised view
Cereals and potatoes	+ 4.78	+ 3.63
Meat and milk	− 0.73	− 3.28
Net increase	+ 4.05	+ 0.35
1909–13 output	16.872	21.10
Increase as per cent of 1909–13	24.0	1.7

Even with the efforts of the FPD, there was still a danger of serious food shortage. Since the military diet was more generous than that of civilians, the expansion of the armed forces led to a rise in overall food demand. The extent of this rise is uncertain, but it may have been as much as 8 per cent above pre-war at its peak in 1918.[10] In the same year, total food supplies (home and imported) were 3 per cent below the pre-war average, and had fallen rather more in comparison with the high levels of 1914 and 1915.

The explanation for the avoidance of more serious shortage in 1917–18 rests not so much with the food production policy, but with the policy of food control. There were two aspects to this. The first, which has attracted most attention, was rationing. This was not designed to ease the food problem *in toto*, but to redistribute supplies more equitably. The second aspect was food economy, the aim of which was to obtain more nutrition from a given supply of food. It was the food economy policy which played the greatest part in overcoming the potential food shortage.

The main way in which such measures contributed to solving the problem was to permit substantial economies in the use of cereals in making bread. The first method of economising was to raise the extraction rate, that is, the proportion of grain entering flour mills which emerged as flour. In peacetime the extraction rate was about 70 per cent. At its wartime peak in April 1918 it was 91.9 per cent. Thereafter it was allowed to fall to about 87 per cent, where it remained for the rest of the war. Grain supplies were also eked out by diluting wheat flour with flour derived from other materials –

principally barley, but also maize, beans, and potatoes. In the cereal year 1917–18 alone, according to the Wheat Commission: '. . . dilution saved us the equivalent of 6,000,000 sacks of flour, and in the same period lengthened extraction rates saved a further total of 4,000,000 – in all thirteen weeks of bread supply during the most critical period'.[11] The result was that the 'war bread' of 1917–18 differed considerably from the usual product. While the rates of extraction and admixture varied so much that it is not possible to estimate the average composition of bread flour in 1917–18, an example will indicate the economies achieved. In April 1918, out of every 100 lb of flour produced, 54 lb represented that part of the wheat which had always gone to human consumption, 17 lb that part of the grain which had formerly gone to animal feed, and 29 lb came from admixture with other cereals or potatoes.[12]

The economies achieved through these devices were substantial enough for bread to remain the only major food left unrationed. More importantly, they proved the most efficacious means available of minimising the food shortage. An approximate measurement of the extent to which food supplies were augmented by these policies may be obtained from Beveridge's estimates of wartime consumption. He provided data on the amounts of grain milled in each war year, and of the resultant supply of flour (including diluents).[13] Since it is possible to calculate how much flour would have been produced in 1917–18 had extraction rates stayed at their pre-war level (and there had been no dilution), we can estimate how much extra flour was produced by the twin policies of higher extraction and dilution. The resulting calculation indicates an increase in food supply of 1.8 billion calories in 1917, and 3.7 billion in 1918.[14]

The extra nutrition provided by the breadstuffs policies in 1917–18 was substantially greater than that provided by the food production policy. The relative importance of imports, home production, and the breadstuffs policy in maintaining total food supply is summarised in Table 15.5.

Thus the final pattern of food supply emerges: a fall by 1916 to the pre-war level, and a slight rise thereafter to about 4 per cent above it, so that the extra demand due to the expansion of the armed forces was to some extent met. This table also permits a conclusion to be drawn on the degree of self-sufficiency achieved in

Table 15.5: Food supply in the UK, 1914–18 (billion calories)

	1909–13	1914	1915	1916	1917	1918
Home production	21.1	21.4	21.9	19.4	20.6	21.2
Imports	29.6	34.2	31.8	31.1	29.2	27.9
Food control	–	–	–	–	1.8	3.7
Totals	50.7	55.6	53.7	50.5	51.6	52.8
Per cent	100	110	106	100	102	104
Home production as per cent of total	41	38	41	38	43	47

Note: [a] Including food control effect

– = not applicable

food supply. With the aid of the new policies, the UK found 47 per cent of its supply of calories from home sources in 1918, compared with 41 per cent in 1909–13. This was not a very substantial increase, being of the order of one-seventh, and was clearly very far from the dreams of total self-sufficiency which inspired some officials.[15] The rise in self-sufficiency was, again, largely due to food control; without it, home agriculture would have contributed only 43 per cent of total food supplies in 1918.

After 1916, the greater role in offsetting food shortage (actual and potential) was played by the food economy measures. The food production policy played a relatively minor role. In retrospect, this is less surprising than it may seem. The scope for increasing food supplies through a policy of food production was considerably less than through a food economy programme such as the breadstuffs policy. This may be seen by comparing the relative contribution to national food supply of imports and home production. By the First World War, home production only contributed about 40 per cent of the total food supply. Thus to raise the total supply by (e.g.) 10 per cent, solely through a food production policy, would require home food production to rise by a quarter. Such a rise would be far greater than the normal variation to be expected from a good harvest, and proved to be well outside the reach of the food production policy. On the other hand, the potential gains from a breadstuffs policy were both greater and more easily realised. The consumption of grain had contributed almost as much energy to the national pre-war diet as the whole output of home agriculture (18.4 billion calories, as opposed to 21.1 billion), and the food economy measures allowed the grain supply (both home and imported) to yield an extra 2.6 billion calories in 1918, as compared to pre-war.[16] Nor was this difficult (or costly) in practice, since it required the minimum of technical adaptation and administrative regulation. In comparison with gains which were so large and so easily realisable, those achieved by the Food Production Department were bound to play a minor role in offsetting the potential food shortage of the First World War.

NOTES

1 Although the discussion so far has been in British terms, this chapter on food supplies has to concern itself with the UK. The reason for this is that it is not possible to accurately separate UK food imports from British food imports.

2 Beveridge, *Food Control*, 321.

3 The early sugar losses entailed a loss of carbohydrate, but not protein or fat. In so far as the FPD policy repaired the carbohydrate loss, it was justified. Since it also yielded an extra supply of protein (if of second-class quality), it provided a bonus.

4 R. H. Rew, 'The progress of British agriculture', *JRSS*, LXXXV (1922), 19.

5. Ernle, *Land*, 151.

6 Middleton, *Food Production*, 322.

7 E.g., S. J. Hurwitz, *State Intervention in Great Britain; a study of economic control and social response, 1914–1919* (Columbia, 1949); A. W. Ashworth, *An Economic History of England, 1870–1939* (1960), 281.

8 Middleton, *Food Production*, 319–22.

9 Murray, *Agriculture*, 242.

10 This is a maximum estimate, and includes the provisioning of armed forces overseas. Beveridge considered that food demand was virtually constant during the war, but he did not take overseas troops into account; Beveridge, *Food Control*, 392; Dewey, 'Food production', 80.

11 Quoted in Beveridge, *Food Control*, 100.

12 Ibid., 99.

13 Ibid., 360–1.

14 These quantities have been reduced by 50 per cent from those originally calculated, to take account of the lesser digestibility of the bread thereby produced; Royal Society, *Food Supply*, Cd. 8421 (1916), 25; Dewey, 'Food production', 87.

15 E.g., Sir Charles Fielding, *Food* (1923), which argued for *total* self-sufficiency as a future policy; Fielding had succeeded Lord Lee as Director-General of the FPD in June 1918.

16 Derived from Beveridge, *Food Control*, 360–1.

Chapter Sixteen

FARMER, LANDOWNER, AND LABOURER

It is evident that there is more than one way of assessing how well British agriculture responded to the difficulties of the First World War. So far, we have seen that the real output of the industry declined slightly, although food production in terms of calories recovered to the pre-war level. We now attempt to measure the financial implications of the war for the three main groups in the agricultural industry – farmers, landowners, and labourers – in the shape of profits, rental income, and wages.

The starting-point for this process is the estimate already made of the physical output ('gross output') of agriculture during the war. So far, this has been presented in constant-price terms, to give an idea of the 'real' output of the industry. However, by valuing it at current market prices, we shall have an estimate of the current income of the industry. If we also estimate the main categories of farm expenditure, we shall have the basis for a view of the changing relative fortunes of the three groups involved. At current prices, the income of the agricultural industry may be estimated as in Table 16.1.[1]

Table 16.1: Gross income of British agriculture at current prices, 1914–18
(£ million)

	1909–13	*1914*	*1915*	*1916*	*1917*	*1918*
	166.2	175.8	216.8	265.5	325.3	348.0
As per cent	100	106	130	160	196	209

Source: Appendix E

The main sources of income had changed their relative import-

229

ance by the end of the war. The largest change was the decline in income from livestock and livestock products as compared to crops. This is a trend which is apparent by 1916, but it became more pronounced subsequently, especially in 1918, when income from livestock actually fell, and by a large amount. Since this was a fall in current values, at a time when inflation was still well over 10 per cent p.a., this represented a sharp fall in real terms. On the crop side, the increasingly important items were cereals (especially oats and wheat), potatoes, hay, and straw. These reflect the impact of the food production policy and military demand. Amongst minor products, one may note the fluctuations in income from horse sales, the rapid rise in income from vegetables, fruit, and eggs in 1918, the continuously depressed income from hops, and the decline in income from wool in 1917 and 1918. Much the largest dairy item was milk; this rose roughly in line with gross income until 1917, when it fell behind to some extent.

The rise in gross income reflected two forces: inflation and price control. The former held sway until 1917, when its operation began to be affected by price control. In 1916, the War Office had fixed prices for the requisitioning of wool, hay, and straw. The first important commodity to be given a fixed price was milk (December 1916). Cereals followed in April 1917, and by the end of the year most agricultural products were subject to price control. As a result, the rate of growth of farmers' gross income slowed down.

Having considered variations in farmers' gross incomes, we shall consider their current costs. These are indicated, as far as it is possible to calculate them, in Table 16.2. The main categories of expenditure remained the same in war as in peace. The only additional item is an allowance for 'government supplies', which consists of labour supplied, and cultivation work done, by the ECs in 1917–18; it must, however, be regarded as a rough estimate.

Before the war, farm costs were dominated by three items: wages, rent, and feedstuffs, accounting for 80 per cent of total costs. Thus the course of wartime costs would be largely determined by what happened to these items. In particular, the stasis of the rent bill is largely responsible for the outstanding feature of wartime costs; the fact that they rose much more slowly than gross farm income, thus permitting a high level of profit. Comparison of gross income with current costs shows that the former doubled by 1918, while the latter only rose by one-half.

Table 16.2: Farmers' current costs, 1914–18 (£ million)

	1909–13	1914	1915	1916	1917	1918
Wages	38.3	40.3	42.8	47.5	52.8	67.2
Rent	33.3	33.5	33.5	33.9	34.0	33.4
Feedstuffs	20.4	21.7	28.2	33.5	35.6	20.5
Irish livestock	6.8	5.8	6.9	9.6	13.7	11.0
Fertilisers	4.1	4.6	4.2	4.8	6.2	9.2
Machinery	3.5	3.8	4.0	5.1	4.9	10.5
Government supplies	0	0	0.7	1.3	2.8	5.5
Miscellaneous	8.1	8.4	9.6	11.0	12.2	13.7
Totals	114.5	118.1	129.9	146.7	162.2	171.0
As per cent	100	103	114	128	142	149

Source: Dewey (1984/1), 376 and Appendix II

The static rent bill reflected the fact that there existed no institutional mechanism for adjusting rents to rapid inflation. Changes in rent were usually confined to changes of tenancy; it was not customary to raise the rent on a sitting tenant. In addition, the Corn Production Act made it difficult for landowners to justify raising rents. An AWB enquiry in 1918 concluded that about 25 per cent of all farms had been subject to rent rises in the war, and that these rises averaged about 18 per cent, so that a rise in the national rent bill of only 4.5 per cent (18% × 25%) is implied. A larger enquiry by Ashby and Rhee showed the national rent bill as almost static; we have used their estimates to provide a weighted index of rents. While their estimates may be atypical, being heavily influenced by the data from one very large estate, even the 4.5 per cent implied by the AWB enquiry would only entail a rise in the national rent bill of £1.5 million by 1918.[2] Since the rental income of landowners remained almost fixed in money terms, and the general price level roughly doubled in the war, this implied a fall in their real income of roughly one-half. This severe squeeze was compounded by the fact that they customarily paid large sums from their gross income for new investment and maintenance on their farms. Thus their pre-war net income had been much below their gross income; Feinstein estimated for the UK that a gross rental income of £43 million (in 1908) became £25 million net.[3] To preserve this level of expenditure in wartime would be difficult. There is a strong presumption that landowners responded to the fall in their rental income (in real terms) by cutting down on maintenance. Two estates studied by McGregor (4,200 and 10,000 acres) showed that maintenance costs in 1910–14 had absorbed 42 per cent of rental income, but that this fell in 1915–19 to 26 per cent.[4]

In considering farmers' costs, we have estimated the variations in the wartime wage bill. From this, it appears that wage costs rose more slowly than inflation and farm product prices in 1914–17, although the gap was narrowed in 1918. The growth of this gap until 1918 partly reflects the decline in the civilian labour force as a consequence of recruiting and conscription. However, it also reflects the failure of wage rates to keep up with inflation.[5]

A contributory element in holding down costs was the sharp fall in the feed bill in 1918. This, however, had risen much more rapidly than other costs in 1914–17. Among the lesser items, machinery costs rose more or less *pro rata* for most of the war, and then increased substantially in 1918, presumably as farmers tried to meet the demands of the food production programme. The cost of Irish livestock varied, but on the whole tended to rise faster than total costs. Fertiliser costs rose more slowly than total costs until 1917, when they began to rise more rapidly. The rise was very rapid in 1918, as the plough policy took effect. The new category, government supplies (for which farmers had to pay), is not negligible by the end of the war, although the estimate must be regarded as very approximate.

The fact that gross income rose faster than farm costs meant that the net income of farmers rose very rapidly (Table 16.3).

Table 16.3: Farmers' net income, 1914–18 (= gross income LESS current costs, £ million)

	1909–13	1914	1915	1916	1917	1918
	52	58	87	119	163	177
As per cent	100	112	168	230	315	342

Since current costs had absorbed most (69 per cent) of pre-war gross income, it followed that net income would benefit disproportionately from any relative reduction in current costs. In financial terminology, farmers' net income was 'highly geared'. Thus it rose in the war at a rate which was considerably greater than the rate of inflation, whether measured by retail or wholesale prices, or by the prices of farm products.[6]

The rise in farmers' net income formed the basis for the sharp rise in profits which contemporaries thought existed. The feeling that profits were high prompted an enquiry by the AWB in 1918, held jointly with an enquiry into the cost of living of rural workers. The work on profits proved disappointing. The Committee distributed about 1,500 questionnaires to farmers, but only 119 were returned, and eventually the Committee was only able to base its conclusions on an analysis of the accounts of 26 tenant farms. These showed a sharp rise in profits, which reached their maximum in 1915–16, when they were 11.5 per cent of farmers' capital.[7]

Our estimate of farmers' net income does not amount to the same as farmers' profits during the war. Two further deductions must be made before a positive statement on the level of profit in the commercial sense can be made. Profit is here defined as the residual sum left after the full opportunity-costs of all factors of production used in producing the output of an enterprise have been deducted from the revenue accruing from the sale of the output. This formulation differs from the lay definition of profit in two ways. First, it takes account not only of the current costs of an enterprise for which payment has to be made, but also of the hidden costs which are entailed by the use of the entrepreneur's own capital and labour. Since, had these factors not been used in the enterprise, they could have earned economic returns in an alternative use, they may be said to incur opportunity-costs. Here, the terminology of current costs and opportunity-costs will be retained; the latter term will cover the farmers' use of his own capital and the manual labour of himself and his family. The second distinction is that, in this formulation, zero profit includes an allowance for 'normal' profit, that is, that profit which is just sufficient to keep the entrepreneur engaged in the business. Any profit above zero represents 'supernormal profit'.[8]

The final problem before assessing the level of profit is to decide on the number of farmers and their relatives employed in farming, since this affects the estimated opportunity-costs of using their labour.[9] There are two sources for this information: the 1908 *Census of Production*, and the 1911 *Census of Population*. Since these give different results, which cannot be reconciled, it was thought advisable to use both, unchanged, to provide two alternative estimates of farm profit (Table 16.4).

Table 16.4: British farming profits, 1914–18 (£ million)

(I) On 1908 Census of Production basis:						
	1909–13	*1914*	*1915*	*1916*	*1917*	*1918*
(A) Net income	51.7	57.7	86.9	118.8	163.1	177.0
(B) Opportunity-costs:						
Interest on capital	13.4	14.6	20.0	28.5	39.3	41.8
Farmers' labour	18.7	18.7	21.0	23.6	26.2	35.4
Relatives' labour	17.9	17.9	20.0	22.5	25.1	33.8
(C) PROFITS (A−B)	1.7	6.5	25.9	44.2	72.5	66.0
Profits as percentage return on farmers' capital	0.5	1.9	6.2	8.2	10.3	8.5

(II) On 1911 Census of Population basis:						
	1909–13	*1914*	*1915*	*1916*	*1917*	*1918*
(A) Net income	51.7	57.7	86.9	118.8	163.1	177.0
(B) Opportunity-costs:						
Interest on capital	13.4	14.6	20.0	28.5	39.3	41.8
Farmers' labour	11.3	11.3	12.7	14.2	15.8	21.4
Relatives' labour	6.7	6.7	7.5	8.4	9.4	12.7
(C) PROFITS (A − B)	20.3	25.1	46.7	67.7	98.6	101.1
Profits as percentage return on farmers' capital	6.3	7.4	11.2	12.6	14.1	13.1

Source: Appendix E and Dewey (1984/1), 378

During the war, it is apparent that super-normal profits were achieved in every year. Whichever of the two bases of calculation is preferred, the rate of profit growth is highest in 1914–15, and the highest rate of return is achieved in 1917. The average wartime rate of return on the 1908 basis is 7 per cent p.a., and 11.7 per cent p.a. on the 1911 basis. The AWB estimate averaged over the four war years covered in the survey falls between these two estimates, at 7.9 per cent. Whether one judges by the rate of rise in net income, or the rate of return on capital employed, farmers as a whole were clearly substantially better off during the war than before it. It may be added that our estimates of profit have been framed on a conservative basis, and may have erred on the side of underestimate. There is also the possibility that the profit estimates have been depressed by our use of the wholesale price index to revalue farmers' capital during the war. While this index had risen by 142 per cent by 1918, Somerville estimated that the cost of re-equipping a farm had risen only by 82 per cent by 1918.[10] If this is nearer the truth, then our profit estimates have been unduly depressed in two ways: by overestimating the opportunity-cost of farmers employing their own capital, and by depressing the final profit figure when expressed as a rate of return on farmers' capital.

If farming as a whole was more profitable during the war than formerly, this is not to say that all farms were equally profitable. It was suggested early on in the war that its initial impact had been more favourable for the cereal rather than the livestock producer.[11] It may be that the later stages of the war saw a reversal of this trend as the new policies of food production and control pushed farmers into less profitable lines of business. It is noticeable that the imposition of the food production programme was accompanied by a decline in the rate of return on farmers' capital when it became effective in 1918. Overall, there seems little doubt that the combined effect of the policies of food production and food control in 1917–18 was to reduce farmers' potential rate of return. While there is no satisfactory way of estimating the extent to which profits were thus squeezed after 1916, a rough indicator of the sums involved may be had by assuming that gross incomes and current costs continued to rise at the same rate in the second half of the war as during the first. On this assumption, net incomes would have been higher by £7 million in 1917 and £41 million in 1918; these are equivalent to a return on farmers' capital of 1 per cent in 1917 and 5 per cent in 1918.

It may finally be enquired whether these high war profits were effectively taxed by the state to any extent. It was certainly suggested in the House of Commons that farmers should be made subject to Excess Profits Duty, but since most farmers did not keep suitable accounts, such an exercise would have been doomed to failure.[12] It was this very inability to keep accounts which before 1914 had led to farmers being permitted to have their income tax assessed on the basis of their rent rather than their income; they were taxed on the assumption that their 'profits' (taken to mean net income) were one-third of the annual rental of the farm. Even before 1914, it was widely felt that this figure was too generous to farmers, especially since, when certain permitted deductions and exemptions had been taken into account, it meant that most farmers paid no income tax at all.[13]

The war spurred the government to raise farmers' taxation, but no new tax was introduced for this purpose, and the income tax yield from farmers did not rise sufficiently to make much impact on profits. In September 1915, the basis of assessment was raised to the full annual rental, and in 1918 to twice the rental.[14] Coupled with the higher wartime rates of income tax, this meant that farmers' income tax assessments rose many times over in the war, but even so, profits were not thereby greatly reduced. The total income tax bill for the whole war came to about £15 million, of which £7.3 million fell in the last year of the war, when inflation had in any case reduced the real burden of taxation.[15]

The rapid rise in farmers' net income, the stasis in rents, and the slowly rising wage bill meant that the balance of financial advantage in the industry had shifted heavily in favour of the farmer during wartime (Table 16.5).

Table 16.5: Division of income of the agricultural industry, 1914–18 (per cent)

	1909–13	1914	1915	1916	1917	1918
Landowners[a]	27	25	20	17	14	12
Farmers[b]	42	44	53	60	65	64
Labourers[c]	31	30	26	24	21	24
Total income (£ million)	123	131	163	199	250	277

Notes: [a] Gross rent (Table 16.2) [b] Net income (Table 16.3)

[c] Farmers' payments to non-family labour (Table 16.2)

Thus farmers were able to raise their share of the income of the industry from about two-fifths before the war to almost two-thirds in 1917–18. This took place chiefly at the expense of landowners, and partly at the expense of labourers. This was accompanied by a severe fall in the real incomes of landowners, and a lesser fall in that of labourers. Neither of these groups could effectively resist these processes. The landowners suffered from the lack of an institutional mechanism with which to raise rents in line with inflation, and fell foul of the rent restrictions of the Corn Production Act. The labourers, whose bargaining position was not strong before the war, found it eroded further during it, as trade union membership fell; that of the largest union, the National Union of Agricultural Workers, having been only about 9,000 in 1914, was down to 7,000 in 1916.[16] This organisational weakness made it difficult to oppose the bringing in of government supplies of replacement labour, which reached high levels in 1917–18. However, the erosion of real incomes was largely made good by the actions of the government in 1917–18, with the inception of the minimum wage and the work of the AWB. In general, it may be said that farmers benefited financially from the war because they were in a seller's market. In addition, the fall in their real level of current costs was not accompanied by a proportionate fall in their revenues. The other two groups were either not in a seller's market (as seems likely in the case of labour, given that the labour shortage was not especially acute), or found institutional barriers to joining it; for the landowners, these took the form of sitting tenants and rent restrictions.

NOTES

1 See Appendices A, C, and E for an analysis of the components of farm income, and of the sources and methods used in their estimation.
2 Agricultural Wages Board, *Financial results . . .*, Cmd. 76 (1916), 9–11; A. W. Ashby and H. A. Rhee, *The Rent of Agricultural Land in England and Wales, 1870–1939* (Oxford, 1946), 10.
3 C. H. Feinstein, *National Income, Expenditure and Output of the United Kingdom 1855–1965* (Cambridge, 1972), 41.
4 J. J. MacGregor, 'The economic history of two rural estates in Cambridgeshire, 1870–1934', *JRASE* 98 (1937), 148–56.
5 Cmd. 24, para. 272; Ashby, 'The work of the AWB in 1918', 139–55.
6 Dewey, 'British farming profits', 377.
7 Cmd. 76, para. 192.
8 R. G. Lipsey, *An Introduction to Positive Economics* (5th edn, 1979), 240.
9 Since estimates of the sums paid by farmers to their relatives are rare, it is of interest that Feinstein calculates that UK farmers paid £12 million to their relatives in 1908 (*National Income*, 41).
10 Cmd. 76, 61.
11 R. H. Rew, 'Farming and food supplies in time of war', *JBA* (1915), 218.
12 J. Stamp, *Taxation During the War* (1932), 71.
13 Ibid., 46.

14 Ibid., 46, 124.
15 Dewey, 'British farming profits', 386.
16 R. Groves, *Sharpen the Sickle! The History of the Farm Workers' Union* (1949), 245.

Chapter Seventeen

THE LEGACY

To contemporaries, the significance of the history of British agriculture during the First World War seemed clear; it was that it had contributed substantially to the avoidance of food shortage. This is not a view which finds support here. The efforts of the Food Production Department were severely undermined by the shortage of animal feed. The result was that home food production was merely restored to the pre-war level, having fallen slightly in the first half of the conflict. While this was a useful contribution, it was a minor one. The contribution of the FPD was also dwarfed by the addition to the supply of food brought about by the breadstuffs policy. The effects of this, coupled with the extra food produced by home agriculture in 1917–18, meant that there was no shortage of any essential food during the war. It could even be suggested that the work of the FPD was unnecessary. Given the impact of the breadstuffs policy, and that home production had been particularly depressed in 1916 by poor harvests, the supply of food would have revived in 1917–18 even without the plough policy.

The reduction in meat and milk output in 1918 was largely due to the shortage of imported feed, and serves as a reminder that the rationale behind the plough policy was not only to produce more domestic food, but to save shipping space, with a view to bringing USA troops and materials to the European front. In this, it was successful. It must also be borne in mind that the plough policy was as much an insurance against future shortage as a remedy for immediate needs. T. H. Middleton, while making considerable claims for the success of the policy, also referred to it lightly as 'The Country's War Risks (Food) Insurance Policy'.[1] This may have been the longer-term intention, and if so it was a prudent one in the uncertainties of 1917. But one doubts whether the intention could have been fulfilled; the policy was running out of steam after the call for recruits in April 1918, and had been effectively abandoned before the Armistice.

Policy apart, the most striking feature of wartime agriculture was its stability. This is seen in several ways: the comparatively slight fall in real output over the whole war period; the comparatively slight fall in food production to 1916, and the more or less equally slight recovery to 1918; and the fact that the structure of output remained almost unchanged until 1917, under conditions of some difficulty. Structural change thereafter was quite substantial, but produced by policy rather than the free decisions of farmers. How farmers managed as well as they did in conditions of increasing factor scarcity up to the end of 1916 is something of a mystery. While it is argued here that in the important case of labour supply the position was much more favourable than was assumed at the time, there was still a labour shortage, as well as a fertiliser and feed shortage. That these were largely obviated speaks volumes for the adaptability of the farming system, of farmers and of the labour force.

In the longer run, it seemed that the war had left few marks on agriculture. True, the government was for the time being committed to the maintenance of the system of price guarantees initiated by the Corn Production Act. This encouraged the proponents of a permanent plough policy, who thought that the time had come to make the country as self-supporting in food as possible. An extreme representative of this school was Lord Lee's successor, Sir Charles Fielding. His suggestion was that the UK should become entirely self-supporting in food, by means of the ploughing of 16 million acres for cereals – over half as much again as the acreage of 1918.[2] But such hopes were dashed when the government abandoned the price guarantees after the sharp fall in agricultural prices in 1921. Thereafter, agriculture was left to find its own salvation with little government support, until the depression of the 1930s forced a reconsideration.[3]

Nor was it the case that the war permanently altered the economic position of agriculture within the British economy. In all important respects, pre-war trends reasserted themselves after a few years. Thus the proportion of males in the UK labour force occupied in agriculture, which had been 27.3 per cent in 1851, had fallen to

11.1 per cent in 1911; after the war it continued to fall, to 9.8 per cent in 1921, and to 8.7 per cent in 1931. The proportion of the national income accounted for by agriculture also continued to shrink, as it had done in the nineteenth century; having been 8.6 per cent in 1891, it was down to 4.1 per cent in 1924.[4]

There were, however two important legacies of the war. The first lay in the lessons of policy. When the international situation deteriorated in the 1930s, and it became apparent that Britain would face a military position similar to, but even more serious than, that of 1914–18, official thoughts turned once more to the question of home food supply. In spite of the slight gains registered by the FPD (which were not apparent at the time), the policy had been soundly based on scientific and military grounds. It had also been demonstrated that such a policy could be carried out with a considerable degree of administrative smoothness. Thus the ECs were reconstituted, and the policy of 1917–18 replayed in 1939–45, to much greater effect. In terms of calories, UK food output (net of the contribution of imported feedstuffs) rose by 91 per cent between 1938–9 and 1943–4.[5]

The other, longer-term, legacy concerned the structure of landholding. Although the beginnings of a tendency on the part of landowners to divest themselves of their agricultural estates had been discerned immediately before 1914, it had not gone very far before the war intervened. The deterioration of the landowners' financial position during the war was very considerable. By the Armistice, their real incomes from rents had been roughly halved, and arrears of maintenance and repair waited to be overcome. Some landowners met the new situation by raising rents, particularly on a change of tenancy, but many preferred to take advantage of the high land prices of the time and sell, leaving their successors to incur the odium of raising rents. There was also a taxation incentive; in 1919, a change in the method of calculating death duties gave heirs an incentive to sell land rather than other assets in order to pay death duties. From the point of view of the tenants, their high wartime incomes, which continued until 1921, provided the means with which to buy the holding. The stasis of rents provided an incentive to purchase, since tenants could only foresee a large increase in rent if they continued as tenants, either with the original owner or a new purchaser. A. G. Street, taking over his late fathers' farm in 1918, was faced with an increased rent demand from the estate agents of nearly 100 per cent, on a 'take it or leave it' basis. He took it, borrowing the working capital (from his mother) at 5 per cent, a move he regretted shortly afterwards, in the depression of 1921–3.[6]

The depression of 1921–3 was a brief interruption in a process of land sales which began before the war, reached feverish levels in 1919–21, and then resumed in a more modest way in 1924–6. By 1927, when reliable estimates are available, the proportion of agricultural holdings occupied by their owners had risen to 37 per cent, having been only 13 per cent in 1909. The bulk of these sales had occurred in 1919–21.[7] This enormous transfer of land, which between 1909 and 1927 may have amounted to between six and eight million acres, has been described as probably the largest since the Norman Conquest. It was certainly a watershed in the history of landownership and rural life.[8]

Finally, the experience of agriculture during the war lends support to some generalisations. Firstly, the dominant theme was of continuity rather than dramatic change. Thus the danger of food shortage in wartime was much exaggerated, as were the achievements of the Food Production Department; nor did the war permanently alter the structure of agricultural production, or check the long-term decline of agriculture as a part of the national economy. In all these instances, the truth was less dramatic and more prosaic than it seemed to contemporaries. Secondly, the fact that British agriculture maintained output comparatively well in the face of considerable shortages of factors of production (even if they were not as serious as many assumed) suggests that farmers and their labour force were capable of considerable ingenuity, most of which has eluded historians. Lastly, the successful administration of the food production policy speaks volumes for the comparatively high degree of political and social unity in British society. Although the policy was soundly based in scientific terms, and executed with tactful efficiency by the county Executive Committees, it could not have achieved even its limited success without the intelligent co-operation of the local farmers and administrators.[9]

NOTES

1 Middleton, *Food Production*, 309.
2 Fielding, *Food* (1923), 251.

3 See, e.g., A. Webber, 'Government policy and British agriculture, 1917–1939', unpublished Ph.D. thesis, University of Kent, 1982.
4 Mitchell and Deane, *Abstract*, 60–1, 366; figures are for agriculture, horticulture, and forestry.
5 Murray, *Agriculture*, 242 (1943–4 is an unofficial estimate).
6 Street, *Farmer's Glory*, 219.
7 S. G. Sturmey, 'Owner-farming in England and Wales, 1900–1950', in Minchinton, *Essays*, II, 287–96.
8 F. M. L. Thompson, *English Landed Society in the Nineteenth Century* (1963), 332–3.
9 Compare French and German experience in the First World War, in Dewey, thesis, chs 26 and 27.

APPENDICES

(All appendices refer to Britain)

APPENDIX A: TOTAL AGRICULTURAL PRODUCTION, 1914–18
('000 tons unless otherwise stated)

	1909–13	1914	1915	1916	1917	1918
Crops						
Wheat	1,598	1,706	1,961	1,559	1,634	2,428
Barley	1,329	1,367	986	1,110	1,189	1,299
Oats	2,050	2,033	2,168	2,100	2,280	2,965
Beans ('000 qrs)	1,038	1,113	919	889	466	922
Peas ('000 qrs)	604	373	300	261	277	439
Potatoes	3,604	4,031	3,830	3,036	4,451	5,360
Turnips and swedes	21,524	19,762	19,340	18,882	20,217	17,532
Mangolds	8,578	7,961	7,890	7,382	8,535	8,280
Hay	8,817	8,135	7,352	9,872	8,461	7,604
Cabbages	918	789	759	716	587	589
Hops ('000 cwt)	295	507	255	308	221	130
Dairy produce						
Milk (mn galls)	1,149	1,243	1,175	1,104	1,026	915
Livestock						
Horses ('000)	79	127	94	27	59	59
Cattle ('000)	1,803	1,895	1,751	1,845	1,909	1,769
Sheep ('000)	10,972	9,489	9,309	9,657	10,120	9,982
Pigs ('000)	3,663	3,337	3,779	3,566	2,617	1,623
Other products						
Wool (mn lb)	121	108	110	113	113	107
Poultry[a]	55	55	55	55	48	48
Eggs (mn)[a]	1,139	1,139	1,139	1,139	1,014	934
Fruit[a]	365	405	365	330	400	270

[a] Based on consumption figures in Beveridge, *Food Control*, 360–1

Sources and methods:

Crops: Acreage and yields per acre obtained from the annual *Agricultural Statistics*. Fruit, poultry and eggs output was estimated by use of the 1908 census of production, and production estimated as proportionate to the estimates of UK consumption in Beveridge, *Food Control*, 360–1. For straw, see Appendix C.

Animals: Annual production of livestock was estimated on the basis of a disappearance formula from an enquiry by the Oxford Agricultural Economics Research Institute (Agriculture and Industry Enquiry: Research Papers on the Gross Output of Farm Products in the United Kingdom, 1867–1938; unpublished typescript, 1954–5), of the form:

$$Or = (Mo - Mi) + i + b - d$$

where

Or is the realised gross output (i.e., the output which is realised by being sold off farms or consumed in farm households),

Mo is the total population at the beginning of the year,

Mi is the total population at the end of the year,

i is the number of imported store stock,

b is the number of births during the year,

d is the number of deaths during the year.

Information on death rates was taken from the 1908 census of production, the 1913 census of production (PRO, MAF 38/94), and the article by Guild, *JRSS* LXXXIII (1920). It may be noted that this procedure gives numbers of animals slaughtered which are much lower than those implied (for the UK) by Prest and Adams or Beveridge.

Milk: Based on the 1908 census; wartime estimates from the final report of the Committee on Production of Milk (Astor Committee), 1919. The 1908 estimate of yield per cow was amended in accordance with the suggestions in the 1925 census of production for England and Wales (PP 1927, XXV), 62.

Poultry and eggs: Pre-war production taken as that in 1908, and wartime production assumed proportionate to the variations in UK consumption in Beveridge, *Food Control*, 360–1.

Wool: Sheep populations from the *Agricultural Statistics*; wool yields per animal from the 1908 census. Skin wool production calculated from the estimated number of slaughterings, and the estimate of the weight of skin wool per carcass in the 1908 census.

APPENDIX B: FARM SELF-SUPPLIES

	1909–13	*1914*	*1915*	*1916*	*1917*	*1918*
Milk (mn galls)	79	81	75	74	72	72
Butter ('000 cwt)	176	176	164	160	157	157
Cheese ('000 cwt)	24	24	22	22	21	21
Eggs (mn)	465	465	432	423	414	414
Poultry (mn birds)	23	23	23	23	20	20
Beef and veal (mn lb)	45	47	44	46	46	38
Mutton and lamb (mn lb)	33	29	28	29	28	24
Pigmeat (mn lb)	29	27	30	29	19	11
Potatoes ('000 tons)	43	43	43	43	43	43

Farm self-supplies were valued at the market prices used to value gross output

Sources: Prest and Adams, *Consumers' Expenditure*. Their estimate for meat used by farm families in the UK is rather rough, viz., 5 per cent of total production, but in default of more precise information, it has been adopted for Britain. Potato consumption has been estimated by applying Beveridge's figure of UK consumption per head to the agricultural population in 1908 as recorded at the census of production.

APPENDIX C: GROSS FARM OUTPUT (PHYSICAL QUANTITIES)

(= Total production, LESS seed, farm animal feed, and farm family self-supplies)

('ooo tons)	1909–13	1914	1915	1916	1917	1918
Wheat	991	1,058	1,216	967	1,013	1,505
Barley	545	560	404	455	487	533
Oats	697	793	954	861	1,118	1,482
Beans ('ooo qrs)[a]	1,038	1,113	919	889	466	922
Peas ('ooo qrs)[a]	604	373	300	261	277	439
Potatoes	2,443	2,772	2,651	1,923	2,952	3,836
Hay	3,705	3,818	4,130	4,490	4,850	4,970
Straw	2,014	2,075	2,225	2,440	2,636	2,701
Cabbages	918	789	759	716	587	589
Hops	295	507	255	308	221	130
Wool: fleece (mn lb)	90	82	85	86	85	80
Wool: skin (mn lb)	30	26	26	27	28	27
Milk (mn galls)	803	886	831	767	708	613
Butter ('ooo cwt)	509	529	529	524	476	434
Cheese ('ooo cwt)	500	500	500	485	485	510
Cream ('ooo galls)	931	1,089	931	773	521	130
Cattle ('ooo)	1,713	1,800	1,663	1,753	1,814	1,680
Sheep ('ooo)	10,423	9,015	8,844	9,174	9,614	9,483
Pigs ('ooo)	3,480	3,170	3,590	3,388	2,486	1,542
Horses ('ooo)	79[a]	127	94	27	59	59
Poultry	32	32	32	32	28	28
Eggs (mn)	674	674	707	716	600	520
Apples[b]	135	155	130	110	150	105
Other fruit[b]	230	250	235	220	250	165

Notes: [a] 1911–13
[b] Based on variations in UK consumption

Method: Deductions of farm self-supplies (above) were made. For seed and feed, deductions were made following the calculations of the AERI, amounting to 38 per cent of wheat production, 59 per cent of barley, and 63 per cent of oats production. For potatoes, the AERI suggestions of 17 cwt per acre for seed and 17 per cent of total production for feed were adopted. For straw, the estimate is for consumption by non-farm horses, civilian and military; numbers of horses were obtained from *Agricultural Statistics* and War Office, *Statistics of the Military Effort* (1922); straw consumption was estimated at roughly 1.3 tons per head p.a., derived from *Stephen's Book of the Farm* (1908) and H. J. Webb, *Advanced Agriculture* (1894).

APPENDIX D: GROSS FARM OUTPUT AT 1909–13 PRICES
(£ million)

	1909–13	1914	1915	1916	1917	1918
Wheat	7.7	8.2	9.5	7.5	7.9	11.7
Barley	4.1	4.2	3.0	3.4	3.7	4.0
Oats	4.8	5.5	6.6	5.9	7.7	10.2
Potatoes	9.4	10.7	10.3	7.4	11.5	14.9
Milk	23.8	26.2	24.6	22.7	20.9	18.1
Butter	2.8	2.9	2.9	2.9	2.6	2.4
Cheese	1.4	1.4	1.4	1.4	1.4	1.4
Cream	0.2	0.2	0.2	0.2	0.1	a
Cattle and calves	26.2	27.6	25.4	26.9	26.6	22.0
Sheep and lambs	21.9	18.7	18.4	19.1	18.3	15.3
Pigs	15.7	14.3	16.3	15.3	10.2	5.2
Horses	2.8	4.4	3.3	0.9	2.1	2.1
Hay	16.1	16.6	17.8	19.5	21.1	21.6
Straw	5.7	5.8	6.3	6.9	7.4	7.6
Hops	2.3	4.0	2.0	2.5	1.8	1.0
Wool	5.2	4.6	4.7	4.8	4.8	4.6
Peas	0.9	0.6	0.5	0.4	0.4	0.7
Beans	1.7	1.8	1.5	1.4	0.7	1.5
Cabbages	1.0	0.8	0.8	0.8	0.6	0.6
Poultry	3.8	3.8	3.8	3.8	3.4	3.4
Eggs	3.4	3.4	3.6	3.7	3.1	2.7
Fruit	5.3	5.8	5.4	4.9	5.8	3.9
Totals	166.2	171.5	168.3	162.3	162.1	154.9
As per cent	100.0	103.2	101.3	97.7	97.5	93.2

Note: a <£0.1 million

Method: Gross output at 1909–13 market prices (derived from the annual *Agricultural Statistics*).

APPENDIX E: GROSS FARM OUTPUT AT CURRENT PRICES,
1914–18 (£ million)

	1909–13	1914	1915	1916	1917	1918
Wheat	7.7	8.6	15.0	13.2	17.9	25.5
Oats	4.4	6.0	10.3	10.3	20.0	26.2
Barley	4.1	4.3	4.2	6.8	8.8	8.8
Potatoes	9.4	11.0	12.7	15.8	28.5	30.6
Milk	23.8	29.5	32.2	38.3	44.0	47.2
Butter	2.8	2.9	3.7	4.2	4.9	5.2
Cheese	1.4	1.5	1.8	2.1	2.9	3.3
Cream	0.2	0.2	0.2	0.2	0.2	0.1
Cattle	26.2	29.4	34.9	42.7	55.0	43.0
Sheep	21.9	22.3	24.7	30.9	37.0	30.3
Pigs	15.7	15.1	20.5	25.5	22.8	13.9
Horses	2.8	5.1	4.7	1.6	4.1	4.7
Hay	16.1	13.1	19.6	31.3	34.9	41.9
Straw	5.7	4.6	6.2	10.6	10.1	13.9
Hops	2.3	1.9	1.4	2.2	1.7	2.2
Wool	5.2	5.3	7.8	9.0	8.3	8.4
Peas	0.9	0.5	0.4	0.5	0.8	2.5
Beans	1.7	1.8	1.9	2.1	1.7	5.8
Cabbage	1.0	0.8	0.9	0.9	1.2	1.6
Poultry	3.8	3.6	4.3	5.2	5.6	8.6
Eggs	3.4	3.8	4.8	6.0	6.6	9.4
Fruit	5.3	4.5	4.6	6.1	8.3	14.9
Totals	166.2	175.8	216.8	265.5	325.3	348.0
As per cent	100.0	105.8	130.4	159.7	195.7	209.4

Source: Gross output (Table C), in current prices from the *Agricultural Statistics*

APPENDIX F: 'CONVENTIONAL' FARM LABOUR SUPPLY,
1915–18
('000 man-units)

	Pre-war (1908)	1915	1916	1917	1918
1. Farmers and their families					
Farmers	480	482	477	472	468
Males >18 yrs	229	213	203	197	198
Males <18 yrs	50	47	44	43	43
Females >18 yrs	115	108	116	118	124
Females <18 yrs	22	21	22	23	24
(Totals)	(896)	(871)	(862)	(853)	(857)
2. Hired labour (regular)					
Males >18 yrs	465	400	358	335	340
Males <18 yrs	67	58	51	48	49
Females >18 yrs	56	49	57	59	65
Females <18 yrs	12	10	12	12	14
(Totals)	(600)	(517)	(478)	(454)	(468)

Appendix F, cont.

3. Hired labour (casual)

Males >18 yrs	26*	21	17	17	12
Males <18 yrs	3	3	2	2	1
Females >18 yrs	7	8	9	10	8
Females <18 yrs	1	1	1	1	1
Irish males	8	8	8	–	–
(Totals)	(45)	(41)	(37)	(30)	(22)
Totals	1,541	1,429	1,377	1,337	1,347

Notes: Farmers are assumed all male

Farmers on holdings 'not farmed for business' are excluded (5–6 per cent of all holdings in 1908)

Source: Board of Trade Z8 surveys 1914–18, and assumptions above, p. 44–5.

APPENDIX G: REPLACEMENT LABOUR IN FARMING, 1915–18

('000 man-units)

	1915	1916	1917	1918
Village women	0	6	25	30
Soldiers	11	14	28	66
Prisoners of war	0	0	3	14
Women's Land Army	0	0	3	8
Miscellaneous	4	10	15	17
Totals	15	30	74	135

Sources:

PRO, MAF 59/1, L. 29047, L. 29369.

MAF 42/8, 40171/D.

NATS 1/53, R. 105, 8/232/3, L. 1/627.

CAB 23/2, 135(10).

CAB 23/3, 170(1).

Imperial War Museum; Women's Land Army archive, LAND IV, V.

War Cabinet, *Annual Report of the War Cabinet, 1917*, PP 1918, XIV, 260; *Annual Report of the War Cabinet, 1918*, PP 1919, XXX, 236–7.

Board of Agriculture, *Wages and Conditions of Employment in Agriculture*, Pt. II, Cmd. 25, PP 1919, X.

Board of Education, *School Attendance and Employment in Agriculture*: Cd. 7881 (1915) PP 1914–16, L, 4; Cd. 7932 (1915), PP 1914–16, L, 5; Cd. 8202 (1916), PP 1916, XXII, 4; Cd. 8302 (1916), PP 1916, XXII, 4; Cd. 8171 (1916), PP 1916, XXII, 4.

I. O. Andrews and M. A. Hobbs, *Economic Effects of the War upon Women and Children in Great Britain* (New York, 2nd edn, 1920), 29, 47, 74.

Lord Ernle (R. E. Prothero), *English Farming Past and Present* (6th edn, 1961), 398.

S. J. Hurwitz, *State Intervention in Great Britain, 1914–1919* (2nd edn., 1968), 219.

D. Lloyd George, *War Memoirs* (1934), III, 1310–16.

T. H. Middleton, *Food Production in War* (Oxford, 1923), 144, 185–6, 208, 223, 231, 235, 239, 266.

APPENDIX H: THE BOARD OF TRADE Z8 EMPLOYMENT
SURVEYS, 1914–18

Surveys were conducted for these months:

1914 October, December.
1915 February, April, July, October.
1916 January, April, July, October.
1917 January, April, July, October.
1918 January, April, July, November.
1919 January,[a] April.

Note: [a] Combined with Nov. 1918

Results were taken for the end of the month. The result for November 1918 is for Armistice Day. A report for July 1917 was written, but has not survived; July 1917 results have been taken from subsequent surveys.

When stated, the numbers of replies received at each survey (in England and Wales) were:

1915		*1916*		*1917*		*1918*	
April	6,150	January	4,626	January	4,934	January	5,297
July	6,240	April	4,780	April	4,433	April	5,870
October	5,350	July	4,071	July	?	July	5,504
		October	5,032	October	4,299	November	3,395

The November sample was perhaps untypical. Leaving this aside, the results may be compared with the 228,788 farmers in Britain returned at the 1911 population census, or the 430,081 occupiers of agricultural holdings returned at the 1908 census of production. On the 1911 basis, the sample achieved is 1.8–2.7% of the total farmer population, and on the 1908 basis it is 0.95–1.5% of the total population.

In Scotland the rate of response was much higher. The first information is for April 1915, when 'over 6,000' forms were sent out, eliciting 'nearly 3,000 return'. The number of replies given on other occasions was:

1916		*1917*		*1918*	
April	2,101	January	2,288	April	3,006
July	2,350	April	2,218	July	2,802
October	2,327			November	2,297[a]

Note: [a] And Jan. 1919

These samples correspond to 4.1–5.9% of the number of farmers (including crofters) returned at the population census of 1911, or 2.7–3.8% of the number of holdings in 1908.

Appendix H, cont.

Characteristics of the sample achieved

1. Average farm size of survey respondents:

England and Wales:

Annual averages

	acres
1915	351
1916	342
1917	341
1918	341

Scotland:

1915	490
1916	494
1918	549

2. Area under crops and grass (mn acres):

England and Wales:

	Total acreage	Z8 acreage	per cent
1915	27.05	2.08	7.6
1916	27.07	1.57	5.8
1917	27.08	1.55	5.7
1918	26.99	1.71	6.3

Scotland:

	Total acreage	Z8 acreage	per cent
1915	13.91	1.47 (Apr.)	10.2
1916	13.94	1.15 (Oct.)	8.2
1918	14.30	1.53 (July)	10.7

APPENDIX I: FERTILISER CONSUMPTION, 1914–18

	1909–13	*1914*	*1915*	*1916*	*1917*	*1918*
1. Quantities ('000 tons)						
Sodium nitrate	90	122	62	17	0	0
Ammonium sulphate	60	(70)	(80)	80	150	230
Superphosphate	694	799	579	558	476	801
Basic slag	263	263	263	262	258	238
2. Value at						
1909–13 prices (£ '000)						
Sodium nitrate	905	1,299	660	181	0	0
Ammonium sulphate	807	941	1,076	1,076	2,017	3,093
Superphosphate	1,894	2,037	1,476	1,422	1,309	2,042
Basic slag	452	452	452	451	444	409
Totals	4,058	4,729	3,664	3,130	3,770	5,544

Appendix I, cont.

3. Value at
current prices (£ '000)

Sodium nitrate	905	1,247	779	299	0	0
Ammonium sulphate	807	762	1,119	1,356	2,400	3,557
Superphosphate	1,894	2,098	1,801	2,389	2,945	4,819
Basic slag	452	452	551	735	835	814

Source: Dewey, thesis, 81

APPENDIX J: PURCHASED FEED CONSUMPTION, 1914–18
('000 tons)

	1909–13	*1914*	*1915*	*1916*	*1917*	*1918*
Cereals						
Wheat offals	2,000	2,100	2,150	1,800	1,800	900
Barley meal and flour	300	250	200	250	0	0
Maize products	350	350	400	300	200	100
Totals	2,650	2,700	2,750	2,350	2,000	1,000
Oilcake						
Cotton cake:						
Imported (net)	200	179	211	192	132	3
Home produced	328	335	259	172	114	176
Totals	528	514	470	364	246	179
Linseed cake:						
Imported (net)	78	44	67	74	77	8
Home produced	239	316	274	324	129	169
Totals	317	360	341	398	206	177
Rapeseed cake:						
Imported (net)	27	37	8	1	1	0
Home produced	27	40	25	48	39	37
Totals	54	77	33	49	40	37
Total cake:	899	951	844	811	492	393

Feed consumption at pre-war (1911–13) prices (£ million)

	1909–13	*1914*	*1915*	*1916*	*1917*	*1918*
Wheat offals	10.2	10.7	10.7	9.2	9.2	4.6
Barley meal and flour	2.3	2.3	1.6	1.6	0	0
Maize products	1.8	1.8	2.4	1.8	1.2	0.6
Cotton cake	3.0	2.9	2.6	2.0	1.4	1.0
Linseed cake	2.8	3.1	3.0	3.5	1.8	1.5
Rape cake	0.3	0.4	0.2	0.2	0.2	0.2
Total value	20.4	21.2	20.5	18.3	13.8	7.9

Feed consumption at current prices (£ million)

	1909–13	1914	1915	1916	1917	1918
Wheat offals	10.2	11.1	14.7	17.1	23.6	11.9
Barley meal and flour	2.3	2.3	2.2	2.9	0	0
Maize products	1.8	2.3	4.0	3.8	3.4	2.1
Cotton cake	3.0	2.7	3.4	3.9	3.9	2.6
Linseed cake	2.8	2.9	3.7	5.4	4.2	3.4
Rape cake	0.3	0.4	0.2	0.4	0.5	0.5
Total value	20.4	21.7	28.2	33.5	35.6	20.5

Source: Dewey, thesis, 86–9

The supply of power in agriculture, 1914–18

This has been roughly estimated (Table 14.3) by adding the HP supplied by agricultural horses and the tractor, on the basis of 1 horse = $2/3$ HP, and each tractor being rated at 25 HP. It is assumed that the average number of tractors at work was 3,000 in 1917 and 7,000 in 1918.

SELECT BIBLIOGRAPHY

DOCUMENTARY MATERIAL

Imperial War Museum, Women's Land Army archive
Public Record Office, files of the Board of Agriculture, Ministry of
National Service and War Cabinet
Bodleian Library, Oxford; Selborne Papers
Institute of Agricultural History, Reading University, archives of
Ransomes Sims and Jefferies, and Fowler and Co.

County Record Offices:

Bedfordshire	Huntingdonshire	Somerset
Cheshire	Lancashire	East Suffolk
Essex	Lindsey (Lincs.)	West Sussex
Gloucestershire	Norfolk	Wiltshire
Herefordshire	Oxfordshire	Worcestershire
Hertfordshire	Salop	

With the exception of East Suffolk, these ROs were consulted for their
holdings of County War Agricultural Committee or Agricultural
Executive Committee material.

JOURNALS AND NEWSPAPERS

Title	Abbreviation
Agricultural History Review	*AgHR*
Economic History Review	*EcHR*
Farm Economist	
Farmer and Stockbreeder	*FSB*
Implement and Machinery Review	*IMR*
Journal of the Board of Agriculture	*JBA*
Journal of (Proceedings of)	
the Agricultural Economics Society	*JPAES/JAE*
Journal of the Board of Trade	

Journal of the Highland
    and Agricultural Society of Scotland   JHAS
Journal of the Royal
    Agricultural Society of England   JRASE
Journal of the Royal
    Statistical Society   JRSS
The Labourer
Mark Lane Express
    and Agricultural Journal   MLE
The Times

PARLIAMENTARY PAPERS

Agriculture, Board of, *The Agricultural Output of Great Britain: report on enquiries made in connection with the Census of Production Act 1906*, Cd. 6277, PP 1912–13, X.
—— *Agricultural Statistics*, 1909–18.
—— *Interim Report of the Departmental Committee appointed by the President of the Board of Agriculture to consider the Production of Food in England and Wales* (Milner Committee), Cd. 8048 (1915), PP 1914–16, V. Final Report, Cd. 8095 (1915).
—— *Committee on the Production and Distribution of Milk* (Astor Committee), Interim Report, Cd. 8608, 2nd Interim Report, Cd. 8886, Final Report, Cmd. 483.
—— *The Recent Development of German Agriculture*, by T. H. Middleton, Cd. 8305 (1916).
—— *Report on Wages and Conditions of Employment in Agriculture* (1919), Cmd. 24, 25, PP 1919, IX.
—— Committee of the Agricultural Wages Board: *Report of the Enquiry into the Financial Results of the Occupation of Agriculture and the Cost of Living of Rural Workers*, Cmd. 76 (1919), PP 1919, VIII.
Agriculture, Ministry of, *Report of the Departmental Committee on Agricultural Machinery*, Cmd. 506 (1919), PP 1919, VIII.
—— *The Agricultural Output of England and Wales 1925*, Cmd. 2815, PP 1927, XXV.
Agriculture, Scotland, Board of, *Annual Reports, 1912–18*.
Agriculture and Technical Instruction (Ireland), Department for, *Report . . . on Irish migratory agricultural and other labourers*, Cd. 8036, PP 1914–16, LXXIX; Cd. 8386, PP 1916, XXXII.
Annual statement of trade of the United Kingdom, 1909–18.
Census of Population 1911.
Census of Population (Scotland) 1911.
Departmental committee on sulphuric acid and fertiliser trades, *Report on the post-war position of the sulphuric acid and fertiliser trades*, Cmd. 29, PP 1919, XXIX.
Education, Board of, *School Attendance and Employment in Agriculture, 1915–16*, Cd. 7881, Cd. 7932 (PP 1914–16, L), Cd. 8202, Cd. 8302, Cd. 8171 (PP 1916, XXII).

—— *Correspondence relating to school attendance . . . (1915)*, Cd. 7803, PP 1914–16, L.

—— *Annual Reports, 1914–19.*

Inland Revenue, Board of, *Annual Reports, 1914–18.*

Royal Commission on Agriculture, *Interim Report*, Cd. 473, PP 1919, VIII.

Royal Commission on the Supply of Food and Raw Material in Time of War, *Report*, Cd. 2643, PP 1905, XXXIX.

Royal Society, *The Food Supply of the United Kingdom*, Cd. 8421, PP 1916, IX.

Trade, Board of, *Report on the State of Employment in the United Kingdom in October 1914*, Cd. 7703; *. . . in February 1915*, Cd. 7850; subsequent reports 1915–19 not published.

War Cabinet, *Women in Industry*, Cmd. 135, PP 1919, XXXI.

—— *Report for the year 1917*, Cd. 9005, PP 1918, XIV.

—— *Report for the year 1918*, Cmd. 325, PP 1919, XXX.

War Office, *Allowances and pensions in respect of seamen, marines and soldiers and their wives, widows and dependents.* Cd. 7662, PP 1914–16, XL.

Working classes cost of living committee (Sumner Committee), *Report*, Cd. 8980, PP 1918, VII.

BOOKS AND ARTICLES

(Place of publication is London unless stated otherwise)

Agricultural Engineers' Association, *Report on trade conditions in the agricultural machinery and implement industry* (1924).

Agriculture, Ministry of, *A Century of Agricultural Statistics* (1968).

Amos, Arthur, 'Motor ploughs and motor ploughing', *JRASE* 76 (1915).

Andrews, I. O. and Hobbs, M., *Economic Effects of the War upon Women and Children in Great Britain* (New York, 2nd edn, 1920).

Ashby, A. W., 'Agricultural conditions and policies, 1910–38', in *Agriculture in the Twentieth Century. Essays presented to Sir Daniel Hall* (Oxford, 1939).

—— 'The work of the Agricultural Wages Board', *JRASE* 79 (1918).

—— *The Agricultural Labourer in Great Britain during the War* (unpublished typescript, 1921).

—— and Davies, J. L., 'Farming efficiency and the agricultural depression', *JPAES* 1 (1929).

—— and Evans, I. L., *The Agriculture of Wales and Monmouthshire* (Cardiff, 1944).

—— and Rhee, H. A., *The Rent of Agricultural Land in England and Wales, 1870–1939* (Oxford, 1946).

Ashby, M. K., *Joseph Ashby of Tysoe, 1859–1919; a study of English village life* (Cambridge, 1961).

Barnett, C., *Britain and her Army 1509–1970; a military, political and social survey* (1970).

Barnett, L. M., *British Food Policy during the First World War* (1985).

Bellerby, J. R. 'Distribution of farm income in the United Kingdom 1867–1938', *JPAES* X, 2 (1954).

—— and Boreham, A. J., 'Farm occupiers' capital in the United Kingdom before 1939', *Farm Economist*, VII, 6 (1953).

Beveridge, (Sir) W. H., *British Food Control* (1928).

Bonnett, H., *Saga of the Steam Plough* (1965).

Bowley, A. L., *Prices and Wages in the United Kingdom 1914–1920* (Oxford, 1921).

Brigden, R., *Ploughs and Ploughing* (Princes Risborough, 1984).

Clark, A. (ed.), *'A Good Innings': the private papers of Viscount Lee of Fareham* (1974).

Dale, H. E., *Daniel Hall, Pioneer of Scientific Agriculture* (1956).

Dewey, P. E., 'Agricultural labour supply in England and Wales during the First World War', *EcHR* XXVIII (1975).

—— 'Food production and policy in the United Kingdom, 1914–1918', *Transactions of the Royal Historical Society* 30 (1980).

—— 'British farming profits and government policy during the First World War', *EcHR* XXXVII (1984).

—— 'Military recruiting and the British labour force during the First World War', *Historical Journal* 27 (1984).

Ernle, Lord (R. E. Prothero), *English Farming Past and Present* (6th edn, 1961).

—— *The Land and its People: chapters in rural life and history* (1925).

Feinstein, C. H., *National Income, Expenditure and Output of the United Kingdom 1855–1965* (Cambridge, 1972).

Fraser, C., *Harry Ferguson, Inventor and Pioneer* (1972).

Fielding, (Sir) C., *Food* (1923).

Fussell, G. E., *The Farmer's Tools* (1952).

Garrad, G. H., 'The work of the motor tractor', *JRASE* 79 (1918).

Gollin, A. M., *Proconsul in Politics: a study of Lord Milner in opposition and in power* (1964).

Guild, J. B., 'Variations in the numbers of live stock, and in the production of meat in the United Kingdom during the war', *JRSS* LXXXIII (1920).

Horn, P., *Rural Life in England and Wales in the First World War* (Dublin, 1984).

Hutchinson, G. T., 'Government tractor cultivation in England and Wales', *JBA*, Dec. 1918.

Jones, C. B., 'The breaking up of permanent grass in 1918', *JRASE* 79 (1918).

Jones, D. T. et al., *Rural Scotland during the War* (1926).

Kirkpatrick, W. H., *The Seasonal Distribution of Farm Labour Requirements*, University of Cambridge Department of Agriculture, Farm Economics Branch, Report 14 (Cambridge, 1930).

Lloyd George, D., *War Memoirs* (1934).

McConnell, P., *Notebook of Agricultural Facts and Figures for Farmers and Farm Students* (1910).

257

MacGregor, J. J., 'The economic history of two rural estates in Cambridgeshire, 1870–1934', *JRASE* 98 (1937).

Middleton, (Sir) T. H., *Food Production in War* (Oxford, 1923).

—— 'Systems of farming and the production of food – the need for more tillage', *JBA*, Sep. 1915.

—— 'Farming of the United Kingdom in peace and war: the plough policy and its results', *Journal of the University College of Wales Agricultural Department*, IX (1920).

Minchinton, W. E. (ed.) *Essays in Agrarian History* (2 vols, Newton Abbot, 1968).

Mitchell, B. R. and Deane, P., *Abstract of British Historical Statistics* (Cambridge, 1962).

Montgomery, J. K., *The maintenance of the agricultural labour supply in England and Wales during the war* (Rome, 1922).

Munitions, Ministry of, *History of the Ministry of Munitions* (12 vols, n.d.).

Murray, K. A. H., *Agriculture* (1955).

Olson, M. *The Economics of the Wartime Shortage: a history of British food supplies in the Napoleonic War and in World Wars One and Two* (Durham, North Carolina, 1963).

Orr, J., *Agriculture in Berkshire* (Oxford, 1918).

Orwin, C. S. and Whetham, E. H., *History of British Agriculture, 1846–1914* (rev. edn., Newton Abbot, 1971).

Prest, A. R. and Adams, A. A., *Consumers' Expenditure in the United Kingdom 1900–1919* (Cambridge, 1954).

Rew, (Sir) R. H., 'Farming and food supplies in time of war', *JBA*, Sep. 1915.

—— 'The progress of British agriculture', *JRSS* LXXXV (1922).

Russell, (Sir) E. J., 'On making and storing farmyard manure', *JRASE* 77 (1916).

Sheail, J., 'The role of the War Agricultural and Executive Committees in the Food Production Campaign of 1915–18 in England and Wales', *Agricultural Administration* I (1974).

—— 'Land improvement and reclamation; the experiences of the First World War in England and Wales', *AgHR* 24 (1976).

Sorenson, C. E. and Williamson, S. T., *Forty years with Ford* (1957).

Stamp, (Sir) J., *Taxation during the War* (1932).

Street, A. G., *Farmer's Glory* (1932).

Sturmey, S. G., 'Owner-farming in England and Wales 1900–50', *Manchester School* XXIII (1955) and Minchinton, *Essays*, II.

Thompson, F. M. L., *English Landed Society in the Nineteenth Century* (1963).

—— 'The Second Agricultural Revolution 1815–1880', *EcHR* XXI (1968).

Thompson, R. J., 'An enquiry into the rent of agricultural land in England and Wales during the nineteenth century', *JRSS* LXXX (1907), and Minchinton, *Essays*, II.

Venn, J. A., *Foundations of Agricultural Economics* (2nd edn, Cambridge 1933).

SELECT BIBLIOGRAPHY

War Office, *Statistics of the Military Effort of the British Empire during the Great War, 1914–20* (1922).

Whetham, E. H., 'The mechanisation of British agriculture 1910–45', *JAE* 21 (1970).

—— 'The Agriculture Act 1920 and its repeal – the "Great Betrayal" ', *AgHR* 22 (1974).

Winter, J. M., *The Great War and the British People* (1985).

Wolfe, H., *Labour Supply and Regulation* (Oxford, 1924).

Wright, P. A., *Old Farm Tractors* (1962).

THESES AND DISSERTATIONS

Beard, M., 'The impact of the First World War on agricultural society in West Sussex' (M.Litt., Cambridge University, 1985).

Cooper, A. F., 'The transformation of agricultural policy 1912–1936: a study in conservative politics' (D.Phil., Oxford University, 1979).

Dewey, P. E., 'Farm labour in wartime: the relationship between agricultural labour supply and food production in Great Britain during 1914–1918, with international comparisons' (Ph.D., Reading University, 1978).

MacGregor, J. J., 'History of landownership since 1870, with special reference to conditions in Cambridgeshire' (M.Litt., Oxford, 1938).

Webber, A. R., 'Government policy and British agriculture, 1917–1939' (Ph.D., University of Kent, 1982).

PERSONAL COMMUNICATIONS

Broome, Viscountess, 4 May 1972.

Davies, Mr J. L., 1 July 1973.

INDEX